Deciding in Unison

Themes in Consensual Democracy in Africa

Edited by

Emmanuel Ifeanyi Ani
University of Ghana
Edwin Etieyibo
University of the Witwatersrand

Series in Politics

VERNON PRESS

www.vernonpress.com

In the Americas:
Vernon Press
1000 N West Street,
Suite 1200, Wilmington,
Delaware 19801
United States

In the rest of the world:
Vernon Press
C/Sancti Espiritu 17,
Malaga, 29006
Spain

Series in Politics

Library of Congress Control Number: 2019950175

ISBN: 978-1-64889-030-7

Also available: 978-1-62273-853-3 [Hardback]; 978-1-62273-923-3 [PDF, E-Book]

Cover design by Vernon Press. Cover image designed by Freepik.

Table of contents

Foreword

Barry Hallen

Southern Crossroads Academic

The issues relating to consensual democracy offer unique insights into precolonial and postcolonial Africa. What makes consensual democracy important is that it is said to arise from indigenous African beliefs and practices with regard to human relations generally and governance in particular. Governance in precolonial Africa did not involve factional political 'parties' or occasional 'elections' in which people are supposedly 'free' (making an 'X' mark on a ballot) to exercise their political will. Consensual democracy is meant to restore the right (not privilege) of people to govern themselves on a constant basis.

In modern times, consensual democracy is first said to have been systematically expressed by noteworthy political figures at the time of African independence in the 1960s. More recently, its most important advocate is the Ghanaian philosopher, Kwasi Wiredu. Wiredu has published no less than ten major essays articulating, elaborating, and defending it as a political alternative that will save the nation-states of Africa from the perils of the liberal democratic forms of government they were obliged to adopt by the European powers at the time of independence.

For Wiredu it is a gross mistake to attribute the problems and instabilities of African nation-states to endemic corruption and incompetence. The liberal democratic form of government championed by the West has proved to be incompatible with the political and moral values and practices of Africa's indigenous cultures. That is why it has ended up causing more problems than it has solved. In a consensual democracy, ethnic bias is to be controlled via the absence of political parties. Candidates who seek office are to be evaluated solely on the basis of their professional qualifications rather than party affiliation. Regular 'town meetings' of the electorate with their representatives to arrive at a consensus on pertinent issues will be frequent and foundational. Consensual democracy thereby restores the right of the individual to participate directly in governance.

Wiredu recognizes that he alone is not competent to give a complete picture of the consensual democratic state. He, therefore, appeals to colleagues to help him with that task. That is at least one way the ten essays that constitute this volume should be regarded. They are written by colleagues involved with political philosophy in the African context who are concerned to review the merits and demerits of consensual democracy as a political alternative for the Africa of today.

With that in mind, the introductory chapter to this volume provides a history and synopsis of consensus theory, prioritizing the thought of Kwasi Wiredu. In subsequent chapters, some contributors endorse Wiredu's views overall, but with substantive revisions and additions. Others disagree entirely with consensual democracy and argue that adjustments can be made to the liberal democratic model that will make it compatible with contemporary Africa. Still, others focus on Wiredu's overall philosophy and the status and role of consensus in it.

All contributors recognize that consensual democracy is not to be treated as the product of a purely theoretical thought experiment. It is said to have roots in the cultures of Africa that can be empirically demonstrated. Consensual democracy, therefore, becomes an example of applied philosophy. It is meant to be of indigenous origin and a real-life political alternative that can be adopted by the nation-states of Africa. As far as Wiredu and the contributors to this volume are concerned that makes the assessment of its merits and demerits relevant to problems that should demand the attention of all.

Introduction

The chapters in this edited volume open up new vistas in the debate about how we could fashion a consensual democracy that minimizes the adversarial element of the majoritarian democracy African countries inherited from their colonial masters. In the main, the contributions set the stage for new frontiers by linking traditional African consensus decision making with knowledge production, epistemology, and the building of resistance movements. The volume also features a frontier breaking piece seeking to demonstrate that Wiredu's consensus proposal is consistent with his views about the relativity of truth, and how we should handle this relativity. But there are chapters demonstrating that the non-party system proposed by Wiredu is unsuitable for practice, and other chapters tracing the problems associated with transferring consensus-supporting values such as communalism into the contemporary Africa setting.

The collection is presently composed of eleven chapters. The first is a summary of the consensus debate so far, and aims to introduce the reader into what has happened in the literature. This chapter, written by Emmanuel Ani and Edwin Etieyibo, explains that the debate is a broad one that encompasses different debates, which have been going on regarding different aspects of Kwasi Wiredu's proposal, or/and different ramifications of his proposal. The sub debates that are currently active are on the role of rationality, the question of interests, the question of models of democracy, the communitarian question, the issue of the structure of the party system, and the consensus potential of different issues. This chapter devotes separate sections to summarizing these sub debates and developments in these sub-areas.

In chapter two, Husein Inusah argues that current attempts at identifying an African epistemology fail because they do not consider what could pass as justified belief and knowledge. Inusah argues that they do not give us the opportunity to study how an epistemic subject stands in relation to a proposition, or study the doxastic attitudes of epistemic agents constructed upon the epistemic canons of truth and objectivity. Inusah suggests that consensus provides a possible platform for meeting these requirements in determining an African definition of knowledge and furthermore providing the resource to reconstruct African epistemology.

In the next chapter, Martin Asiegbu and Victor C. Nweke contend that Kwasi Wiredu's argument for an African model of democracy that operates in the absence of political parties is consistent with his conception of truth. They argue that there is a link between Wiredu's understanding of truth and what has come to be known as consensual democracy in African political philosophy. Their approach is expository, critical, and argumentative. They present an analysis of both Wiredu's theory of truth as well as his position on the place of democracy and consensus in the intellectual heritage of Africa. Their central submission is that Wiredu's conception of truth as 'considered opinion' is fundamentally deliberative. They explain that a careful reading of Wiredu's idea of consensus and democracy in connection with his epistemological standpoint will reveal that Wiredu advances a specific variant of deliberative democracy that is consistent with his conception of truth. They thus conclude that Wiredu is a foremost theorist of a variant of deliberative democracy that stems from the African intellectual heritage.

The fourth chapter by Dennis Masaka takes issue with Wiredu's thesis that a non-party system of democracy is a realistic possibility in solving the political crises inaugurated in Africa through the imposition of majoritarian democracy. Whilst Masaka agrees with the thesis that liberal or majoritarian democracy has led to some significant problems in Africa thereby justifying the need to rethink the possibility of a return to the "traditional" consensual democracy model, he thinks that multi-party politics might still be viably pursued within the framework of a consensual democratic model. His general point is that the existence of political parties might turn out to be necessary for a viable consensual democratic system of governance in Africa in present times.

In chapter five, Bernard Matolino argues that supporters of consensus have to strike a balance between its rooting in traditional communalist societies, its modern conceptual defence and its possible application. He explains that this balance is necessary to bolster the claimed desirability and conceptual superiority of democracy by consensus vis-à-vis majoritarian democracy. He points out that the juxtaposition of these two modes of democracy is partially a historical and partially a conceptual battle. The historical factors present themselves as a mirror image of the contest between accounts of the conceptual vitality of traditional politics and the unsuitability of forcibly imposed Western liberal multi-party democracy. However, as Matolino observes, the sticking problem for supporters of consensus is the correlation between the past, in which consensus worked, and the present theorization of its superiority. In this chapter, Matolino attempts to show that the latest attempt by Martin Ajei at supporting consensus does not work as it fails to transcend the tension between consensus' rootedness in communalism and its supporters' attempts to cast it as conceptually superior to its rival.

We then see the sixth chapter by Vitumbiko Nyirenda, in which he examines Kwasi Wiredu's proposal of an alternative to the majoritarian system of democracy in Africa. In this article, Wiredu had argued against majoritarian democracy as a system of governance that fails to deal with most of Africa's political problems — problems that arise as a result of the need for parties to retain power and lack of substantial representation of the electorate. To deal with these problems, Wiredu had proposed consensual democracy as an alternative form of governance. In this chapter, Nyirenda demonstrates that Wiredu's consensus democracy does not avoid the issues of elections that are central and problematic to majoritarian democracy. Nyirenda's central argument is that as long as consensus democracy involves elections, it will lead to the same problems in one way or another.

In chapter seven, Emmanuel Ani shows that Wiredu's proposal for a reading of consensus democracy as unanimity in decision making did not earn the agreement of scholars generally. Ani then shows that the feasible way for advancing the consensus democracy project is to re-read it as a democracy by compromise. Ani delves into the concept of compromise, explaining three types of compromise. First, we have proportional compromise (when we compromise in terms of degrees, quantity, scales, qualities). We do this when we bargain over what quantity of time to invest in meetings or projects with other people, when we bargain over the prices of goods, and so on. Second, we have strategic compromise (when we compromise to resolve a conflict over strategy and method, and over strategic interests). Third, we have normative compromise (when we compromise to resolve a conflict over normative values such as religious beliefs and moral principles). Ani compares this taxonomy of compromise to Chiara Lepora's three kinds of compromise (substitution, intersection, and conjunction compromise), and draws lessons. Ani argues that Lepora's taxonomy is about what we lose and gain, and Ani's is about the content or item upon which we wish to compromise. Going beyond this, Ani explains that the most important denominator between the two taxonomies is that the proportional and strategic compromises (as well as the substitution and intersection compromises) offer veritable prospects for practice, whilst the normative compromise (and Lepora's conjunction compromise) is the most challenging. Ani argues that scholars exploring the prospects and challenges of a democracy by compromise would need to take in stock these kinds and sheds of compromise to figure what practitioners in such a democracy are up against, as well as how, in what ways, and in which situations they could maximize the material and psychological benefits of compromising, as well as reduce its psychological costs to compromisers.

The eight chapter is the contribution by Munamato Chemhuru, who seeks to foster what he calls 'Afro-consensual' democracy as a plausible basis for inclusive democratic political practice in post-colonial Africa. He provides reasons why Afro-consensual democracy guarantees participation, inclusivity and freedom, which the multi-party system of liberal democracy is thought to represent. Overall, he concludes that Afro-consensual democracy is more appealing when compared to the Western multi-party constitutional style of democracy as it is currently being understood and practiced in post-colonial Africa.

In chapter nine, Edwin Etieyibo discusses consensus in the context of dissensus, especially in the form of resistance movements. Etieyibo explores the implications of the idea of dissensus *qua* resistance to Wiredu's proposal for a consensus democracy. He acknowledges that although Wiredu's consensual democracy recognises dissensus as the starting point for consensus, and allows for suspension of disbelief by parties or representatives, the role and value of opposition or dissensus *qua* resistance appear to be compromised given Wiredu's claim that consensus leads to genuine reconciliation and abstention from further disputation and recrimination. Etieyibo argues that although Wiredu acknowledges dissensus and proposes a suspension of disagreement in order to reach consensus, the idea of opposition seems lost by the very nature of consensus and Wiredu's claim that consensus leads to genuine reconciliation, as well as abstention from further disputes and recrimination.

In chapter ten, Alexander Kwakye looks at what he considers some of the defects that some scholars have identified with multiparty democracy, a political order widely adopted in Africa. In particular, he examines the positions of Kwesi Wiredu and Kwame Gyekye on multiparty democracy. Kwakye accepts the position that in order for democracy to thrive in Africa, it ought to be tailored contextually to meet the socio-political needs of Africa. However, he rejects the ontological view that partisan extremism is a *sine qua non* of multiparty democracy. He argues in support of Gyekye's view that partisan extremism is a product of people's behaviour rather than a necessary consequence of multiparty democracy.

The book concludes with the eleventh chapter, which is Helen Lauer's analysis of democracy and good governance in comparing Kwasi Wiredu and Emmanuel Chukwudi Eze. Lauer explores what she describes as 'the widely read controversy' between these two scholars of African governance systems. Lauer argues that we should re-read these two scholars on a more careful reading as compatible rather than opposing. As part of this, she revisits some of Eze's critique of Wiredu in order to revise them. Lauer notes that Wiredu is concerned with effective distributive justice whilst Eze is concerned with the entitlements of individuals to recognition and opposition, and Lauer argues that there is 'a basic congruity between these divergent yet complementary foci of West African political heritage and their relevance to our current economic and demographic conditions.'

Overall, the contributions in this book further the debate on consensual democracy in Africa by criticizing objectionable features of the consensus proposal whilst affirming the general value of a consensual variant to African politics. We hope this book provides material for research that seeks to bring new dimensions to the consensus project.

Emmanuel Ifeanyi Ani	*Edwin Etieyibo*
Accra, Ghana	*Johannesburg, South Africa*

Chapter 1

The Consensus Project: The Debate So Far

Emmanuel Ifeanyi Ani

University of Ghana

Edwin Etieyibo

University of the Witwatersrand

Introduction

This chapter summarizes the debate that has so far greeted Kwasi Wiredu's proposal for a non-party system of democracy based on consensus. Wiredu's proposal is inspired by the traditional consensual practices of his native Akan of West Africa. We survey the support his proposal has received, as well as the opposition. The debate is a broad one that encompasses different debates, which have been going on regarding different aspects of Wiredu's proposal, or/and different ramifications of his proposal. The aspects or ramifications are the role of rationality, the question of interests, the question of models of democracy, the communitarian question, the issue of the structure of the party system, and the consensus potential of different issues. We devote separate sections to summarizing the debates and developments in these sub-areas.

Wiredu's Rejection of Multiparty Democracy

The debate about the propriety of democracy by consensus in Africa (which we shall henceforth call the consensus debate) began with a proposal by Kwasi Wiredu, a prominent African philosopher who argued that the multiparty system of competitive democracy is inappropriate for African countries. Wiredu argued that the multiparty system exacerbates political conflicts in an especially divisive way. According to him, it is not the case that political conflict is foreign to Africa; rather, it is the claim that conflict that emanates from the activities of political parties is not indigenous to Africa (2011: 1060). Wiredu calls this system of democracy "an epiphenomenon of colonialism" (Ibid) and argues that it is dangerous to practice in face of the ethnic configurations and other kinds of conflicts in Africa because it exacerbates pre-existing tensions, including the marginalization of smaller ethnic groups by larger ones (2011: 1064).

Wiredu argues that the raison d'etre of political parties is to wrestle other parties for political power, which he sees as institutionalizing conflict or making it officially permissible and laudable. Electoral outcomes are sometimes very close, with the result that when one party wins and forms government, it wins by a slight majority, and those who support the opposition is often as numerous as those who support the party in power, resulting in what Wiredu refers to as a relative disenfranchisement of a section of the population (Wiredu 2011: 1060). He points out that this arrangement is backed by the constitution, amounting to what he calls a pre-established disharmony (Ibid). He writes that when a party wins power, others lose and stay out of it, and their ideas normally do not receive attention (2011: 1061). Wiredu asks us to think about the psychological infelicities of losing power, and the fact that the winners are keen to show their power to reach decisions to the exclusion of losers (Ibid).

It does not stop here. The multiparty system specifies that the political opposition is supposed to act as a check on the ruling party. But Wiredu argues that checks become unbalanced when one party has the presidency and another party the legislature, because the political opposition uses the legislature to turn opposition into obstruction of meaningful government initiatives (2011: 1059). Wiredu thinks the central idea is simply uncooperativeness, and a consequent adversarial spirit in politics (Ibid).

Wiredu also takes another shot at elections in the multiparty system. He begins by reminding us that the only way of seeking the consent of the governed is through rational persuasion, and argues that this is not what we see in elections. He notes that elections are so expensive that only those rich enough can participate, and much of the money goes into kinds of campaigning that do not aim at rational persuasion (2011: 1062). These are the kinds of processes that give us democratic leaders, including the President of the United States of America, as well as in many African countries where bribery and deception are among other darker methods of getting votes (Ibid).

In contrast to the multiparty system, Wiredu proposes a democracy by consensus. He argues that such a system could be inspired by traditional consensual practices. For an example of a traditional consensual system, Wiredu presented an account of the consensual political system of the Ashanti of Ghana.

Wiredu's Presentation of Traditional Consensual Practices

Wiredu asks us to take a refreshing look at the consensual systems of governance that were used by some traditional African societies. Wiredu cited Kenneth Kaunda as saying, "In our original societies, we operated by consensus. An issue was talked about in solemn conclave until such time as agreement could be achieved" (Wiredu 1996: 182). Wiredu also cited Julius Nyerere as saying, "… in African society the traditional method of conducting affairs is by free discussion" and Guy Glutton Brock as saying, "The elders would sit under the trees, and talk until they agree" (Ibid). Wiredu then notes that consensus was not merely a political phenomenon, but was "an immanent approach to social interaction" and generally regarded as axiomatic, although this did not mean that consensus was always achieved (Ibid). There was indeed conflict in African society, but the important issue for Wiredu was that the aim of resolving issues was to achieve reconciliation "rather than a mere abstention from further recriminations or collisions" (Ibid). This is not the same as the usual scenario in which disputes could be settled without the achievement of reconciliation. And reconciliation is for Wiredu "a form of consensus", because it restored goodwill by a reappraising of "the importance and significance of the initial bones of contention" (1996: 182-183). Wiredu clarifies that consensus need not entail an agreement on moral or cognitive issues, what is important is that all parties felt that their positions were considered on the issue at hand, neither does consensus "entail total agreement" (1996: 183). Wiredu, in fact, reminds us that consensus actually presupposes (at least initial) diversity, and since issues do not always polarise along the lines of strict contradictoriness, dialogue could be used to smoothen edges and produce compromises that all agree to.

Wiredu argues that we might avoid value-laden issues and dwell more on agreeing over practical issues. He writes, "where there is the will to consensus dialogue can lead to a willing suspension of disagreement, making possible agreed actions without necessarily agreed notions. This is important because certain issues do, indeed, precipitate exhaustive disjunctions which no dialogic accommodations can mediate" (1996: 183). Here, Wiredu seems to be saying that certain issues are quite intractable to discuss. And when he prescribes that we should limit our consensus drive to action-related issues, he appears to be suggesting that intractable issues are more in the value-laden category. Wiredu tells us that the suspension of disagreement is usually to be done by "the residual minority" (Ibid). But what is special about consensus is that "the majority prevails not over, but upon, the minority" "… to accept the proposal in question", instead of simply living with it as we see in majoritarian democracy (1996: 190). He adds that a minority is expected to acquiesce in a consensus system in order for a decision to be reached (Ibid).

Wiredu, however, points out that this process depends on the patience and persuasiveness of the right kind of people.

Wiredu distinguishes between two categories of traditional African societies: those with a centralized authority exercised through the machinery of government, and those without centralized government-like authority. He noted that life in the second category was just as orderly as life in the first (Ibid). Wiredu then tells us that consensus was practised by those in the first category, who were among the most centralized and warlike ethnic groups in Africa, and he cited the Zulus and Ashantis as examples (Ibid 183-184). Wiredu then muses that, by contrast, less militaristic societies also manifested less enthusiasm for consensus. Wiredu sees this contrast as 'paradoxical', but does not reflect on it.

Having mentioned the Zulu and the Ashanti as two prominent examples of traditional societies whose political systems were based on consensus, Wiredu writes that, in the Ashanti kingdom, lineage was a basic political unit, and every such unit had a head, elected through consensus. The qualifications for such a position were "seniority in age, wisdom, a sense of civic responsibility, and logical persuasiveness" (1996: 184). Wiredu narrates that where these qualities united in one person, election was routine, but where they were scattered among different persons, discussions were often more prolonged but aimed at consensus. Indeed, Wiredu reports that there was never an act of formal voting, and no longstanding word for voting in the Ashanti language. All elections were done through consensus. The lineage head represented the lineage in the village or town council, which in turn elected someone to represent it at the regional council, which in turn elected someone to represent them at the national council headed by the king of the Ashantis, the *Asantehene*. Decisions (presumably both electoral and substantive) were by consensus at all levels (Wiredu 1996: 185).

Wiredu tells us that consensus was not an accidental method to the Ashantis, it was a premeditated option because they considered voting to be too easy a way to reach decisions (1996: 185), and voting side-lined minorities (1996: 183, 186, 190). Minorities are represented in consensus, and Wiredu tells us that there are two concepts of representation. We have formal representation (the representation of a given constituency in council), and substantive representation (the representation of the will of a constituency in the making of a decision). Wiredu observes that formal representation could exist without substantive representation, even though the formal is desired for the sake of the substantive (1996: 186). He writes that the Ashanti considered substantive representation a fundamental human right, that each individual should not only be represented in council but also in counsel on any matter that is relevant to her interests or those of her group, and that this is why consensus is important (Ibid). Wiredu concedes that consensus may not always be had, but argues that we could always aim at it, and that a system dedicated to such an ideal "must be institutionally different" from a system that depends on the sway of the majority, however, such a system is hedged around with checks and balances (1996: 186).

All this is made easy by the Ashanti belief that, ultimately, all human interests are the same, that it is only the perceptions of those interests that are different, and that rational discussion has the capacity to dig down to the rock bottom of the identity of interests (1996: 185). Wiredu writes that this belief in the power of reason to resolve interests is depicted by an Akan motif of a crocodile with one stomach and two heads locked in a struggle over food. Wiredu tells us that the Akan believe that if the two heads could but see that the food in contest was destined for one stomach, "the irrationality of the conflict would be manifest to them" (Ibid).

Non-Party Democracy by Consensus

Wiredu proposes a non party system of democracy based on consensus. He writes that, although the kinship traditional system cannot be re-invoked today, it is still a practical proposition to fashion a non-party system based on consensus. Presenting the central merit of consensus, Wiredu argues that the point of consensus is not the absence of disagreement or conflict but the willingness to compromise to reach agreements and decisions that will enable group action, and Wiredu thinks we need to find this attitude in institutions different from today's democracies (2011: 1058).

Wiredu argues that cooperation does not easily come to "political parties", and we should instead have "political associations", which need not have the adversarial attitude. According to him, conditions that are conducive to cooperation and compromise and, consequently, consensus would be present if political bodies such as political associations operate under a constitution whereby the aim or goal is not (a) the winning of a certain number of seats or votes in a general election and (b) where this does not authorize the group that wins these seats to form a government which excludes other groups (2011: 1062).

Going further, Wiredu suggests that we may do away completely or, at least, partially, with elections. He writes that associations need not officially contest elections, to decrease the partisan nature of assembly deliberations (2011: 1062). If we cannot eliminate elections completely, we could at least minimize them. Wiredu concedes that although we may not totally obviate elections, occupational groups "could select supplementary representatives by some agreed procedure that minimizes adversarial competition as much as possible" (2011: 1065)

As seen from the above quotations, Wiredu proposes a democratic system that does not see elections as a defining mark of democracy. But he does not think that voting would disappear. He conceded that a vote could be used to break an impasse in rare cases of an intractable division. But he argued we have to judge the success of the system through the rarity of such votes (1996: 190). He also conceded that voting could be used for electing representatives because choice is, "determined by superior numbers in terms of votes". But Wiredu argued that even here, the representatives need to address all opinions in their constituencies in order to work out a representation that is as consensual as possible (Ibid). Here, Wiredu prescribes that even if we are to continue with voting, we need to minimize the partisanship that comes with it, such as the tendency of representatives to represent only those that voted in favour of them in the constituency, whilst trying to punish those voters who did not

Support for Wiredu's Proposal

Edward Wamala, Joe Teffo and Kwame Gyekye broadly support Wiredu's proposal and agree with his descriptions of traditional African consensual practices. Wamala narrates the consensual system of government practised by the traditional Ganda (of present-day Buganda) along the general lines of Wiredu's narrative of that of the Akan of West Africa. Like Wiredu, Wamala argues that the Ganda consensus system was democratic, that the decision of the chief's council was more powerful than the personal opinion of the chief, that the (power of the) monarchy was limited, and so on (Wamala 2004: 435-440). Like Wiredu, Wamala also argues that the multiparty system is inhospitable to the democratic (consensual) values of traditional Ganda society (Wamala 2004: 440-441).

In support of Wiredu, Teffo argues that we should seek "to retrieve and preserve what is logically sound and empirically justified from the African tradition and to try to perpetuate it" (Teffo 2004: 445). He argues that the South African traditional system of governance was democratic even though it was a monarchy, it was founded on solidarity, it was a "domesticated democracy", that consensus was a hallmark of traditional political decision making, that it (consensus) manifested a deeper sense of democracy compared to majority rule, a chief was a chief only because of his people, and so on (Teffo 2004: 443-448). He argues that a contemporary democracy could be fashioned "based on an institutionalized quest for consensus", and that such a system "cannot, logically, be a party system, whether it features one party or two parties or any number of them" (Teffo 2004: 448).

One could therefore see that Wiredu, Wamala and Teffo are united in faulting the multiparty system of democracy and questioning its relevance for African countries. They also share in the view that the traditional consensual systems of governance were genuinely democratic, and the powers of traditional leaders were limited.

Kwame Gyekye supports the notion of consensual democracy, but he does not entirely discard the idea of the multiparty system, or even of majoritarianism. Gyekye admits that he is worried about what he calls the "excessive political partisanship" we see in a multiparty democracy. He describes it as "a political behaviour that makes members belonging to one political party refuse to amend their opinions, positions or perspectives despite robust and cogent arguments and criticisms that should make them amend their views and positions" (Gyekye 2013: 243). Gyekye thus observes that this kind of behaviour makes politicians refuse to accept important proposals and convincing ideas from their opponents, and to integrate such input into their own positions for the good of the society. This, in Gyekye's view, eliminates negotiation and compromise. Gyekye, therefore, also calls for consensus since, in his view, it "nurtures the ethos of negotiation" and "may leave every participant in a decision-making assembly satisfied, to a degree, without entertaining the feeling that he or she has been left in limbo (2013: 244). Gyekye, however, thinks that consensus will not always be achieved, and therefore, "absolute consensus is nearly always impossible to attain" (Ibid 245). He therefore opts for a midway between consensus and simple majority, what he calls a super majority. This is the method of taking decisions by a two-third majority. Gyekye observes that this method is already used in the American democracy to decide on certain matters, such as "amendment to the Constitution, overriding a presidential veto, impeaching the president and some other matters" (Ibid). Gyekye argues that two-third majority implies that near consensus is ideal. According to him, "two-thirds majority is certainly nearer to consensus formation than the simple majority of fifty-one percent" (Ibid).

Opposition and Debate

The history of the consensus debate was inaugurated by two early responses to Wiredu's proposal. These are the articles of Emmanuel Chukwudi Eze (2000) and Carlos Jacques (2011). Eze argued that Wiredu's depiction of traditional consensual practices contained a lot of romanticism, reification, and exaggerations that made it quite difficult to know how to adapt the practice for contemporary society. He also raised the issue of the identity of human interests and how they could impact on consensus. Jacques observed that Wiredu's arguments are the same as those of the African despots who operated one-party systems (Jacques 2011: 1025-1026). The issues raised by Eze and Jacques have led to debate involving Bernard Matolino (2009, 2013, 2016), Helen Lauer (2011), Martin Ajei (2016) and Emmanuel Ani (2014a, 2014b, 2018a, 2019). For the purpose of clarity in discussing the broad debate, we would partition it into several sub-areas, such as the question of the role of rationality in deliberation and achieving consensus, the question and role of interests, the sub-debate about Wiredu's non-party proposal, as well as its comparison with the multi-party and one-party systems. Let us look at how the debate is shaping up in each of these areas.

On the Role of Rationality in Deliberation and Consensus

Chief among the opposition is Eze's observation that Wiredu points out but does not explore the several sources of political power enjoyed by the Akan king or chief. Eze thought that Wiredu was being rationalistic in listing the chief's moral authority, religious authority, capacity for rational persuasion, and yet arguing that the chief's only source of legitimate influence is his capacity for rational persuasion (the intrinsic persuasiveness of his ideas). Eze contends that if Wiredu wants us to believe that the chief's only source of legitimate influence is the persuasiveness of his ideas, and that his moral and religious authority did not contribute to giving him more influence, then Wiredu should have clarified "the relations – distinctions, similarities, and, especially, overlaps – that may exist or occur between the enunciated sources of moral legitimation and the normative justification of the exercise of political power. Eze argues that "it is rarely, and perhaps never, the case that one of the sources of legitimation of authority listed by Wiredu exists solely and cleanly independent of the others" (2000, par 14). He therefore wondered why the Ashanti chief, and especially his subjects, would think that the chief's only source of legitimate influence is only the intrinsic persuasiveness of his ideas. But Eze was grateful to Wiredu for listing these varied sources of influence, since Eze believed that clarifying them is important for considering consensus in the much more secularized and religiously plural African countries.

Eze also observed that Wiredu's description of the Akan consensual practices was populated with terms such as "faith", "belief", "reconciliation", "restoration of good will", "moral opinions", and others. Eze questions how these concepts would make sense to contemporary Africans today without appealing to mythological, ancestral and religious scaffoldings.

Eze noted that Wiredu's rationalistic presentation is hinged on the Akan belief that all interests are ultimately the same, that it is only the perception of those interests that are different, and that rational dialogue would dispel the differences in perception. Eze, however, wonders whether it is the belief in the power of reason that led the Ashantis to believe that all interests are ultimately the same, or the power of their belief in a shared and common past and future (carried forward in the myth of origins) that "leads them to employ reason and rational discussion as a means of achieving and sustaining this shared life form" (Eze 2000, par 17).

Eze questions Wiredu's thesis that it is logic that makes one political idea more persuasive than another, and argues that political ideas and governance rely heavily on mythologies and symbols such as "the flag," "God," "freedom," "the Motherland," "the Party," and so on (Eze 2000, par 18). Eze argues that these fantasies frequently succeed in achieving their effects "with little or no reason", and that using them enables people to collaborate and "see reason" with one another and to act together (Ibid).

Responding to Eze's critique of Wiredu, Bernard Matolino supports Wiredu's thesis that the Akan king's legitimate influence lies only in his ability to marshal logical and persuasive arguments, and that his moral and religious authority have no impact on his legitimate influence. To make this argument, Matolino distinguishes what he sees as the king's moral and religious authority and functions on the one hand, and the king's exercise of 'real' power on the other hand. The 'real' power comes from logical and persuasive arguments. The religious functions are only procedural requirements for public office, they merely indicate who the king is. They are just authority indicators, but they are not that authority. As such, for Matolino, religious authority does not need to interfere in the exercise of a king's powers of logical persuasion, and "does not as a matter of course diminish or enhance his prowess in constructing logical and persuasive arguments" (Matolino 2009: 37).

In an article on traditional African consensual rationality, Emmanuel Ani disagrees with Matolino's argument that the Ashanti king's influence originates solely from his capacity for logical persuasion, and that his religious authority is not a source of influence. Ani agrees with Matolino that the king's religious authority does not need to enhance or diminish his ability to marshal logical and persuasive arguments, but Ani argues that the king's religious authority does not *need* to make him more logical in order to be more persuasive. Ani argues that the king's religious authority has its own influence "quite apart from his logical arguments" (Ani 2014: 349). To demonstrate his position, Ani cites Aristotle's three components of persuasion, namely, perceived character (ethos), emotions or experience (pathos), and word or logic (logos). When we receive an argument or message, we are persuaded not just by the logic but also by the perceived character or trustworthiness of the messenger as well as the messenger's attitude in delivering the message. Matolino strives to show that the perceived social image of the king has no influence in his deliberative input, but Ani cited a study of deliberative dynamics within American juries showing that jury members with higher status jobs, higher education, higher income and so on talk more and are more likely to be perceived as accurate. The study shows that higher status members are given more opportunities to make suggestions, and routinely treated as if their contributions to group problem-solving are better (Hastie et al. 1983; Stodtbeck et al. 1957 cited in Ani 2014: 350). Ani argues that these modern social statuses are the modern equivalents of the king's religious authority, although, in societies that are still highly religious, religious leaders still speak authoritatively on even political issues (Ani 2014: 350-351). Ani argued that if deliberation were purely rational, it would not have been interrupted by colonialism (a non-rational factor) and we would not be striving to resuscitate it (Ani 2014: 347). The argument about whether deliberation depends on only the logical power of arguments and whether non-rational factors can influence deliberation has led to further exchanges between Matolino and Ani (see Matolino 2016 and Ani 2018a). What is at stake in this debate is that if deliberation were not purely rational, then scholars would be compelled to acknowledge that deliberation was aided by the common ancestry, homogeneity and solidarity of traditional societies, to acknowledge that these advantages are absent in contemporary plural societies, and to locate the non-rational factors that could facilitate contemporary deliberation and consensus in the absence of the sociological advantages found in traditional societies.

On the Question of Interests

Wiredu had argued that consensus was so viable in traditional Akan society because of the Akan belief that the interests of all members of society are *ultimately* the same, only immediate perceptions of those interests are different, and rational deliberation reconciles the perceptual differences (1996: 185). Wiredu tells us that this thought is expressed in an art motif depicting a crocodile with one stomach and two heads locked in struggle over food. Wiredu tells us of the Akan belief that if the two heads could but see that the food was destined for the same stomach, the irrationality of the conflict would be made manifest to them (Ibid). In response, Eze argues that the art motif assumes that there is no rational basis for the two crocodile heads to fight over who masticates the food. But Eze argues that before we declare such a conflict irrational, we would have to rule out the possibility of extra-nutritional reasons such as aesthetic pleasure, "the sheer joy of chewing food, in fact, the joy of eating! – which could accrue to one head independently of the other" (2000, par 25). Eze points out that if there is a possibility of such head-specific primal masticatory pleasure, then the only way of declaring irrational the struggle between the heads is to ensure they chew equal amounts of food. Eze argues that if there were no individuated desire to chew the food, then there would be no conflict over the food, and no conflict over power as we know it today. As such, for Eze, human interests are ultimately reconcilable if the two heads have no reason to struggle for food. Eze gives an example with international capitalism. He wonders how the commercial interests of a multinational company seeking to simply get oil out of the ground as quickly as possible coincide with the political and survival interests of the host community. He also wonders how the interests of 95 percent of Americans who share only as much wealth as another one percent of the same population coincide (Eze 2000, par 21).

Responding to Eze, Matolino agrees that competing human interests is natural, and that Wiredu is mistaken about the ultimate identity of all human interests. But Matolino argues that consensus is still possible in situations of conflicting interests, and reminds us of Wiredu's claim that consensus presupposes divergent interests (Matolino 2009: 40). Matolino then advocates a mutual-adjustment model of consensus. In a later article, Matolino argues that the primary goal of political parties in a democracy is not to reconcile interests but to actualize the plans for which they set up themselves (Matolino 2013: 147, 149-151).

The Question of Democracy Models

In responding to Wiredu, Eze argues that a democracy is one of those arrangements set up to "mediate the struggles and the conflicts that *necessarily* arise from the necessarily *competitive* nature of individuated identities and desires", or "the legitimation – and "management" – of this always already competitive (i.e., inherently political) condition of relativized desires" (Eze 2000; par 29 [Emphasis in the original]). As such, for Eze, consensus or unanimity of positions "cannot be the ultimate goal of democracy, but only one of its moments" (Ibid). The contract of democracy, for Eze, are rules for agreeing and disagreeing, not the simple elevation of agreement alone to the axiomatic. He adds that disagreements are cherished for their sakes and benefits, and therefore are as valuable in a democracy as are agreements. Going further, Eze argues that the only consensus that is primary to democracy is to play by a set of rules, and the most distinguishing mark of democracy is in the processes themselves – the debates, and the refrain from using force – rather than in a specific nature of outcome (Eze 2000; par 31).

Eze asks if it is his notion of democracy as protecting both agreement and disagreement, or Wiredu's notion of democracy as privileging only agreement, that is suitable for African states. He notes that the appeal of his notion is a greater sense of freedom, inventiveness, pluralism, whilst the appeal of Wiredu's notion is greater stability, although without a guarantee that such a stability is driven by pursuits of the common good. Eze then notes that neither of the notions is intrinsically Western or African, and concludes that the best form of democracy is "one that culturally reconciles both centripetal and centrifugal political forces of its constituents – while preserving each current in its most vital *élan*" (2000; par 33).

Matolino argues that Eze "does not succeed" and is grossly wrong in his characterization of democracy as only the management of agreement and disagreement, and faults Eze's view of the fundamentally competing nature of human interests. He accuses Eze of arguing that democracy has "nothing to do with consensus" (Matolino 2009: 41). Just as Eze argued that consensus is not the whole of democracy but only a moment in it, Matolino argued that management of competing desires is also only a moment in a democracy, and accused Eze of propagating only one model of democracy (Ibid).

In a later article, however, Matolino, shifts from this position, and advocates a position similar to that of Eze. There, he argued that parties₁ (people with similar interests, and can include political parties) bind their members in a way that excludes other parties₁ in a serious way. He argues that the ultimate aim of parties₁ is not to attain reconciliation but to pursue the objectives they formed when they constituted themselves as parties₁ (Matolino 2013: 147). He writes, "It is quite inconceivable to imagine a party1 organising itself on the strong belief that seeking consensus is its ultimate quest in its political programme and existence" (Ibid). This is a departure from his support of Wiredu's notion of democracy as aiming for consensus.

The Communitarian Question

Supporters of a consensual democracy in Africa are united in observing that consensus in traditional society was founded on communalism (also communitarianism or the communal ethos). Wiredu argues that consensus is reflective of the communal way of living, and that the essential ingredient of this lifestyle is that the individual adjusts his interests to those of the community (2011: 1056-1058). To support the idea of communitarianism, many African scholars share the idea of the primacy of the community over the individual, and since this idea is a favourable foundation for proposing consensus, we find that most supporters of consensus are also supporters of the idea of communitarianism. Mogobe Ramose sums up this ideological connection by claiming that there is a foundational link from communalism through solidarity to consensus (Ramose 1999: 139f). Those who are critical of the consensus ideal also have their reservations about the idea of communitarianism. Commenting on the consensus project in the context of the communalistic ethos, Dirk Louw (2001: 21) argues that the consensus ideal aims for a sameness that is oppressive. Michael Eze argues that the idea of the primacy of the community over the individual is incorrect. According to him, "To argue that the community pre-exists the individual is to argue that we can indeed have a community without a person for the community is *necessarily* constituted by persons. And to argue that an individual pre-exists the community is ontologically contradictory for a person is necessarily a social subjective" (Eze 2008: 109). Eze is also not comfortable with the consensus ideal. He argues that it "neither accommodates autonomy nor alterity", and "banishes any room for difference" (2008: 111). Eze argues that "the community can only develop and flourish through the ripples of different subjective autonomies", and this leads him to argue that consensus "obscures and does not promote our constitutive development" (Ibid).

Carlos Jacques also takes exception to the communitarian assumptions driving the argument for consensual democracy. He argues that Wiredu and the nationalists share some naïve dissatisfaction with political diversity and love for unity. For instance, Jacques cites Kenneth Kaunda (a nationalist) as arguing that institutionalized opposition is foreign to Africa (Kaunda 1975: 476; cited in Jacques 2011: 1026). Jacques also cites Sekou Toure as arguing that it is the obligation of a "national democracy" to surmount "the minor and irrational antagonisms, dividing every society" (Toure 1975: 493; cited in Jacques 2011: 1026). Indeed, for Jacques, these scholars and politicians are common in their assumption "that *unity* is distinctly African, whereas division is foreign, something brought with colonialism..." (Jacques 2011: 1026). Jacques recalls that Paulin Hountondji called it "the *unanimist illusion,* presupposing as it does that unanimity among Africans was both a fact before colonialism and a goal to be sought after independence" (2011: 1027). Responding, Helen Lauer argues that these critics did not consider that Wiredu wrote about "sharp disagreements that prevailed at all levels" and "various loci of disagreement and conflict...even within traditional councils" (Wiredu 1998: 246; cited in Lauer 2011: 177). She argues that Wiredu did not exaggerate the harmony that existed in traditional society (Ibid). The critics, however, appear to be concerned about the very idea of communitarianism, especially in contradistinction to individualism, rather than about the amount of conflict or disagreement that actually existed.

The Structure of the Party System

Wiredu's dissatisfaction with the multiparty system leads him to propose a non-party system based on consensus. But Jacques observes that Wiredu employs the same arguments as those despotic nationalist African leaders who argued for a unitary democracy based on consensus as a foundation for their one-party tyrannies. Jacques does not see any originality in Wiredu, and concludes that there is only "a very thin difference" (Jacques 2011: 1025) or a difference only in name (Jacques 2011: 1026) between Wiredu's arguments and those of these tyrants.

Responding to Jacques, Helen Lauer argues that Jacques' grouping of Wiredu with the despotic nationalists is unfair. To substantiate this, she cites Wiredu's own criticisms of the one-party systems, as well as Wiredu's disclaimer that his proposal should not be confused with the one-party proposals (Lauer 2011: 1032). She reassures us that Wiredu is aware of the danger of oligarchy in the one-party and multi-party systems (Lauer 2011: 33), and concludes that scholars ought to interpret other scholar's writings accurately before criticizing them (2011: 1034-1035). But Matolino writes that one party polities and consensual polities are both intolerant of opposition as they see it (opposition) as a distraction from the core duty of attaining consensus (Matolino 2013: 150). Wiredu had distinguished between three senses of parties. He writes that the first sense of party means all groups with some interest, the second means parties to any group decision, and the third means political parties (Wiredu 2001: 238). According to Wiredu, then, parties$_1$ are those with a particular interest, parties$_2$ are parties to a decision, and parties$_3$ are political parties. Wiredu says that the aim of a consensual democracy is to transform parties$_1$ (interests) and parties$_3$ (political parties) into parties$_2$ (parties to consensus decisions). But the party$_2$ project is what Matolino argues is intolerant of opposition.

Kibujjo Kalumba makes a similar observation when he argues that Wiredu did not consider the human rights implications of transforming political parties into political associations that jettison their aspirations to power and simply put heads together for the common good. Kalumba writes, "any laws enacted by the system to contain the political associations' aspirations to acquire political power are arguably infringements on their right to pursue self- chosen goals in a peaceful manner" (2015: 110). Kalumba argues that unless these decision-making bodies are nonrepresentational, they will still end up "being dominated by members of the largest ethnic groups" (Ibid). Kalumba also doubts if Wiredu's proposed non-party system could get "typical African decision making bodies any closer to consensus and its desired outcomes of peace and stability than its multiparty competitor" (Ibid). He then argues that Wiredu's proposed non-party system still begs the question of why the ethnic majority would want to bend over to cater for the interests of the minority instead of simply pursuing their goals. Kalumba also argues that Wiredu may have been "too quick to debunk the multiparty system as a framework for pursuing consensus", and reminds us that Wiredu had written that in Switzerland and Belgium, "there are constitutional arrangements that have pointed away enough from majoritarianism to attract the designation "consensual'" (Wiredu 2011: 1064; cited in Kalumba 2015: 112). And Switzerland and Belgium are multiparty democracies. We may expect more scholarly contributions regarding the structure of the party system.

The Consensus Potential of Different Issues

Wiredu is aware that it is more difficult to achieve consensus on normative beliefs. He therefore argues that we could focus more on agreeing on action without necessarily agreeing on beliefs or notions. Ani has cautioned the use of this instrument by showing that some seemingly action-related decisions are, in fact, value laden, and to decide on action implies also deciding on value. In such a situation, it may be better for us to entertain value differences than to relegate them to the background or underground, where they may continue to simmer and probably become dangerous (2014a). More recently, Ani has written an article in which he partitioned issues according to their various potentials for consensus. According to this taxonomy, deliberating on mathematical, empirical, logistical, and scientific issues easily lead to consensus because the consensus is more or less guaranteed through calculation (Ani 2019: 304-313). Ani categorized these kinds of issues as type one issues. But higher up the ladder are values, some of which lack empirical or logical handle, making consensus a bit more difficult and whimsical. Ani categorized all value-laden issues as type two issues. The easier-to-deliberate values are logistic values, values related to items in the empirical world. These include material interests, preferences regarding schedule and timing, differences in work ethic, and other kinds of action-related values. Since logistic values are related to the empirical world, disagreements involving them could be settled by appealing to evidence. They are thus a bit amenable to consensus. A bit higher up the difficult ladder are normative values. These are metaphysical beliefs, articles of faith, religious beliefs, beliefs about the general nature of man, certain political ideologies and worldviews (far left, moderate left, moderate right, far right and so on), ethnic allegiance, the desire to dominate, and so on. Concrete examples include views about God, abortion, gay marriage, the afterlife, and so on. It is difficult to achieve consensus on these issues because our relationship with these aspects of life is not always rational (Ani 2019: 310-312). Ani notes that most small groups achieve consensus routinely because they are united by interests or common values prior to deliberation, and deliberate mostly on type one issues regarding how to concretely achieve their common interests. By contrast, larger groups such as national parliaments may find routine consensus more difficult because they are less frequently united by a common interest, and often deliberate to pass laws on normative values. Ani concludes that any desire to bring the unanimity rule to national bodies such as parliaments must be the result of empirical investigation to find out the types of issues normally deliberated upon, and the frequency with which various issues are deliberated. According to him, such a study is needed "so we see what a parliament is really up against when operating with consensus as a general stopping rule" (Ani 2019: 319). In another essay, Ani argues that it is time for empirical researchers (Ani 2018b: 824) to step in and begin testing and concretizing the arguments made by theorists in the field.

Conclusion: Summing the Debate

The debate about fashioning a democracy of a consensual sort, which was kick-started by Wiredu and Eze, has so far lasted for two decades. This debate has progressed to a stage where the unanimity notion of consensus has generally fallen out of favour among scholars. This fall is obvious when Kibujjo Kalumba, a critical sympathizer of consensual democracy, argues that unanimity is "too high of a moral requirement" (Kalumba 2015: 106). The debate is thus beginning to see a transition from pursuing the unanimity notion to the idea that instruments of compromise could be built into the otherwise adversarial system of multi-party majoritarian democracy being practised by many African countries. Incidentally, Wiredu had also emphasized compromise as a cornerstone of consensus (Wiredu 2011: 1057). The hope is that such compromise instruments could encourage parties to agree on vital issues in spite of their party affiliation, to treat issues with the genuine concern they deserve, and to reduce the tendency to becloud issues needing grave attention with partisan politics. This currently appears to be the general challenge in the debate, and the hope is that scholars may emerge with proposals that take the African context into adequate consideration.

References

Ajei, M. O. 2016. Kwasi Wiredu's Consensual Democracy: Prospects for Practice in Africa. *European Journal of Political Theory* 15(4): 445-466.

Ani, E. I. 2014a. On Agreed Actions without Agreed Notions. *South African Journal of Philosophy* 33(3): 311-320.

Ani, E. I. 2014b. On Traditional African Consensual Rationality. *Journal of Political Philosophy* 22(3): 342-365.

Ani. E. I. 2018a. The Question of Rationality in Kwasi Wiredu's Consensual Democracy. In Edwin Etieyibo (ed.). *Method, Substance, and the Future of African Philosophy*. London: Palgrave Macmillan, pp. 251-274.

Ani, E. I. 2018b. Africa and Deliberative Politics. In Andre Bachtiger, John Dryzek, Jane Mansbridge, and Mark Warren (eds.). *The Oxford Handbook of Deliberative Democracy*. Oxford: Oxford University Press.

Ani, E. I. 2019. The Consensus Project and Three Levels of Deliberation. *Dialogue: Canadian Philosophical Review* 54: 299-322.

Eze, E. C. 2000. "Democracy or Consensus? Response to Wiredu." *Polylog*. Available at http://them.polylog.org/2/fee-en.htm.

Eze, M. 2008. What is African Communitarianism? Against Consensus as a Regulative Ideal. *South African Journal of Philosophy* 27(4): 106-119.

Gyekye, K. 2013. *Philosophy, Culture and Vision.* Legon-Accra: Sub-Saharan Publishers.

Hastie, R. et al., 1983, *Inside the Jury.* Cambridge, MA: Cambridge University Press.

Jacques, C. 2011. "Alterity in the Discourse of African Philosophy: A Forgotten Absence." In Lauer H. and Ayidoho K. (eds.). *Reclaiming the Human Sciences and Humanities through African Perspectives Vol II.* Legon-Accra: Sub-Saharan Publishers, pp. 1017-1030.

Kalumba, K. M. 2015 Consensus and Federalism in Contemporary African Political Philosophy. *Philosophical Papers* 44(1): 103-119.

Lauer, H. 2011. Negotiating Precolonial History and Future Democracy: Kwasi Wiredu and his Critics. In Helen Lauer (ed.). *Identity meets Nationality: Voices from the Humanities.* Legon-Accra: Sub-Saharan Publishers, 174-189.

Louw, D. J. 2001. 'Ubuntu and the Challenges of Multiculturalism in Post-Apartheid South Africa', *Quest* XV (1-2): 15-36.

Matolino, B. 2009. "A Response to Eze's Critique of Wiredu's Consensual Democracy." *South African Journal of Philosophy,* 28 (1): 34–42.

Matolino, B. 2013. "The Nature of Opposition in Kwasi Wiredu's Democracy by Consensus." *African Studies, 72* (1): 138-152.

Matolino, B. 2016. "Rationality and Consensus in Kwasi Wiredu's Traditional African Polities." *Theoria* 146: 36-55.

Ramose, M. B. 1999. *African Philosophy through Ubuntu.* Harare: Mond Books.

Stodtbeck, F. L. et al. 1957. "Social Status in Jury Deliberations" *American Sociology Review* 22: 713-19.

Teffo, J. 2004. Democracy, Kingship and Consensus: a South African Perspective. In Kwasi Wiredu (ed.). *A Companion to African Philosophy.* Maiden: Blackwell Publishing Ltd, pp. 443-449.

Wamala, E. 2004. Government by Consensus: An Analysis of a Traditional Form of Democracy. In Kwasi Wiredu (ed.), *A Companion to African Philosophy.* Maiden: Blackwell Publishing Ltd., p. 435-441.

Wiredu, K. 1996. *Cultural Universals and Particulars.* Bloomington and Indianapolis: Indiana University Press.

Wiredu, K. 2001. Democracy by Consensus: Some Conceptual Considerations. *Philosophical Papers* 30 (3): 227–244.

Wiredu, K. 2011. 'The State, Civil Society and Democracy in Africa' in Lauer H. and Ayidoho K. (eds.). *Reclaiming the Human Sciences Vol II.* Legon-Accra: Sub-Saharan Publishers, pp. 1055-1066.

Chapter 2

Consensus as Model for Re-conceptualizing African Epistemology

Husein Inusah

University of Cape Coast

Introduction

In this paper, I will attempt to show that our present conceptualisation of African epistemology rests on a mistake and the mistake is the lack of an apt abstraction of an African concept of knowledge upon which we can construct a comprehensive epistemological enterprise that is consistent with the core features of mainstream epistemology namely, how an epistemic subject stands in relation to a proposition, or the study of the doxastic attitudes of epistemic agents constructed upon the epistemic canons of truth and objectivity. Furthermore, I shall show that a primary criterion for any epistemology is that it should study propositional knowledge, a criterion that our present abstraction of African epistemology does not take into account. Finally, I shall recommend traditional African consensus as a model from which we can abstract an appropriate concept of African epistemology that is consistent with the idea that studies the relation an epistemic subject stands with a given proposition on the bases of the epistemic canons of truth and objectivity. So, I put forth two criteria for judging the appropriate format for such an epistemology.

1. It must study propositional knowledge.

2. It must study the doxastic decision making of epistemic agents (how a subject stands in relation to a proposition).

Note that I will not delve deep into the process of abstracting the concept of knowledge from traditional African consensual practice since such further illumination is beyond the scope of this paper. However, I shall endeavour to defend the proposal that traditional African consensual practice is knowledge-producing just like other forms of consensual practices, and further recommend it as a resource from which we can abstract an African concept of knowledge, and upon which we can subsequently construct an African epistemology.

Some Preliminary Remarks

In this essay, I will refrain from using the phraseology "Western epistemology" and instead use "mainstream epistemology" in its place. The strategy is intentional and a brief explanation will suffice to clarify this. Most African scholars are inclined to refer to mainstream epistemology as "Western epistemology",[1] a description that commits the fallacy of false dichotomy. This is a fallacy we commit when we create a dichotomy that does not exist to defend a conclusion. By this, we seem to have endorsed the view that there are only two alternative ways of doing epistemology; i.e., either you are committed to doing African epistemology or you are committed to doing Western epistemology, there is no middle ground. However, this dichotomy is completely false. What we call Western epistemology is not in any form Western. That is to say, it is not bound by demography or culture. It is not a version of cultural epistemology; it is universal in nature and transcends cultures. However, there are sub-fields of mainstream epistemological enterprise which focus on social epistemology. It is within this domain that African epistemology falls. It is possible to stumble on Chinese epistemology (see Jana Rosker 2014), Arabic epistemology (see Black 2006), Persian epistemology (see Peykani and Khalili 2014) and so on, all these constituting a special compartment of mainstream epistemology that we now call social epistemology. Furthermore, this assumption that traditional mainstream epistemology is western commits the genetic fallacy because it considers epistemology mainly based on its origin rather than its constitution. As noted, this is a palpable misconception arising from the failure to assess mainstream epistemological enterprise on its merit. The bulk of this essay relies on the assumption that African epistemology is not an alternative paradigm to mainstream epistemology and that the latter is not bounded by demography or culture.

The Concept of Human Knowledge

The concept of human knowledge may seem a nebulous concept. It could refer to knowledge of acquaintance- something like "knowledge of something". For

---

[1] See F. A. Airoboman and A. A. Asekhauno (2010); Amaechi Udefi (2014). These are few works that label traditional main stream epistemology as western epistemology.

instance, to say, "I know the devil's pool" is a type of knowledge of acquaintance. There is also knowledge of competence (knowledge-how) usually deployed to describe a subject's competence in a relevant field such as "He knows how to play football". Finally, there is propositional knowledge, usually dubbed "knowledge that". Propositional knowledge is knowledge that expresses a propositional attitude of a subject – the relation that the subject stands with a proposition. The entire epistemological enterprise as a sub-field of philosophy deals with this type of knowledge, and this buttresses the reason why mainstream epistemology is strictly defined to reflect the concept of propositional knowledge. Propositional knowledge is informative and so can be true or false. For example, when a subject asserts her belief that "Accra is the capital of Ghana", this proposition is informative and could be true or false.

It is this kind of knowledge that is primary to human cognition and vital to theoretical speculations. Propositional knowledge is useful in all scientific endeavours, deliberations and decision making as well as experimental and logical enquiries because in obtaining information one must be able to tell whether this information is true or false. This is the type of knowledge that is required of an adult human being, it is a type of knowledge that distinguishes us as adult cognizers from other creatures and things.

Propositional knowledge goes beyond just obtaining and possessing any information. It involves separating credible information from false or dubious ones. It is about being justified or having reasons to believe only true information and avoiding false beliefs as much as possible. It is a kind of knowledge built on our capacity to distinguish truth from falsity. This is the kind of knowledge that is significantly required for every strand of epistemology. It is the kind of knowledge that underlines all our scientific accomplishment and our practical successes in life, concerning the worthy decisions we make in practice. Unfortunately, many of the works that come under the label "African Epistemology" fail to consider this criterion for knowledge. In what follows, I shall examine some of these labels that come under the guise of African epistemology to unravel why they cannot be regarded as epistemology.

Some Models of African Epistemology

Three major theoretical styles come under the guise of African epistemology. First, some theoretical styles consist of a group of literature that focuses primarily on a systematic reflection of African experiences embedded in oral tradition, handed down by our ancestors. These oral traditions include bedtime stories, folklores, proverbs and the wise sayings of sages. The second attempt at an African epistemology consists of a group of literature that studies the epistemic values of African ontology and specific belief systems as constituting a brand of African epistemology. The third theoretical style consists of using the African system of divination as a model for studying African epistemology. I shall discuss these styles in the remainder of this section in order to show why they cannot be said to be a kind of epistemology consistent with the tenets of mainstream epistemology. I have left out some works that also come under the tag "African Epistemology" such as the works that appear to do analysis of the components of the contemporary conception of knowledge (see Wiredu 1985 and Bedu-Addo 1985). Though these works might be considered aspects of African epistemology, I prefer to omit them because the strategy proponents of these works adopt is a bit closer to the sentiments I share in this chapter. The reason is that these works focus on doing analyses of knowledge – analysis of the necessary conditions of knowledge as seen in mainstream epistemology. The seeming difficulty with this strategy is that it rides on the assumption that there is already a conception of knowledge within the African thought system that needs to be analyzed. This is quite erroneous on the grounds that such a concept of knowledge does not exist. Another difficulty is that even if a certain abstraction of the concept of knowledge is feasible, it may not feature the same necessary and sufficient conditions found in the tripartite definition of knowledge traditionally accepted in mainstream epistemology. However, there is something fascinating about this strategy. It draws so much on the contemporary concept of knowledge that occupies a central position in contemporary epistemology. That is to say, these works are not positioned as an alternative epistemological paradigm against traditional mainstream epistemology.

I will start with the group of literature that uses oral literature as a basis for studying African epistemology. Oral tradition is considered as one of the most essential mechanisms for knowledge acquisition and transmission in African thought systems. It refers to the past events that are passed down from one generation to the other by word of mouth. It may include myths, legends, folklore, songs, customs and traditions, rites, names of places, arts, sacred places, titles, crafts, proverbs and symbols, amongst others. Oral traditional is said to constitute the core of African epistemology because the bulk of our knowledge claims are extracted from a variety of oral tradition. For instance, Uduigwomen remarks…

"…there is no way one can explain African epistemology without a reference to the tradition that is orally expressed. What makes a man acceptable in any given African society is the ability to recount those principles of the society's tradition. It can, therefore, be safely concluded that oral tradition constitutes for Africans a vital source and carrier of knowledge" (Uduigwomen 1995: 77).

The lesson emerging from the remark above is that oral tradition is a kind of epistemology because it is a source of knowledge acquisition and the channel by which information is transmitted from an older generation to the younger generation. However, one must note that not all versions of oral tradition have epistemic value. Even if we were to grant that oral traditions could pass for knowledge, not every event that is handed down to us by our ancestors possesses epistemic value. It is instructive to note that some bedtime stories amongst the Akans, for example, are designed to depict the protagonist, Anansi, as cunning and self-serving to the extent that when he helps other creatures, he does that only to suit his own purpose. And no matter the extent of his cunning strategies and wicked deeds, Anansi always triumphs at the end of the day. On the contrary, our elementary critical thinking lessons have prompted us to be circumspect about the kind of intellectual traits that are worth developing. For instance, traits like egoism, arrogance, deceit, and so on are not virtuous and therefore cannot be said to have epistemic value. So, not all oral traditions have epistemic significance.

A further problem with this way of construing African epistemology is that it conflates the transmission of a body of knowledge handed down to successive generations by word of mouth with the study of the doxastic attitude of the believers of this oral tradition. That is to say, a study of oral tradition as a body of knowledge itself cannot be construed as epistemology unless it is studied in tandem with an agent who asserts a belief in a form of a proposition that results from this oral tradition. In short, it is the study of the doxastic attitude of epistemic agents towards how they form beliefs that are justified by oral tradition within the acceptable parameters of objectivity and truth. Otherwise, just oral tradition alone without a recourse to the conditions under which it leads to justified belief and knowledge will place oral tradition outside the domain of what is standardly construed as epistemology. Thus, there is no denying the point that oral traditions could feature in epistemological consideration in the conceptualisation of African epistemology. However, the fact of the matter goes beyond the mere identification of the fact that "oral tradition constitutes for Africans a vital source and carrier of knowledge" as Uduigwomen will want to suggest. The nuances involved here must be duly clarified in order that we can identify the distinctive role oral tradition plays in epistemology because there are other fields of study that have significant interest in oral tradition. Traditional jurisprudence, history and literature, for example, have significant interest in oral tradition, but they do not focus on the epistemological character and the epistemic implication of oral tradition on the epistemic agent.

The second theoretical approach to African epistemology studies African beliefs systems and ontology as constituting African epistemology. Interestingly, most of the works subsumed under this approach are rarely labelled African epistemology by their authors. It is later scholars that have interpreted these works as falling within the domain of African epistemology and have proceeded to label them as such.[2] Scholars leaning towards this strategy frequently construe African epistemology as an understanding of reality within the African thought systems. This is frequently said to consist of how the African interprets, understands and conceptualises reality within the purview of the African thought systems (Anyanwu 1983: 60). Some earlier works in African philosophy are construed to fall within this domain. For instance, Amaechi Udefi has argued that some earlier scholarly works such as Placide Tempels, *Bantu Philosophy* (1959); E. Bolaji Idowu, *Olodumare: God in Yoruba Belief* (1962); William E. Abraham, *The Mind of Africa* (1966); J. B. Danquah, *The Akan Doctrine of God* (968); John S. Mbiti, *African Religions and Philosophy* (1969) and many others are African epistemologies (Udefi 2014: 108). These works, according to Udefi, focus on the assumption that African epistemology is consequent on African ontology and therefore logically implies that to undertake any project in African epistemology, it is key to understanding African ontology and cultural conceptions of reality. He opines that the "early discourse of African epistemology attempted to link the African mode of knowledge with ontology" while intimating that both cannot be comprehensively understood or studied without the other.

Contrary to this assumption, it needs to be pointed out that works declaring the affinity between ontology and epistemology cannot necessarily be construed as African epistemology merely on the account that the latter is consequent on the former. When a work illuminates the relationship between ontology and epistemology, it is just declaring the obvious – that we cannot construct epistemology without ontology. For any work to qualify as epistemology, it must preoccupy itself among other things with the study of the questions about how reality is constructed so as we can know it as cognitive agents, or how we are constituted such that reality can manifest itself to us. Furthermore, it should describe in-depth the relationship between the epistemic subject and his belief states. It should study the doxastic decision making of epistemic agents ranging from how they form beliefs; how they justify their beliefs or how their beliefs are justified for them, and so on.

Udefi noted further that the rationale for these scholars' position about the affinity between ontology and epistemology was to "ultimately establish that Africans had an idea of God even before Europeans came to Africa", to refute the long-held belief that Africans do not have any conception of God before

---

[2] See Jimoh and Thomas (2015); Udefi (2014); Airoboman and Asekhauno (2010).

the coming of Europeans (Udefi 2014: 108). As I noted earlier, this does not, in any way, study how we justify beliefs or how our beliefs get justified for us. It does not even show how the *belief* that Africans know God before the advent of Europeans is validated. More specifically, it does not demonstrate how our belief that we know God before the advent of the Europeans in Africa gets justified on the basis of our ontology. These considerations account for the reasons why this brand of epistemology cannot be construed as epistemology.

One other problem that emerges from this theoretical approach to doing African epistemology is that it takes the way the African interprets, understands or conceptualizes reality as a form of epistemology. Again, this conception presupposes that any form of interpretation has a positive epistemic value. In contrast, interpretation without epistemic normative ideals (reliability of the source of the belief, the act of epistemic dependence and the epistemic trust of the source of the belief and so on) that guide the way we form beliefs of our ontology from this interpretation is highly likely to result in forming dubious beliefs about our ontology. There should be some epistemic constraints that ought to guide our epistemic practices. That is to say, we should subscribe to the idea of epistemic responsibility, doing epistemic due diligence before giving any belief a credibility taking cognizance of the fact that human beings are disposed to biases, egocentric tendencies and prejudices when dealing with beliefs. Otherwise, any doxastic attitude towards our ontology might be dubious. Any type of epistemology should be able to formulate objective and empirically accessible criteria such as those indicated above for epistemic evaluation of human doxastic states. So a mere abstraction of knowledge from one's ontology does not necessarily pass for knowledge.

Furthermore, this approach to conceptualizing African epistemology endorses the view that knowledge is embedded in African ontology. That is to say; it regards ontology as knowledge in itself. However, this is a mistaken assumption. The human being is the source of human knowledge. Ontological entities are not necessarily humans and cannot possess knowledge. To say that one knows is to say that one has a propositional attitude towards certain ontology or an environment of which s/he abstracts. Such knowledge is rooted in and abstracted from the person's ontology, but this abstraction is usually conveyed to the mind via either or a combination of the following: perception, introspection, memory, intuition, testimony, and so on. So, ontology has something to do with knowledge but ontology is not knowledge.

The third approach to doing African epistemology usually draws on the African system of divination as constituting a distinct kind of African epistemology. According to Mutombo Nkulu-N'Sengha, "divination stands at the core of African epistemology as a valid cognitive mode. It exemplifies well the way African epistemology integrates scientific and religious knowledge, natural cognitive faculties and supernatural powers" (Nkulu-N'Sengha 2014: 41). The detail of this approach is esoteric, but I shall endeavour to offer a brief explanation by using the Yoruba concept of divination as a case model. The Yoruba notion of divination, *Ifá*, according to Olufemi Táíwò, consists of three agents: the god, *Ifá*, who is regarded as repository of wisdom and knowledge (Táíwò 2004, p. 305); the supplicant, the individual who seeks to consult *Ifá* on some problems (Táíwò 2004, p. 306); and the Babalawo, the priest, who interposes between *Ifá* and the supplicant because *Ifá* does not speak directly to the supplicant (Táíwò 2004: 306).

The process of divination involves the following sequence, according to descriptions Táíwò borrowed from Wande Abimbola's understanding of the process of *Ifá*.

> When the client [supplicant] enters the house of the *Ifá* priest [*babaláwo*], he salutes him and expresses a wish to "talk with the divinity." The *Ifá* priest then takes out his divining chain and lays it on a mat or a raffia tray in front of the client. The client whispers his problem to a coin or a cowry shell and drops it on the *Ifá* instruments. Alternatively, the client could pick up the divining chain or the *ìbò* and whisper his problem to it directly. In either case, it is believed that the wishes of the client's *orí* (God of predestination who knows what is good for every person) have been communicated to *Ifá* who will then produce the appropriate answer through the first *Odù* which the *Ifá* priest will cast when he manipulates his divining chain (2004: 307).

This process has several epistemological implications. One of them is that knowledge does not depend on empirical inference alone (here I refer to the empirical inference drawn from the reading of the cowries from the priest), a considerable chunk of the knowledge generated in the process of divination "rest on the cognitive resources of the omniscient entity, namely *Ifá*" (Ibid, 10). Another crucial epistemological concern is that the justification and clarification of this knowledge obtained from *Ifá* is grounded on the "unsurpassed knowledge" attributed to *Ifá* (Ibid).

As seen from the above, the process of divination is a sophisticated practice and quite esoteric but may be useful in several ways with regard to ways of knowing. It may allow us to know things that are not humanely available to us since it may generate knowledge that emerges from a transcendent or an omniscient Being. Despite these feats, the practice of divination as a form of epistemology has inherent features that distance it from the core tenants of mainstream epistemology. One of such setbacks is that, at the empirical level, it deals with a personal interpretation of the priest in connection with what is communicated to him/her by *Ifá*. This information is inaccessible to others or not open to others for critical evaluation. The second setback is a consequence of the first – once this form of knowledge is initially only privately known to the priest, it may become quite vulnerable to personal misconceptions and distortions.

One of the core attributes of mainstream epistemology is that it deals with empirical facts. Matters involving justification and truth are frequently discussed within the purview of physically accessible facts – facts that can be evaluated by others outside the views of the epistemic subject. Mainstream epistemology grounds knowledge on publicly accessible facts.

Another way the practice of divination parts ways with mainstream epistemology is that with the former, knowledge is seen to emanate from a transcendental/divine/omniscient entity. On the contrary, mainstream epistemology studies, among other things, human knowledge. It focuses on the nature, the scope and limitations of human knowledge. Given that divination as a form of epistemology does not study human knowledge, it cannot qualify as a form of mainstream epistemology.

Now we appear to have a rough sense of the various conceptual models that fall under the guise of African epistemology and why they fail to conform to the core tenets of mainstream epistemology. What I have done is to argue that such conceptual models fall short of being construed as African epistemology that is consistent with mainstream epistemology. This notwithstanding, there is a major setback that plagues all these conceptual models of African epistemology, namely that they presuppose the existence of the concept of knowledge within the African thought system. However, such a concept seems non-existent so far as I know because if we are to ask the question: *how can we define knowledge from the African perspective*, an appropriate answer will elude us. It is inappropriate to begin to conceptualize African epistemology without a well-defined conception of an African concept of knowledge. Such a mistake may seem a clear breach of the conventional order of things. We cannot begin to develop and study a comprehensive account of African epistemology if we have not yet developed a comprehensive account of an African concept of knowledge.

Thus far, I have stated that the various works that come under the tag African epistemology face, among other things, two major setbacks. I have argued that this group of works departs from the core tenets of mainstream epistemology because (1) each of these works takes for granted the conception of knowledge within the African thought system and (2) they do not make it as a matter of central focus, the study of *how we know*. I shall, in the following pages, argue that what we label as African epistemology is a cultural or social epistemology and should not be construed as an alternative epistemological paradigm to mainstream epistemology.

African Epistemology as Social Epistemology

Before the 2000s, mainstream epistemology was occupied with the study of human knowledge and justified belief that was profoundly individualistic. It focused on evaluating people's beliefs, disbeliefs and judgment suspensions without consideration of their social environment. This, of course, as noted by Alvin Goldman and Thomas Blanchard, led to a one-sided and inaccurate picture of human knowledge that is usually shaped by the environment and social situations (Goldman and Blanchard 2015).

Social epistemology was promoted to check this imbalance by studying the epistemic implications of social and cultural systems on the epistemic agents(s). Social epistemology started to gain currency around the 2000s when Alvin Goldman published his seminal book, "*Knowledge in a social world*" (1999). Since then, social epistemology has become a vast field of study under mainstream epistemology. According to Goldman (2010: 1), social epistemology is a branch of mainstream epistemology that studies the epistemic properties of individuals that arise from their relations to others, as well as *the epistemic properties of groups or social systems* (my emphasis). Goldman (2010) identifies three major sub-aspects of social epistemology in order to show why social epistemology is related to mainstream epistemology.

These conceptions of social epistemology, according to Goldman, include the revisionist, preservationist and expansionist approaches. Revisionist social epistemologists reject some of the core aspects of mainstream epistemology, such as the objectivity of truth and rationality. Goldman argues that this position denies revisionism a slot under mainstream epistemology (Goldman 1999: 2). Preservationist social epistemologists stay glued to the core tenants of mainstream epistemology. This is because they study the decision-making strategies of individual epistemic agents in the light of social evidence. The expansionist social epistemologists widen their coverage of social epistemology while heading the same path as mainstream epistemology. The expansionist social epistemological projects cover topics such as the study of the epistemic properties of collective doxastic agents and the influence of alternative social systems on epistemic outcomes.

The lesson drawn from the above illustration is that mainstream epistemology has now assumed an expansionist and preservationist epistemological project that spans across social and demographic space. It has currently distanced itself from the individualistic epistemology of the past. However, this widespread approach seems not apparent to most proponents of African epistemology who appear to reject mainstream epistemology as Western because of its individualistic focus and its western origin.

This widespread approach of social epistemology has significant implications on the conceptualisation of African epistemology. It is evident from the texture of the literature reviewed above that what we call African epistemology is a cultural epistemology because it deals with ways of understanding reality and what constitutes knowledge based on this reality within a specific cultural milieu. According to Molefi Kente Asante, the African perceives reality in several ways. He notes that the African makes cognitive claims based on inclusiveness, collectivism and the value of personal relationship (Asante 2000: 126). This may buttress the idea that cultural and environmental factors have greater import on cognitive claim about reality, and further buttresses the argument that African epistemology is a cultural epistemology.

Note that if we grant that African epistemology is a cultural epistemology, then it is inherently social. This further implies that African epistemology is a variant of social epistemology because it focuses on the cognitive framework of a group of people to define what constitutes knowledge and justified belief, and what constitutes doxastic decision making within the parameters of the African system of rationality. Considering the point this way makes it quite imperative to begin to conceptualize African epistemology from a different theoretical tangent rather than the collection of literature we have branded so far as epistemology. It is expedient that we begin to study the doxastic attitude of Africans across the various prominent linguistic groups to abstract the concept of knowledge and justified belief so that our discussions can fall within the theoretical parameters of mainstream epistemology. Furthermore, this approach of conceptualizing African epistemology will place the theory in the right perspective consistent with the other core features of mainstream epistemology.

Consensus as a Model for Abstracting African Epistemology

In other to fashion an African epistemology that will be consistent with mainstream epistemological paradigms, Kwasi Wiredu's conception of consensual democracy quickly comes to mind. Note that one of the consequences of construing knowledge as social falls within the remit of social and political studies. Hence, our safest starting point for this new approach will be to begin to study our social and political theory of collective decision making of what Kwasi Wiredu has called traditional African "Consensual Democracy". Wiredu considers traditional African consensual democracy as an alternative social-political paradigm to the Western-style majoritarian democracies. For Wiredu, consensual democracy is rooted in the social and political style of governance of the traditional African past (Wiredu 2010: 1059-60).

Using the social and political style of governance of the Ashanti, Wiredu notes that evidence abounds on African decision making as being characterized by deliberation with an eye on consensus. On account of this, Wiredu opines that the traditional African model of consensus was widespread across traditional African demography. Wiredu argues that traditional African model of consensus resonates with the core values of the African communal way of life, stressing that it is designed to ensure that deliberations and decisions bind the interest of individuals in the community (Wiredu 2010: 1056-8). Citing Kofi Busia's account of the political and social life of the Ashanti, Wiredu notes that consensus had its foundation in the kingship system. To Wiredu, the traditional African model of consensus is participatory, inclusive and collective (Wiredu 1996: 185-6).

Wiredu's proposal of consensual democracy constitutes an important resource from which we can construct an African epistemology consistent with the core cannons of mainstream epistemology. It offers the resource to study African epistemology as cultural epistemology within the larger purview of social epistemology, which I have shown is a legitimate sub-field of mainstream epistemology. This brand of African epistemology explores the effects of sound interactions for knowledge and justified belief among a group of people. This will fit pretty well into the expansionist approach of social epistemology, which ventures further into the epistemic properties of group doxastic decision making and the influence of social systems and policies on the epistemic output while departing from the individualistic conception of mainstream epistemology.

As noted, we can deploy Wiredu's model of consensual democracy as a resource for abstracting an African epistemology consistent with mainstream epistemology though Wiredu's discussions on deliberation and consensus focus largely on democratic authority with the aim of showing how deliberation can foster legitimate political decision (Wiredu 2010: 1057-8). Contrary to the political reading of Wiredu, this approach will focus on the epistemic features of traditional African model of deliberation with an eye on consensus, while pitching the entire discourse within the larger purview of mainstream epistemology. So, there is a rich epistemological resource that we can unpack from studying our traditional models of deliberation that have an eye on consensus.

To this end, we may have to interrogate how deliberation in an African consensual democracy is supposed to produce knowledge, and this will involve unpacking the normative and rational ideals of consensual democracy by examining its normative ideals, such as inclusiveness, pluralism and collectivisms, which are supposed to yield epistemic outcomes. With this, we can also examine how true beliefs are isolated from false beliefs taking cognizance of the view that when collective ideas are brought together under the spirit of inclusiveness and pluralism, true and false beliefs may be muddled together. Therefore, one may argue that collectivity and inclusiveness of consensually driven deliberation may not yield any epistemic outcome especially in situations where there is a tacit pressure from the majority to epistemically oppress the minority to follow their line of reasoning or where the parties involved in the deliberation have specific egoistic interest (see Ani 2014: 354).

However, this may not be entirely correct. There are cases where consensual driven deliberation produces justified belief and knowledge, that is, when the parties in the deliberation observe and commit to the objective norms of deliberation without recourse to extraneous factors that may impede the epistemic outcome of the deliberation. Thus, a critical look at the epistemic dimensions of African consensual democracy will enable us to sieve true beliefs from dubious beliefs and offer the model of how group verdict justifies beliefs within cases where consensus-driven deliberation yields justified beliefs. This approach will offer us the means to begin to conceptualize knowledge and justified belief upon which we can conveniently construct an African epistemology as a variant of social epistemology that is consistent with mainstream epistemology.

Furthermore, because deliberation with an eye on consensus involves agents producing decisions or conclusions that become beliefs, it may be argued that deliberation is knowledge-producing. During deliberation, the discussants share ideas with others, they verify their already deeply held conviction about the issues under discussion while they expand and strengthen their understanding of the issue in play. In so doing, the final product that emerges as a result of the deliberation, indeed becomes more refined. This belief becomes more refined because it encapsulates all the relevant points put forward by the discussant and eschew the irrelevant ones.

Another important reason why consensual driven deliberation is useful for the conceptualization of African epistemology is that it addresses the social and cognitive underpinnings of evaluation strategies usually deployed in deliberation. It indicates an objective process we rely upon to produce knowledge and justified belief. Deliberation makes it quite expedient to develop these epistemic evaluation mechanisms that are grounded on one's ontology which usually become the ideal epistemic norms that guide argumentation and doxastic decision making. This makes it possible to examine the mental process and the cognitive capacities of agents at work in the production of beliefs that results from deliberation.

Another reason why deliberation and consensual practice will provide the framework to abstract an African epistemology is that it offers the opportunity to justify our beliefs since some of the beliefs obtained as a result of consensus may be justifiable. Here, the question "what justifies our acceptance of consensual verdict" may be posed and agents will have to rely on the epistemic evaluation strategies endorsed by the group to put this putative belief to test. This can only be provided by agents in a consensual driven deliberation. More so, consensual driven deliberation is the only belief-producing social phenomenon that can be studied *together* with the social phenomenon that produces the belief, instead of simply studying a belief that has already been produced in the past without knowing *how* the belief was generated or how that belief can be justified. Thus, it is within a consensual practice that oral tradition such as folklores, proverbs and sage ideas can be studied, understood and justified so that beliefs justified based on that can become epistemically credible. Finally, the beliefs (decisions and conclusions) produced in consensus-ended discussions are not esoteric, unlike the products of divination.

How the crux of the project is to be cashed out is beyond the scope of this paper. However, it is my fervent wish that this direction may provide a fresh model of an investigation into what actually constitutes African epistemology with the hope of directing our intellectual path towards an appropriate conceptualisation of African epistemology.

Conclusion

African epistemology is one of the core sub-fields of African philosophy that appears theoretically inadequate because it generates so many questions that require answers. Many kinds of literature that come under the guise of African epistemology frequently lack the resources to abstract the concept of knowledge within the African perspective. I have argued that these assumptions resonate with ideas that are not in conformity with the core tenets of mainstream epistemology and therefore need to be rejected as forms of epistemology. My alternative is the suggestion that we can begin to construct an African epistemology from traditional African consensual democracy. This approach will help carve out a distinctive epistemology that is cultural in outlook and will conform to social epistemology, which has now become an integral sub-field of mainstream epistemology.

References

Abraham, W. E. 1962. *The Mind of Africa*. Chicago: University of Chicago Press.
Airoboman, F. A. and A. A. Asekhauno. 2010. Is there an African Epistemology? *JORIND* 10(3): 13-17.

Ani, E. I. 2014. On Traditional African Consensual Rationality. *The Journal of Political Philosophy* 2(33): 342-365.

Anyanwu, K. C. 1983. *The African Experience in the American Market Place: a Scaring Indictment of Western Scholars and their distortion of African Culture*. New York: Exposition Press.

Asante, M. K. 2000. *The Egyptian Philosophers: Ancient Voices from Imhotep to Akhenatem*. Chicago, Illinois: African American Images.

Bedu-Addo, J. T. 1985. On the Concept of Truth in Akan. In P. O. Bodunrin (ed.) *Philosophy in Africa, Trends and Perfectives*. Ile-Ife: University of Ife Press, 68-90.

Black, D. 2006. Knowledge (*'ilm*) and certitude (*yaqīn*) in al-Fārābī's epistemology. *Arabic Sciences and Philosophy* 16: 11–45.

Danquah, J. B. 1944. *The Akan Doctrine of God: A Fragment of Gold Coast Ethics and Religion*. London: Cass.

Goldman, A. I. 1999. *Knowledge in a Social World*. Oxford: Oxford University Press.

Goldman, A. and T. Blanchard. 2015. Social epistemology. *Stanford Encyclopedia of Philosophy*. Retrieved from https://plato.standford.edu/entries/epistemology-social. Accessed on the August 21, 2019.

Goldman, A. I. 2010. Introduction. In A. Haddock, A. Millar and D. Pritchard (eds.) *Social Epistemology*. Oxford: Oxford University Press, 1-28.

Idowu, B. E. 1962. *Olodumare: God in Yoruba belief*. London: Longmans.

Jimoh, A and J. Thomas. 2015. An African Epistemological Approach to Epistemic Certitude and Scepticism. *Research in Humanities and Social Sciences* 5(11): 54-61

Mbiti, J. S. 1969. African Religions and Philosophies. New York: Heinemann.

Nkulu-N'Sengha, M. 2014. African Epistemology. In M. K. Asante and A. Mazama (eds.) *Encyclopedia for Black Studies*. California: Sage Publication, 39-44.

Peykani, J. and M. Khalili. 2014. The Role of Testimonies in Iranian Folk Epistemology. *Journal of Asian Pacific Studies* 33:122-131.

Rosker, J. 2014. Epistemology in Chinese Philosophy. *Stanford Encyclopedia of Philosophy*. Retrieved from https://plato.stanford.edu/entries/chinese-epistemology/. Accessed on 26th of August, 2019.

Táíwò, O. 2004. An Account of a Divination System and Some Concluding Epistemological Questions. In Kwesi Wiredu (ed.) *A Companion to African Philosophy*. Malden: Blackwell Publishing Company, 304-313.

Tempels, P. 1959. *Bantu Philosophy*. Paris: Presence Africaine

Udefi A. 2014. The Rationale for an African Epistemology: A Critical Examination of the Igbo views on Knowledge, Belief, and Justification. *Canadian Social Science* 10(3): 108-117.

Uduigwomen, A. F. 1995. The Place of Oral Tradition in African Epistemology. In Uduigwomen A. F (ed.) *Footmarks on African Philosophy*. Lagos: Obaron & Ogbinaka Publisher, 68-77.

Wiredu, K. 1985. The Concept of Truth in the Akan Language. In P. O. Bodunrin (ed.) *Philosophy in Africa, Trends and Perspectives*. Ile-Ife Nigeria: University of Ife Press, 43-54.

Wiredu, K. 1996. *Cultural Universals and Particulars*. Bloomington: Indiana University Press.

Wiredu, K. 2011. State, Civil Society and Democracy in Africa. In H. Lauer and K. Ayidoho (eds.) *Reclaiming the Human Sciences*. Volume 2. Legon-Accra: Sub-Saharan Publishers, 1055-1066.

Chapter 3

Deliberative Theory of Truth: An Epistemological Approach to Kwasi Wiredu's Theory of Democracy and Consensus

Martin F. Asiegbu

University of Nigeria

Victor C. Nweke

University of Koblenz-Landau

Introduction

Kwasi Wiredu is no doubt a prolific African philosopher with imprints that have generated debates in different subject areas of African philosophy such as philosophy of mind, epistemology, ethics, political philosophy and the history of African philosophy. Of all his salient theories, the most engaged in the twenty-first century is his proposal for consensus as a social and political philosophy (Eze 1997: 313-323; Matolino 2013: 132-152; Ani 2014: 342-365). His views on ethics have also attracted serious interest in the twenty-first century. The rate of interest in Wiredu's proposals in ethics and political philosophy today differs from what attracted the interest of his contemporaries in the twentieth century. Besides the prolonged general debate on the nature of African philosophy, Wiredu and some of his contemporaries, especially Odera Oruka (1997), engaged in an interesting debate on the nature of truth (cf. Oruka 1997: 3-54). We contend that there is a link between Wiredu's conception of truth and his understanding of the nature of African philosophy as an academic discipline. A close reading of his book, *Philosophy and an African Culture,* suggests that Wiredu's conception of the nature of academic philosophy itself has a bias for epistemology and logic.

His distinction between traditional and modern African philosophy, as well as his hope that 'a hundred flowers will bloom' in African philosophy (Wiredu 1980: xiv) could be arguably best understood when approached from the perspective of his conception of truth. Our primary interest in this essay is to explicate the relationship between Wiredu's idea of consensus and his conception of truth. The interest in Wiredu's consensual democracy has suddenly shot up to the forefront of African philosophical discourse, but the subtle thread linking the various facets of his philosophy is often neglected. By pointing this out, we hope to open another area of discussion in Wiredu's philosophy; this new area belongs to another significant area of interest in African philosophy, which is epistemology.

Generally, political philosophy belongs to ethics, while truth belongs to epistemology. Ethics and epistemology are respectively broadly classified as aspects of practical and theoretical philosophy. The strict acceptance of these classifications will immediately reject any possible link between truth and democracy (or consensus). Yet, in *Philosophy and an African Culture*, Wiredu sees truth as a concept that has both theoretical and practical dimensions (1980: xii). His comments on this statement show how his understanding of truth underlines his views on political philosophy in the same book. Our hunch is that Wiredu's idea of truth has a strong influence on his theory of consensus, an influence that has not been explored in extant texts in the field. We argue that, reading Wiredu's theory of "democracy by consensus" (Wiredu 1995a: 53-63; 1996:182-190; 1997: 303-312; 2001: 227-244) in relation to his epistemological position, leads likely to a more profound understanding, interpretation and appropriation of his contributions in diverse areas of African philosophy, especially political philosophy.

The essay is divided into three major parts. The first deals with an analysis of Wiredu's idea of truth. The focus of this section is to explicate Wiredu's perspective through an analysis of primary and secondary kinds of literature, and then, show how his position on truth amounts to a sort of deliberative epistemology. The second part focuses on Wiredu's theory of consensual democracy. Again, we shall rely on both primary and secondary texts to unveil Wiredu's basic propositions and outline some of the critical responses they have generated. Finally, the last part contains our exposition of the relationship between Wiredu's idea of truth and his theory of consensual democracy. We shall portray how Wiredu moves from a deliberative theory of truth in epistemology to a deliberative theory of democracy in political philosophy.

Determining the Meaning and Nature of Truth

The most explicit rendition of Kwasi Wiredu's understanding of truth is perhaps contained in his article 'Truth as Opinion' – originally published in

1972. It was reprinted as chapter eight of his Philosophy and an African Culture. The content of the chapter reflects its seemingly paradoxical title, 'Truth as Opinion' (1980: 111-123). The basic thesis of Wiredu is that "there is nothing called Truth as distinct from opinion" (Ibid 111). In other words, truth is opinion. He repeatedly avers that "to be true is to be opined." Wiredu succinctly expresses his view of truth in several concise statements that tend to contradict established positions. Another typical statement in this regard is this: "truth is nothing but belief or opinion" (1980:189, 125f). This suggests that for Wiredu opinion and belief are synonymous with truth. The contention here is between opinion or belief and truth. It is not between belief and opinion. Whatever Wiredu says about opinion and truth also applies to belief and truth. The striking issue with Wiredu's idea of truth as opinion is that it goes contrary to an influential understanding of truth in the history of philosophy; that is also supported by what Wiredu describes the objectivist theory of truth(Wiredu 1980: 114).

According to Wiredu, the objectivist theory of truth sees truth as logically distinct from opinion or belief. The decisive import of this view is that truth and opinion are logical contraries. Basic features of truth are always contrary to the features of opinion. The objectivist theory posits that truth is eternal, that is, a true proposition is consistently infallible irrespective of time. Truth is independent of historical circumstances (Ibid). The idea of a true proposition as infallible inadvertently excludes fallible propositions from the domain of truth. The objectivist theory of truth sees probable and fallible propositions as opinions. What accounts for this view is the conception of truth as a representation of reality (what is the case) – where reality is understood as static. If truth is a representation of reality, and reality is static, then truth must be static. Richard Rorty (1979) buttresses the prominence of this mode of thinking in the history of Western philosophy from the time of Plato to the contemporary era. Plato expressed it in *Theaetetus*. At the base of both the correspondence and coherence theories of truth is the objectivist thesis that truth is infallible. The realist conception of truth canvassed by William Alston (1996) follows an objectivist bias for an accurate representation of what is the case which is inherent in Plato. By understanding truth as opinion, Wiredu negates the objectivist distinction by showing how every claim to truth can be considered as opinion advanced from a specific point of view (Wiredu 1980:115). Wiredu's negation of the objectivist distinction between truth and opinion attracted criticisms from some of his contemporaries (Omoregbe 1985: 11-13; Blocker 1985: 55-67; Oruka 1997: 3-25). To grasp Wiredu's theory of truth, and the criticisms levelled against it, it is important to ascertain what Wiredu means by opinion. When Wiredu makes the claim that "truth is opinion," or "to be is to be opined," what really does "opinion" stand for in his view? Does Wiredu and his critics ascribe the same attributes to the term, "opinion"? Joseph Omoregbe reads Wiredu's rejection of the objectivist distinction to mean that Wiredu advances a subjectivist theory of truth. For Omoregbe, "Truth is always objective whereas opinion is always subjective. Opinion is always the opinion of somebody, a subjective view of something, but truth cannot be said to be the truth of somebody" (1985: 12). Following his understanding of opinion as always subjective and necessarily opposed to truth, which is always objective, Omoregbe submits that "Wiredu tries to dismiss the distinction between subjectivity and objectivity or to reduce objectivity to subjectivity so that objectivity will disappear" (1985: 12). This conclusion stems from a difference between Omoregbe and Wiredu on the meaning of the term opinion.

Wiredu distinguishes between a weaker sense and a stronger sense of the term. Opinion in a weaker sense refers to uncertainties, imprecisions and mere assumptions that are unreliable. Understood in this sense, opinion smacks of hearsay or rumour. The stronger sense of opinion connotes a logically consistent proposition. A logically consistent proposition is always firm and certain. It is intuitively different from hearsay and rumour (Wiredu 1980: 114-116, 174-175). Omoregbe's idea of opinion falls within a weaker sense of the term. And Wiredu admits that it will "be too patently false" to suggest that truth is opinion in this weaker sense of the term (Wiredu 1985a: 96-97). By truth as opinion, Wiredu means the stronger sense of opinion (1980: 115-116). For Wiredu, a considered opinion is supported by adequate evidence. When an individual holds an opinion, he/she makes a lively attempt to buttress it with valid inference. Besides his elaborate discussions, this point is evident in Wiredu's confession of a strong affinity between his theory of truth and "John Dewey's theory of truth according to which truth is the same with warranted assertibility" (1980: xii). A considered opinion will count as a warranted assertion. It will be helpful to also analyze the perspectives of Odera Oruka on Wiredu's theory before we comment on how Wiredu's theory of truth as opinion cannot be interpreted as a subjectivist theory of truth that necessarily negates objectivity – irrespective of the fact that it negates the objectivist theory of truth.

The criticisms of Odera Oruka are contained in two articles that were originally published in 1975 and 1988, respectively. In the first article, 'Truth and Belief' (reprinted in Oruka 1997: 3-11), Oruka posits that Wiredu's argument in support of truth as opinion is valid but unsound. Oruka advances a form of "coherence, universalist and self-evidence theories of truth" which on the one hand, agrees with Wiredu that if truth is radically different from belief (opinion), then truth cannot be expressed. On the other hand, Oruka objects to Wiredu's conclusion that truth is identical with belief (1997: 9). Oruka contends that "if truth is identical with belief, then no belief or proposition can ever be capable of being false" (9). The underlying view here is that if truth is identical with belief, then there is no criterion for distinguishing a true belief, proposition or opinion from a false one. Oruka maintains that there is a distinction between true belief or true proposition and a false belief/proposition and this distinction is always made by appealing to a criterion which is independent of, and different from, the opinion of the individual(s) that expresses the proposition or belief (1997: 10-11). In the absence of a criterion, "An unconsidered belief or opinion is still a belief and must, in Wiredu's opinion, be considered as true as any other" (Oruka 1997: 8). On this note, Oruka also interprets Wiredu's theory of truth to be subjective as opposed to objective, claiming that Wiredu's view of truth lacks a criterion for truth that is independent of the human point of view. In other words, Oruka takes Wiredu's claim that "truth is merely an opinion advanced from some specific point of view" to mean that truth is relative to a point of view. Wiredu later responded to Oruka's criticisms of his thesis in an article, 'In Defence of Opinion' (published in the next issue of the same journal and reprinted in Wiredu 1980: 174-180), where he made some clarifications on his criterion of truth as opinion.

According to Wiredu, Oruka's main criticisms against his view that truth is opinion, stem from inattention to his conception of opinion and his explanation on the logical relation between truth and point of view (1980: 186). On the issue of opinion, Wiredu maintained that an unconsidered opinion or belief cannot count as opinion in the stronger sense (Ibid 176). As explained earlier, the stronger sense of opinion is a product of reason supported by the rules of rational inquiry. By rational inquiry, Wiredu refers to a "process involving the use of the combined resources of observation, logic and imagination" (Ibid). A belief or opinion is therefore necessarily formed by following universal canons of rational inquiry – specifically, the rules of evidence and formal logic (Wiredu 1993: 450-476). A belief or opinion that is necessarily articulated in line with the rules of formal inference is, in principle, true irrespective of place and time. Wiredu contends that this understanding of opinion saves his idea of truth as opinion from the charge of relativism. Truth is an opinion that is logically (rationally) advanced (inferred) from a specific point of view. "Truth is not relative to a point of view. It is, in one sense, a point of view" (1980: 176-77). In view of these clarifications, Oruka in his second article, 'For the Sake of Truth: A Critique of Wiredu's Thesis' (reprinted in Oruka 1997: 12-25), admits the validity of Wiredu's counter-arguments to most of his objections to truth as opinion. However, Oruka maintained that while he subscribes to a general theory that sees truth as universal and infallible, Wiredu's theory suggests that truth can be contextual and fallible. He then concludes that statements that are universal and infallible, are generally seen as truth, while statements that are contextual and fallible, are taken as opinion or belief. "A confusion between the two may result in identifying truth with belief.

For the sake of truth, this should not be done," he concludes (Oruka 1997: 24). With this admonition, Oruka retains the objectivist distinction between truth and opinion or belief. A crucial question that is still open till now is whether Wiredu's negation of the objectivist theory of truth means the rejection of objectivity, as Omoregbe suggested.

As stated earlier, Wiredu did not accept that his idea of truth as opinion, advanced from some specific point of view, is equivalent to Omoregbe's remarks that "opinion is always the opinion of somebody, a subjective view of something". Wiredu went further to state as follows; "I have anticipated the objection and have tried to meet it by offering explanations of the subjective-objective distinction which show that my view is not prejudicial to the objectivity of truth" (Wiredu 1985a: 97). Wiredu observes that Omoregbe's comments show that he is 'obviously' aware of his explanations but was, perhaps, due to space limitations, unable to raise a specific objection against his idea of objectivity as distinct from objectivism. The objectivist theory of truth that Wiredu repudiates is tied to objectivism, not objectivity. Wiredu draws attention to the difference between objectivity and objectivism by commenting on the objective nature of his conception of truth as opinion (1980: 121-122).

Wiredu elucidates that his conception of truth as opinion is grounded on a naturalistic account of the principles of rational inquiry – the rules of evidence and formal logic. And he avers that these rules are objective. If this is the case, then his idea of opinion as a point of view born out of rational inquiry must be also objective. To argue that "any claim to truth is merely an opinion advanced from some specific point of view" implies that a claim to truth must be consistently inferred from a specific conceptual framework. The citation from Dewey's understanding of truth as warranted assertion was meant to buttress what Wiredu takes to be of "paramount importance" for his idea of truth – the rules of rational inquiry (Wiredu 1980: 197). This idea of objectivity is like the coherent theory of truth which Oruka subscribes to. The crucial difference between them is the idea of infallibility. What lies at the base of the coherent theory of truth is the reference to an infallible basic proposition that is self-evident or axiomatic. What lies at the base of truth as opinion is the reference to a fallible human point of view. As Wiredu maintains, "Epistemology in the Western tradition is replete with implicit claims to infallibility. Truth, for example, is widely supposed to be what is the case independently of any human point of view" (Wiredu 1995b: 127). He explains that upholding the distinction between truth and a human point of view "has seemed crucial for the simple reason that the human point of view is essentially fallible while truth is tautologically devoid of error" (Ibid 127). Note that the human point of view in question refers to opinion. The common sense understanding of truth as infallible and necessarily opposed to every fallible human proposition, which is also adequately argued for in the history of Western philosophy, makes it normal for one to conclude that a fallible human point of view is necessarily a subjective opinion and therefore inherently distinct from the truth. Wiredu thinks otherwise. He understands any theory of truth that ties objective propositions or beliefs to infallibility as objectivism. Wiredu's idea of objectivity as conformity with the principles of rational inquiry does not admit the idea that an objective proposition is infallible. Neither Omoregbe nor Oruka argued against his contention that "a point of view born out of rational inquiry, and the canons of rational inquiry have a universal human application" (Wiredu 1980: 176-77).

Thus, Wiredu characterizes opinion as 'considered' belief, judgment, thought(s), all linked to a point of view. In this way, an opinion must be supported by adequate evidence, information. It is a reasoned belief grounded on a point of view. When an individual holds an opinion, he/she makes a lively attempt to buttress it with valid inference. Consequently, Wiredu's understanding of truth as opinion strictly means truth as considered opinion. A considered opinion is always objectively inferred from a specific point of view, using the rules of valid inference. The formation of every point of view is a process that involves "the use of the combined resources of observation, logic and imagination" in a manner befitting the nature of human beings as rational agents: "If we are rational persons we will not – we cannot – form our opinions anyhow. Confronted with a problem we do not shut our eyes and 'assert' anything that comes into our head". (Wiredu 1980: 176). This suggests that what Wiredu means by a point of view, the human point of view, is something that is intersubjectively formulated and socially shared; "Truth is not relative to point of view. It is, in a sense, a point of view. But a point of view born out of rational inquiry, and the canons of rational inquiry have a universal human application" (Wiredu 1980: 176-77). Wiredu's elucidations contend that truth is not a given; it is always a product of conscious deliberations by individual human beings as epistemic agents that always look and interpret the world from a specific point of view, one that they consider credible (Wiredu 1980: 174-179; 1996: 34-41). An explicit analysis of some of the core features of truth as considered opinion is perhaps necessary.

Features of Truth as Considered Opinion

There are at least two basic characteristics of Wiredu's understanding of truth as an opinion that deserve special attention. The first is that truth as opinion advanced from a specific point of view implies contextuality as opposed to subjectivism. A point of view defines the viewpoint of the subject of experience of truth. When one mentions this characteristic - a point of view -

one needs to refer to the three possible points of view that people often hold, namely, the first person, second person and the third person perspectives or points of view. We are dealing principally with the first and the third points of view. Though significant, second-person point of view is employed mostly in narratives. A principal issue inherent in philosophical debates on the nature of truth borders on whether truth is tied to a first- or third-person point of view. The first-person point of view depicts the perspective of the subject (of experience). It is the first hand, primary and unmediated view of the subject who perceives the action or event. Characteristic of this viewpoint is its dictatorial authority. Since the subject affirms its experience with 'certitude' more than any other participant, this authority is rarely overridden. Hence it is often deemed 'dictatorial' (cf Roepstorff and Jack, 2004: v-xxi; Goldman, 2004; 1-14). The perspective's mainstay is introspective knowledge. Only the subject possesses privileged access to its knowledge since the subject alone can tell its own perceptions and experiences. The subject characterizes such knowledge as error-free, hence the infallibility of first-person knowledge (Stupenberg 1998: 36-58). To tie truth to a first-person point of view is to argue that truth is subjective. That is, truth is relative to the perspective of an individual. Ever since the emergence of Descartes' philosophy, the first-person perspective did gain enormous grounds. Introspection gives the first-person perspective its bite and makes it insurmountable for a knowing subject to consistently deny the possibility of certain knowledge without self-contradiction. A fundamental challenge to the first-person approach to truth is the issue of solipsism and knowledge of other minds. Wiredu's idea of truth as tied to a point of view differs from a first-person point of view which apparently embraces subjectivism.

The third-person point of view depicts the perspective of a detached observer (of an experience). Some scholars argue that it positions itself directly against the first-person perspective. While the first-person point of view suggests a subjective approach to truth, the third-person point of view calls for an objective approach to truth. Thus, the proponents of the third person perspective controvert the first-person point of view vehemently (Dennett 1991; 2006). Not only are both points of view, first and third, distinct and dispute each other, proponents of the third person perspective insist on the impossibility of elaborating any scientific (true) knowledge from a first-person perspective. The approach of the third person point of view to truth is deemed objective, scientific and empirical. It is pliable to the methods of science, much unlike the first-person point of view (Chalmers 1996; Nagel 1979). Hence, to claim that truth stems from a third-person point of view is to presuppose that truth is objective and true propositions are subject to logico-mathematical demonstration. Wiredu's theory of truth as opinion advanced from a specific point of view strictly alludes to this idea of the third-person point of view. What this means is that truth is objective strictly in the sense that it is not a personal view that can only be accessed and attested to by one individual. Note that this idea of objectivity does not necessarily mean that truth is indifferent to social context or that whatever is true is true irrespective of place and time – Thomas Nagel's account of "the view from nowhere" easily comes to mind (Nagel 1986). Every point of view is 'specific' both in terms of time and place. In this connection, to argue that truth is opinion is to claim that a true proposition or belief springs from a specific point of view that is deemed as credible within a specific social and historical context.

For Wiredu, the objectivity of truth does not imply that truth is context-blind. The objectivity of the third-person point of view is always established by reference to a specific context. A typical example is the statement, 'it is raining'. The truth or falsity of this statement is relative to the place and time to which it refers; and the truth or falsity of such a statement can be intersubjectively demonstrated using the canons of rational inquiry. At issue here is this: a true statement must correspond to a specific human point of view in the world. The statement, "it is raining," can only be logically verified when it is properly predicated. Without predication, two contrary statements, which are true, may be dismissed as false. Again, the statement, "it is raining," can be true and false in reference to either different places at the same time or the same place at different times. This is structurally akin to the correspondence theory of truth. The main difference is that what validates a statement is often interpreted to mean 'a view from nowhere', distinct from the human point of view. Wiredu insists that truth, as we humans know it, is always grounded on a specific human point of view. Beneath every third-person point of view is a rational person, a subject that uses the canons of rational inquiry to explore and explain reality from a specific context. The truth or falsity of any proposition or belief can be objectively demonstrated, via the universal principles of formal logic, once the specific point of view from where it is advanced is properly predicated (cf. Wiredu 1995b: 127-128).

Second, truth is advanced from a specific point of view that is seen as credible. What human beings see as credible also differs both in terms of place and time. Wiredu avers that human beings do not come into the world as "masters of the art of inquiry", the art of advancing credible opinions using "the combined resources of observation, logic and imagination". They must learn and keep improving this art through diverse forms of socialization available to them (1980: 176-178). Reflections on the consequences that emerge from a hitherto credible point of view often compel human beings to abandon or reconstruct it (Ibid 60). Wiredu maintains that human beings are fallible epistemic agents capable of advancing truth from a credible, not infallible, point of view. He insists that this is also the truth about any scientific or objective claim to truth (Ibid 122-123). This claim implicates some influences on truth, which influences may be historical, cultural, societal, and possibly economic. These influences do color truth, mitigate it, or even portray it in a brilliant light. While some influences may be purely external and superficial, others may force the society to change its view, presumed as truth. For instance, it took quite some decades to arrest the Trans-Atlantic slavery. For those decades, some people advanced the idea that it was appropriate to enslave others. A change in the context impacts on truth in a significant manner. Scientific truth has undergone a number of revisions too. Advances in science necessitate changes. In his celebrated book, *Structure of Scientific Revolution*, Thomas Kuhn (1970) rightly argues that the history of science is full of such changes. His thesis, according to him, resulted from a study of the history of science. It is a history of the progress and failure of scientists and scientific discoveries. A few examples will help our discourse. Oxygen replaced phlogiston just as vitalism disproved the mystery of life. The last mystery is the mystery of consciousness (Dennett 1991). The dynamism implied in the scientific view of truth not only makes its truths non-authoritarian (anti-dictatorial), it further recognizes the contributions of an individual scientist's point of view, the conditions in which he works, and other influences. In Wiredu's view of truth, dynamism and point of view are tied together. It all implies that truth is not out there. Truth is not static, posted out in the world and remaining immutable to change. Both features - dynamism and point of view - entail the view that truth can be radically influenced as to undergo certain changes. Whatever one terms truth, it is always advanced from a credible human point of view. A considered opinion is credible but fallible. The constant failure of science is instructive. There is no fixed truth but truths. All truths are subject to warranted revisions (cf. Quine 1953: 20-43). What often led to such revisions are the deliberative activities of human beings on their diverse and dynamic experiences as imperfect epistemic agents.

Wiredu's Theory of Truth as a Deliberative Theory of Truth

The major contention of Wiredu's theory repudiates theories of truth that advance the idea that truth is out there as an ensemble, immutable, neither diminishing nor changing and changeable, a hallowed, non-reducible Given. The features of truth as considered opinion suggest that truth is always a product. It is the product of human beings as members of a defined political community. They share certain experiences and a common conceptual scheme that enable them to communicate and make sense of the world through deliberation. Truth, its criteria and nature are ultimately defined and evaluated by human beings as they deliberate on their lived-world. Beyond the epistemic activities of human beings, there is no truth (see Ramose, 2005: 35-46). Yet, the epistemic activities of humans are tainted by their life-world and limited to the quality of their understanding of a given reality within a social milieu. Truth is, therefore, nothing other than a considered opinion that is consistent with the most profound conventional understanding of a given reality in a particular place at a particular time. Above all, this understanding of truth buttresses that what human beings claim to be true is fallible, imperfect and subject to change in the face of a better understanding that may emerge as human beings deliberate on their experiences in the world.

Admittedly, Wiredu's theory of truth is audaciously radical. It breaks away from the traditional distinction between truth and opinion in the history of Western philosophy. Hence, most objections to his view of truth focus on his equation of truth to "opinion." Wiredu's claim has a number of meanings and implications. One may understand it as meaning that truth is the same with the "weaker sense of opinion" as an unsupported assertion. Wiredu's claim is akin to the thesis of Richard Rorty in *Philosophy and the Mirror of Nature*, which negates the traditional, especially modernist, claim that philosophy mirrors or captures reality exactly as it is. Rorty argued, and we think rightly too, that whereas truth or reality itself may be out there, fixed, static and eternal, conceptions of the truth or reality as expressed through language are basically human constructions that are neither fixed, static nor eternal. The elucidations of Wiredu suggest that all theories of truth, as conceptualized by different philosophers, are at best considered opinions that were arrived at through reasoned deliberations in relation to a given context. No knowledge claim or policy should therefore be accepted or rejected without reasoned deliberation to determine its credibility. Wiredu's idea of the canons of rational inquiry (1993: 450-476), the biological foundation of universal norms of thought and cross-cultural communication (1996: 35-44), as well as his account of the affinity between knowledge, truth, and fallibility (1995b: 127-148) evince this view. Blocker (1985: 55-67) notes that Wiredu's theory of truth rides on his attempt to develop a theory that is grounded on human experiences but devoid of dogmatic conclusions and a self-contradictory form of relativism. Blocker submits that he shares the pragmatic and humanistic approach of Wiredu, but he cannot on that ground follow Wiredu to conclude that truth is opinion.

Indeed, Wiredu's theory of truth calls for the humanization of epistemology by grounding truth on a criterion that counts as credible rather than one that passes as infallible. Wiredu affirmed the humanistic focus of his theory of truth in all his writings on truth that we have so far cited in this work. A considered opinion is always advanced from a credible point of view. An infallible point of view in beyond the reach of humans. The fact that a credible point of view is fallible makes every claim to truth open to revisions; revisions that often emerge as human beings deliberate on how to manage their diverse experiences in a dynamic world. We contend that this mode of thinking seems to underline Wiredu's political philosophy, especially what is now commonly referred to as consensual democracy. Before we proceed to buttress this in the next section, it is important to note that Wiredu admits that his theory of truth is advanced from his point of view as an expert in African philosophy (Wiredu 1980: 114; 1985a: 96). Wiredu used concepts in his indigenous Akan conceptual scheme to buttress his view. The title of one of his essays is "The Concept of Truth in Akan Language" (1985b). It is therefore not out of place to describe Wiredu's theory of truth as 'an' African theory of truth. This view is distinct from saying that it is 'the' African theory of truth or 'a theory of truth for Africans'.

On Democracy and Consensus in African Political Philosophy

Enormously wide-ranging as the breadth of Wiredu's interests are, he succeeds often to engage the traditional African culture in his attempt to elaborate a philosophy that seeks a solution to unsettling contemporary African problems. His particularist exemplification of philosophical principles is typical of his consensual democracy or "democracy by consensus," as he puts it. Unlike Nordlinger (1972) and Lijphart (1977) that tend to set out on a search for democratic institutions that best manage ethnic interests (Cohen 1997: 607-630) from elsewhere, Wiredu and other African scholars (Ramose 1992: 62-83; Gyekye 1997: 115-143; Wamala 2004: 435-442) and students sought for such democratic institutions by exploring the consensual practice widespread in indigenous African modes of political and ordinary "social relationships" (Matolino 2013). Wiredu discovers a worthy source of democratic ideal in an indigenous Akan (Ashanti) model of politics and decision-making process. Far from any intent to romanticize about Africa's past, Wiredu (1995a; 1996; 1997; 1998; 2001) perceives the Akan traditional model of politics as an encouraging guide to address contemporary African problems of governance and democracy. That said, we shall now describe the nature of the Akan indigenous model that Wiredu articulates.

The Nature of Wiredu's Akan Model of Democracy

Akan indigenous model recognizes the royal Chief at its apex of a council of elders - representatives appointed from different clans. The Chief's tenure is for life and he is accountable to the community constituted of the living members, the gods, and the ancestors - "living dead" (Nwafor 2017). Consequently, the Chief plays several roles; a spiritual and political leader, a custodian of law, etc. He faces deposition should he act ultra vires and independently, neglecting the joint decisions of the council to pursue a personal will (Wiredu 1998: 242-243). This shows that the Akan indigenous model is non-tenured (in the sense that it is not limited to a specific number of years), and complementary (in the sense that it takes different dimensions of the community into consideration). Even so, the powers of the political leader are not unlimited. For the chief must govern the community through deliberation with the council of elders.

The traditional model typifies a political consensus decision-making approach that operates on the principle of continuously reasoned deliberations on conflicting issues. Strictly, the consensual practice operates with participants, who possess a will to consensus, to agree and to "accommodate" diverse points of view. As significant as the will to agree are the multiple interests at odds with one another and so clash. This diversity is relevant to adequate community representation and consensual agreement. Without the conflicting diversity of viewpoints, there is no need for any quest for a consensus. Wiredu emphasizes, "Deliberations need not always lead to compromise" (1998: 247). Equally, he adds, "consensus need not be the end of all debate" (Ibid). The deliberations that lead to a consensual agreement thrive on conflicting points of view that defend different interests. Wiredu's (1996) pivotal claim about his inspirational model stresses the "will to consensus" of the elders. This renders any hideous manipulation or gang-ups among the elders difficult, though not impossible (Ani 2014). Difficult because a consensual system requires the consent of all members concerned. This is different from a majoritarian system that requires the consent of some members, the majority (Wiredu 1997: 306-7). Wiredu argues that the uncooperative views generally gradually stand down to a joint consensual decision. Yet, to do away completely with recalcitrant views is hardly the primary goal of representation in the Chief's council of elders. The goal is to arrive at a credible opinion "through a reappraisal of the significance of the initial bones of contention" and Wiredu adds that this "does not necessarily involve a complete identity of moral or cognitive opinions". However, "It suffices that all parties are able to feel that adequate account has been taken of their points of view in any proposed scheme of future action or coexistences" (Wiredu 1997: 304).

The search for consensus is a search for a considered opinion through deliberations on conflicting points of view that different representatives present as credible. The challenge of consensus lies in "how a group without unanimity may settle on one political option rather than the other without alienating anyone" (Ibid). For all the elders are direct representatives of their respective clans that constitute the bigger community. As representatives appointed by the living members of their clans, they are accountable to them.

In spite of holding tenaciously to one's view, each elder-representative is prepared to agree to a consensus to put a policy that will ensure the wellbeing of their clan and the community in place. This disposition of the elders to agree on political decisions through reasoned deliberation rests on the idea of interdependence that undergirds the African political system in question. It was a system that prizes the idea that to be is not to be alone, to plan against the wellbeing of the other invariably amounts to planning against the optimal wellbeing of the self (Asouzu 2004; Nweke 2018: 155). Wiredu avers that "adherence to the principle of consensus is a premeditated option. It is based on the belief that ultimately, the interests of all members of society are the same, although their immediate perceptions of those interests may be different" (Wiredu 1997: 306). Undergirded by this understanding of social life, "African traditional systems of the consensual type were not such as to place any one group of persons consistently in the position of a minority" (Ibid 304). This is because it is a system that grounds political legitimacy on the consent of all members rather than the consent of the majority.

Another significant feature of the Akan model is the absence of political parties. Riding on the non-party nature of the Akan model of democracy, Wiredu proposes a non-party consensual democracy "under which governments are not formed by parties but by the consensus of elected representatives" (Wiredu 1995a: 61). He argues that a non-party system will enable representatives to deliberate and reach consensus on issues without the ulterior influence of political parties. In this case, the government will be a coalition of citizens rather than a coalition of political parties (Ibid 61-62). Although Wiredu admits that consensual democracy need not be a system of governance without parties, he, nonetheless, maintains that a "consensual system will naturally be a non-party arrangement" (Wiredu 1998: 227-244). Hence, the version of consensual democracy that he articulates and defends is a non-party system. His view is that within a non-party consensual democracy, it will be difficult for any ethnic, religious or ideological group to be "inflicted with a sense of being permanent outsiders to state power" (Wiredu 1995a: 62). In relation to this, Wiredu submits that the complexities of contemporary African politics make his plea for a return to a non-party consensual democracy necessary rather than negates it.

Reading the Reactions to Wiredu's Consensual Democracy in Relation to his Theory of Truth

Wiredu's theory of consensual democracy has been subjected to critical scrutiny by a number of scholars in African philosophy. Some published works that capture critical comments for and/or against Wiredu's theory includes Emmanuel Eze (1997; 2000), Bernard Matolino (2009; 2013), Helen Lauer (2012),

Emmanuel Ani (2014; 2018) and Martin Odei Ajei (2016). As stated earlier, our goal is neither to respond to existing objections nor present more objections to Wiredu's theory. We simply seek to show that reading Wiredu's theory of consensual democracy against the backdrop of his theory of truth may enable one to understand, and perhaps, interpret, defend or criticize him better. We go on to illustrate this point by outlining some of the objections to Wiredu's political theory and then proceed to show how the knowledge of Wiredu's epistemological theory may affect the quality of some of the objections. Our basic focus will be on the objections raised by Emmanuel Eze.

Our decision to focus on Eze follows from the view that Eze can be seen not just as the most "influential critic" of Wiredu (Lauer 2012: 41) but his most unsympathetic reader in African political philosophy. Eze's critique is also freely accessible online. Besides, while Matolino and Ani do object to some of the propositions of Wiredu's theory, Eze faults the very idea that an appropriate system of governance for modern African states should be modelled after an indigenous non-party system of governance that existed in a pre-colonial African society. The apt summary by Helen Lauer captures this point. According to Lauer (2012: 41):

> Eze's main points of criticism are as follows: (1) Wiredu indulges in misleading romanticism and an excessive rationalism in his normative accounts of pre-colonial Akan society; and (2) Wiredu's arguments in favor of the pre-colonial Akan non-party style of politics can function just as well to defend the single-party platforms of the early nationalists whose monopoly on political power required rigid suppression of democratic freedoms.

Eze (1997; 2000) makes a spot of the traditional nature of Wiredu's indigenous Akan model of consensual democracy. Particularly concerned are the principal guarantors of the legitimacy of the chief-in-council authority. In traditional African society, the community guarantors include its divinities, deities, and ancestors - who, together form the invisible dimension of a community. He joins issues with Wiredu over the traditional worldview underpinning the primordial indigenous African era. Eze insists that such a worldview functions with instrumental mode of thinking, completely inapplicable in the emergent modern African State. So preposterous are the sources of precolonial African society would be, Eze maintains, that should one attempt a merger with the modern African State, the result would be disastrous. Both the outlook of the precolonial era and its model of political practice would fail an adequate test in modern African society. Eze (1997: 318) proposes a reinvention of "traditional mythological origins and justifications of consensual politics." Actually, a new set of mythical beliefs would be needed to sustain the reconstruction. Such a set would typically affect the indigenous Akan model of governance. A modern African State certainly would divest itself particularly of a good part of the primordial African period to make way for the burgeoning attractions of modernity. None of these would offer divinities and ancestors as guarantors of a consensual democracy.

The primary objection here seems to be that Wiredu's association of a traditional Akan model of governance with enormous success loses sight of the differences of such a small Akan world with the current articulation of the world as a global village. Eze attacks Wiredu's indigenous source of inspiration as completely blind since it is largely overtaken by the emergence of modern African States. He also disputes Wiredu's political, nonparty polity as a nonstarter. He classifies Wiredu's nonparty proposal among the writings of early nationalist African scholars and political leaders, to whom African traditions appeal the most - the "return to the source model" of thinkers that support a one-party state.

Accordingly, the two basic objections of Eze presuppose that Wiredu calls for the excavation and use of the precolonial Akan political system in a modern African state exactly as it was. This is clear in the fact that Eze started by showing that he reads Wiredu's account of consensual democracy as something that can be "classify alongside with those African thinkers who advocated a "return" to "the tradition" or a "return" to "the source" as Amilcar Cabral calls it" (Eze 1997: 313). Eze's objections to Wiredu's consensual democracy are mainly advanced from this understanding. We admit that it is possible to return to the source in a critical and creative manner; intellectuals do study the intellectual history of a people to mine novel ideas for addressing contemporary challenges (Matolino 2017: 1). The 'return to the source' approach in African philosophy that Eze refers to bespeaks an uncritical return to adopt a "pristine" African ideal. Such a move will be inconsistent with the dynamic nature of Wiredu's theory of truth. An interpretation that is consistent with Wiredu's theory of truth is that his theory of consensual democracy calls for the reconstruction and use of an indigenous precolonial African political system in modern African states. The said reconstruction is meant to reflect the existing social reality of the African state or any modern society in question. This sense of "a return to the past" is different from the one that Eze attributes to Wiredu.

Eze (1997; 2000) argues against the traditional model since its adoption would compare to a square peg in a round hole, Wiredu realizes that its conscious modification would be an appealing bastion against the inherently problem-infested Western majoritarian or one-party rule. Wiredu's theory of truth kicks against the idea of a perfect and changeless system that can be totally exported across history and cultures without new inputs. Had Eze not read Wiredu's proposal as "a return to the past", he would have perhaps concentrated more on showing why the principle of consensus that Wiredu articulates is inherently problematic. To argue that Wiredu calls for an uncritical return to a precolonial African political system would suggest that Wiredu's political proposal negates a basic principle of his epistemological view – the need for incessant deliberations in search of considered opinions. Raising the charge of romanticism against Wiredu will be stronger if one shows that it contradicts Wiredu's epistemological stance in African philosophy. Otherwise, such objections may appear as uninformed to people who are aware of the critical stance of Wiredu towards both traditional and universal values (Wiredu 1980, 1996; Oladipo 2002). It is, in principle, possible that a philosopher or theorist can contradict herself/himself. Identifying a contradiction in the ideas of a philosopher, even if the ideas were advanced in different works, is a valid observation that often calls for further clarifications.

Experts in African political philosophy such as Bernard Matolino (2009) and Hellen Lauer (2012) are of the view that the objections of Eze (1997; 2000) will become ineffective when one understands how Wiredu approaches the Akan model of consensual democracy to articulate his theory of consensual democracy. The indigenous model serves Wiredu solely as a "normative reconstruction" (Lauer 2012: 42). Wiredu combined the Ashanti political system afforded him by K. A. Busia, with his experiences both as an Akan person and as an academic philosopher living in a changing world, to articulate the political system of consensual democracy (Ani 2018: 5). The indigenous model serves as the starting point, not the product, of Wiredu's reflections (Graness 2002: 254-255). Typically, Matolino (2009: 34-42) is a response to Eze's critique of Wiredu. He drew attention to how Eze reads Wiredu's consensual democracy to mean uncritical 'return to the source' and then explains why this view is apparently wrong. Despite his defense of Wiredu's consensual democracy against the criticisms raised by Eze, Matolino (2013) isolates four principal themes of Wiredu's consensual democracy and disputes Wiredu on them.

Principal among them all is Wiredu's non-party vision of consensual democracy. For Matolino (2013:145ff), Wiredu's objections to one-party system of governance depends, among other things, on Wiredu's conceptualization of the term, "party," which uses in Wiredu's writings generate possible confusion of, at least, three meanings - "party$_{1, 2, 3}$." Indeed, Matolino (2013) disputes Wiredu on "non-party polity." The point here is that unlike Eze, Matolino's objections to Wiredu focus on Wiredu's conceptualizations of the principles and features of his version of consensual democracy. This type of objection is basically consistent with Wiredu's theory of truth as considered opinion that is contextually generated through deliberations. One of the demands of this understanding of truth is that the credibility of every political option is subject to deliberation, and should be deliberated, and where necessary be revised. This understanding of consensual democracy which relates to his theory of truth as considered opinion has its own problems. Matolino raised and analyzed some of the problems in his recent book, *Consensus as Democracy in Africa* (2018), by engaging the perspectives of diverse researchers on the nature of consensual democracy in African political philosophy. Wiredu's consensual democracy has set scholars of African political philosophy on a search for suitable political systems for Africa's contemporary democracy.

Conclusion

Our main contention is that a thorough reading of Wiredu's theory of consensual democracy, with an eye to his theory of truth, shows that Wiredu is among the foremost proponents of deliberative theory in the fields of epistemology and political philosophy. We upheld this argument through an analysis of Wiredu's epistemological theory that ties truth to credible conclusions. We showed how his theory of truth is linked to the deliberations of epistemic agents in their lifeworld over time. Further, we explained the centrality of deliberations in his theory of consensual democracy and also demonstrated how the two theories could both be seen as aspects of deliberative theory. The emphasis on consensus through deliberation is a prominent feature of deliberative democracy. Anke Graness drew attention to the similarities between the idea of consensus in Kwasi Wiredu and Juergen Habermas (2002: 259-262), who is one of the acclaimed proponents of deliberative democracy. It will therefore not be out of place to classify Wiredu as one of the proponents of a variant of deliberative democracy that is articulated from an African lifeworld.

References

Ajei, M. O. 2016. Kwasi Wiredu's Consensual Democracy: Prospects for Practice in Africa. *European Journal of Political Theory* 15(4): 445–466.

Alston, W. P. 1996. *A Realist Conception of Truth*. London: Cornel University Press.

Ani, E. I. 2014. On Traditional African Consensual Rationality. *Journal of Political Philosophy* 22(3): 342–365.

Ani, E. I. 2018. Africa and Deliberative Politics. In Andre Bachtiger, John Drizek, Jane Mansbridge, and Mark Warren (eds.). *Oxford Handbook of Deliberative Democracy*. Oxford: Oxford University Press. www.oxfordhandbooks.com

Asouzu, I. I. 2004. *The Method and Principles of Complementary Reflection in and Beyond African Philosophy*. Calabar: University of Calabar Press.

Blocker, G. 1985. Wiredu's Notion of Truth. In P. O. Bodunrin (ed.) *Philosophy in Africa: Trends and Perspectives*. Ile-Ife: University of Ife Press, 55-67.

Chalmers, D. 1996. *Consciousness in Search of a Fundamental Theory.* Oxford: Oxford University Press.

Cohen, F. S. 1997. Proportional Versus Majoritarian Ethnic Conflict Management in Democracies. *Comparative Political Studies,* 30(5): 607–630.

Dennett, C. D. 1991. *Consciousness Explained.* New York: Little, Brown & Co.

Dennett, C. D. 2006. *Sweat Dreams: Philosophical Obstacles to the Science of Consciousness.* (Jean Nicod Lectures). Massachusetts: MIT Press.

Eze, E. C. 1997. Democracy or Consensus? Response to Wiredu. In E. C. Eze (ed.) *Postcolonial African Philosophy: A Critical Reader.* Oxford: Blackwell, 313-323.

Eze, E. C. 2000. Democracy or Consensus? Response to Wiredu. Revised online, *Polylog: Forum for Intercultural Philosophy.* Available at: http://them.polylog.org/2/fee-en.htm

Graness, A. 2002. Wiredu's Ethics of Consensus: Model for a Global Ethics? In Olusegun Oladipo (ed.) *The Third Way in African Philosophy: Essays in Honour of Kwasi Wiredu.* Ibadan: Hope Publishers, 252-268.

Goldman, A. 2004. Epistemology and the Evidential Status of Introspective Reports I. *Journal of Consciousness Studies,* 11 (7-8): 1-16.

Gyekye, K. 1997. *Tradition and Modernity: Philosophical Reflections on the African Experience.* New York: Oxford University Press.

Kuhn, T. 1970. *The Structure of Scientific Revolutions.* Chicago: University of Chicago Press.

Lauer, H. 2012. Wiredu and Eze on Good Governance. *Philosophia Africana* 14 (1): 41-59.

Lijphart, A. 1977. *Democracy in Plural Societies: A Comparative Exploration.* New Haven: Yale University Press.

Matolino, B. 2009. A Response to Eze's Critique of Wiredu's Consensual Democracy. *South African Journal of Philosophy* 28(1): 34–42.

Matolino B. 2013. The Nature of Opposition in Kwasi Wiredu's Democracy By Consensus. *African Studies* 72(1): 138-152.

Matolino, B. 2017. Return to The Source? Challenges and Prospects. In P. Ngulube (ed.) *Handbook of Research on Social, Cultural, and Educational Considerations of Indigenous Knowledge in Developing Countries.* Hershey PA: IGI Global, 1-14.

Matolino, B. 2018. *Consensus as Democracy in Africa.* Grahamstown: African Humanities Program-NISC.

Nagel, T. 1979. *Mortal Questions.* New York: Cambridge University Press.

Nagel, T. 1986. *The View From Nowhere.* Oxford: Oxford University Press.

Nordlinger, E. A. 1972. *Conflict Regulation in Divided Societies.* Cambridge, Mass.: Harvard University Press.

Nwafor, M. I. 2017. The Living-dead (Ancestors) among the Igbo-African People: An Interpretation of Catholic Sainthood. *International Journal of Sociology and Anthropology* 9(4): 35-42. DOI: 10.5897/IJSA2017.0719

Nweke, V. C. A. 2018. Global Warming as an Ontological Boomerang Effect: Towards a Philosophical Rescue from the African Place. In J. O. Chimakonam (ed.) *African Philosophy and Environmental Conservation.* London: Routledge, 226-243.

Oladipo, O. (ed.) 2002. The Third Way in African Philosophy: Essays in Honour of Kwasi Wiredu. Ibadan: Hope Publications.

Omoregbe, J. I. 1985. African Philosophy: Yesterday and Today. In P. O. Bodunrin (ed.) *Philosophy in Africa: Trends and Perspectives.* Ile-Ife: University of Ife Press, 1-14.

Oruka, O. H. 1997. *Practical Philosophy: In Search of an Ethical Minimum.* Nairobi: East African Educational Publishers.

Quine, W. V. O. 1953. *From a Logical Point of View (Logical Essays by W. V. O. Quine).* Cambridge: Harvard University Press.

Ramose, M. B. 1992. African Democratic Traditions: Oneness, Consensus and Openness: A Reply to Wamba-dia-Wamba. *Quest: Philosophical Discussions-An International African Journal of Philosophy* VI (2): 62-83.

Ramose, M. B. 2005. *African Philosophy through Ubuntu.* Revised ed. Harare: Mond Books Publishers.

Roepstorff, A. and Jack, A. I. 2004. Trust or Interaction? Editorial Introduction. *Journal of Consciousness Studies*, 11 (7-8): v-xxii.

Rorty, R. 1979. *Philosophy and the Mirror of Nature.* New Jersey: Princeton University Press.

Stupenberg, L. 1998. *Consciousness and Qualia.* Amsterdam: John Benjamins.

Wamala, E. 2004. Government by Consensus: An Analysis of a Traditional Form of Democracy. In Kwasi Wiredu (ed.), A Companion to African Philosophy. Maiden: Blackwell, 435-441.

Wiredu, K. 1980. *Philosophy and an African Culture.* New York: Cambridge University Press.

Wiredu, K. 1985a. Reply to Critics. In P. O. Bodunrin (ed.) *Philosophy in Africa: Trends and Perspectives.* Ile-Ife: University of Ife Press, 91-102.

Wiredu, K. 1985b. The Concept of Truth in Akan Language. In P. O. Bodunrin (ed.) *Philosophy in Africa: Trends and Perspectives.* Ile-Ife: University of Ife Press, 43-54.

Wiredu, K. 1993. Canons of Conceptualization. *The Monist* 76 (4): 450–476.

Wiredu, K. 1995a. *Conceptual Decolonization in African Philosophy: Four Essays by Kwasi Wiredu* (selected and introduced by Olusegun Oladipo). Ibadan: Hope Publications.

Wiredu, K. 1995b. Knowledge, Truth and Fallibility In I. Kucuradi and R. S. Cohen (eds.) *The Concept of Knowledge: The Ankara Seminar.* Dordrecht: Springer, 127-148.

Wiredu, K. 1996. *Cultural Universals and Particulars: An African Perspective.* Bloomington: Indiana University Press.

Wiredu, K. 1997. Democracy and Consensus in African Traditional Politics: A Plea for a Nonparty Polity. In Eze E. C. (ed.) *Postcolonial African Philosophy: A Critical Reader.* Cambridge: Blackwell, 303–312.

Wiredu, K. 1998. State, Civil Society and Democracy in Africa. *Quest: An International Journal of Philosophy* XII (1): 241-252.

Wiredu, K. 2001. Democracy by Consensus: Some Conceptual Considerations". *Philosophical Papers* 30 (3): 227–244.

Chapter 4

Towards a "Multi-party" Consensual Democracy in Africa

Dennis Masaka

Great Zimbabwe University

Introduction

In the work titled *"Democracy and Consensus in African Traditional Politics: A Plea for a Non-party Polity"*, Kwasi Wiredu (1997: 303-311) avers that decision-making in "traditional"[1] Africa was principally by consensus. In arguing thus, Wiredu (1997: 308) wants to show that there is a fundamental difference between Africa's consensual democratic paradigm and the liberal or majoritarian type of democracy (Metz, 2012: 64) that initially came as an imposition but has lately been taken, though grudgingly, as the preferred template for governance in present day Africa (Fatton, Jr. 1990: 457; Sklar 1983: 14). Wiredu's (1997: 303-311) thesis is that a return to consensual democracy may prove to be a panacea to myriad of problems that majoritarian democracy paradigm has inaugurated across the African continent.

The comparison that Wiredu (1997: 308) makes between consensual democracy and majoritarian democracy is intended to show that the former is

---

[1] In this chapter, I use the term "traditional" with caution because it has often been understood negatively as that which is unchanging, backward and unscientific, and contrasted with "modernity" that is contestably identified with the Western world alone and conceived as a stage of human development that is characterised by scientific thinking and progress (Gross 1992: 4). Yet, such a clinical dichotomy is untenable because "tradition" mutates into the "modern" and barring any interferences to progress, that which is "modern" today mutates into "tradition" with the passage of time. Following this reasoning, what is "tradition" today was once the "modern" at some point in history. This only serves to show that the portrayal of consensual democracy as "traditional" contentiously sees it as rigid and fixated in the unchanging past: a characterisation that I contest.

more suited to the African condition than the latter given the outcomes of the rather disastrous experimentation with the imposed majoritarian democracy in Africa (Fatton, Jr. 1990: 457; Eze, 1997: 315; Tar 2010: 83-84). In this light, Wiredu (1997: 303-311) outlines the positives that subsist in consensual democracy that are interestingly assumed to be lacking in a majoritarian democracy. Though I support the imperative for African countries to depart from the culture of unqualified dependency on alien paradigms (Mazrui 1975: 88-92; Ramose 1999: 9), and in this case alien paradigm of democracy, there is also need for them to interrogate their traditions in order to establish whether they could be carried forward without transforming them so that they could speak to the present realities.

In this connection, my intention is to analyse Wiredu's (1997: 303-311) thesis for a return to consensual democracy (*see* Eze 1997: 313) that was overtly in use in Africa prior to colonial conquest. I offer qualified support to Wiredu's (1997: 303-311) defense of a consensual polity in Africa for the reason that the current state in Africa is configured in ways that make it significantly different from the "traditional" one where rule by consensus as Wiredu (1997: 303) understands it was a viable paradigm. In other words, my intention is not to totally dispute its suitability as a corrective to the problems that majoritarian democracy has presented to countries in Africa, but to try to suggest some way of improving it so that it might more closely speak to the present circumstances of these countries. More specifically, even though Wiredu (1997: 308) thinks that a consensual polity is not troubled by the problem of the "minorities" as is the case with a simple majoritarian polity, I will argue that the problem of "minorities" is one that cannot be completely avoided by any paradigm of democracy. While I agree with the thesis that majoritarian democracy has led to some significant problems in Africa (Fatton, Jr. 1990: 458) thereby justifying the need to rethink the possibility of a return to the "traditional" consensual democracy model, I would like to defend the position that multi-party politics may still be viably pursued within the framework of a consensual democratic model. However, before pursuing this suggestion, I have to first explore Wiredu's (1997: 303-311) contention that political parties in a majoritarian democracy are more interested in the acquisition of power than in pursuit of the goals that would accrue from a consensual democracy.

Fundamentally, the position defended here is that the existence of multiple political parties, a phenomenon that is often uncritically considered as solely confined to the Western paradigm of democracy and absent in African consensual democracy, might turn out to be necessary for a viable consensual democratic system of governance in present day Africa. In this connection, even though I strongly feel that some form of multi-party system was implicit in African consensual democracy as Wiredu (1996: 187; 1997: 308) seems to imply *albeit* with some qualification; I do not think that it is very improper to imagine the necessity of political parties in a consensual polity that are not necessarily burdened by the negatives of adversarial politics. Nevertheless, a word of caution could be that the African paradigm of democracy ought to remain the basis upon which the "multi-party" consensual democracy paradigm is to be anchored (*see also* Wamba-dia-Wamba 1992: 32; Ramose 1992: 65; 2009: 414; Oladipo 1995: 27; Hountondji 2009: 1). By choosing to defend Wiredu's (1997: 303-311) thesis for African consensual democracy even though with some qualifications, I would want to differ with Uwizeyimana's (2012: 140) claim "...that there could not be a separate African democracy, or a democracy of a special kind, based on African traditions."

The chapter is partitioned into three sections. I present a brief account of Wiredu's (1997: 303-311) defense for consensual democracy in the first section. In the second section, I critique Wiredu's (1997: 303-311) thesis in defense of consensual democracy as a worthy alternative to majoritarian democracy highlighting its possible challenges that may render it in need of reworking for it to be more suited to the current dynamics of countries in Africa. I will also show that even though there are attempts at presenting the consensual and majoritarian polities as polar opposites, there are some similarities between these two. However, I will argue that such similarities do not necessarily downplay the thesis that a consensual polity is more suited for countries in Africa. In the third section, I argue that a multi-party consensual democracy model might turn out to be a viable and refreshing option for countries in Africa in present times. This is my point of departure. I now turn to an exploration of Wiredu's (1997: 303-311) defense for a "non-party polity".

Wiredu's Understanding of Consensual Democracy

Wiredu (1997: 303-311) offers "consensus" as a worthy basis for human life and governance in present-day Africa. The call for a return to government by consensus is considered as a direct response to the present situation in Africa where the governance paradigm in use, that is, majoritarian democracy, is considered alien to Africa (Uwizeyimana 2012: 140) and has been blamed for some of the significant failures of governments in Africa (*see* Sklar 1983: 18). In particular, the majoritarian tendencies of this alien paradigm of democracy has been blamed for inaugurating the clamour for contestations that are primarily driven by the urge to attain power principally for its own sake. Below, I seek to interrogate Wiredu's (1997: 303-311) clamour for a departure from majoritarian democracy and a return to government by consensus in present-day Africa, that is, politics of inclusion that cherishes consensual solutions and not competition, as is the case with multi-party democracy (Gyekye 2010: 241; Uwizeyimana 2012: 140).

In defending the thesis for a return to the rule by consensus in present-day Africa, Wiredu appeals to a system of governance that is viewed to have been the bedrock of governance in "traditional" Africa. The point here could be that if consensus worked well in the past, it could work well in present and future times (Wiredu 1997: 303). With a bit of cautionary statement, Wiredu regards consensus as very much part of life and governance in "traditional" Africa. In defending the position that the rule by consensus was the basis of governance in Africa, Wiredu (1997: 303; *see also* Uwizeyimana 2012: 140) cites the averments by thinkers cum political leaders such as Kenneth Kaunda and Julius Kambarage Nyerere as very much in defense of the position that rule by consensus was the defining character of the "traditional" system of governance. However, as Wiredu notes, ironically, such averments were made in defense of a one-party system, which was considered as an option by some founding leaders of the liberated countries in Africa, though with much resistance from opposition political parties. Wiredu rejects the connection that these one-party despots attempted to establish between consensual democracy and one-party polity (Ibid).

Despite the efforts to implicate consensual democracy in the emergence of one-party polities in Africa, Wiredu considers it as a viable system of governance. In this connection, Wiredu thinks that in interpersonal relationships between adults, consensus was taken as axiomatic or self-evident and necessary in attaining "joint action" (Ibid). However, the use of the term "axiomatic" in this context may appear somewhat prescriptive and confining; because it may not necessarily be reasonably correct to think that, it was the only means by which people attained "joint action". In addition, if it is viable to claim that consensus was "axiomatic" in Africa, it might have been so in principle and not always in practice. In other words, if consensus was axiomatic, it may not follow then to say that it was always attained. In fact, Wiredu reckons the prevalence of occurrences that run counter to the dictates of consensus in "traditional" African societies (1997: 309-310).

However, whenever these conflicts occurred, Wiredu (1997: 304) reminds us that there were always ways of resolving them through "negotiation" with the intention of attaining "reconciliation". He (Ibid) highlights "reconciliation" as the outcome of negotiating contentious issues in "traditional" Africa. In this connection, consensus could be taken as a key in attaining genuine reconciliation whereby contending individuals and or groups are true to themselves that the contentious issues that have been tearing them apart have been honestly settled through negotiation. Wiredu (Ibid) takes this approach to settling disputes and contentious issues between and among people as different from negotiations that adopt, as an end, a mere stop to further disputes and contestations. Below, I comment on Wiredu's idea of consensual democracy.

Responding to Wiredu's Defense for a "Non-party Polity"

The emphasis that Wiredu puts on the need for negotiation between and among contending parties that culminate in reconciliation stems from the fact that, at times, problems and disputes may be solved without attaining reconciliation. Yet, consensus mandates that a negotiated settlement culminates in reconciliation. As Wiredu argues, "reconciliation is, in fact, a form of consensus. It is a restoration of goodwill through a reappraisal of the significance of the initial bones of contention" (Wiredu 1997: 304). However, it remains to be spelt out what the term "consensus" would mean as it is deployed in Wiredu's thesis for a non-party polity. Wiredu (1997: 303-311) might not have sufficiently explored the potential of consensus in contemporary Africa. I will, in the meantime, focus on Wiredu's understanding of this term before I revert to the exploration of the consensual democracy paradigm that is considered an alternative to the alien paradigm of democracy in Africa.

One may discern the idea of consensus that Wiredu seems to hold from his description of the rule by consensus. In this connection, Wiredu (1997: 304) argues that:

> ...consensus does not in general entail total agreement. To begin with, consensus usually presupposes an original position of diversity. Because issues do not always polarize opinion on lines of strict contradictoriness, dialogue can function, by means, for example, of the smoothing of edges, to produce compromises that are agreeable to *all*[2] or, at least, not obnoxious to any.

From this passage, one might come to an understanding of consensus as denoting the attainment of a "common ground" on an issue or issues that are under contestation between individuals or groups. Granted that this is an acceptable rendering of the term "consensus", it remains unclear how such a "common ground" could be attained, let alone ensuring that "everyone" or "all" eventually commit to it. Wiredu alludes to this possibility when he avers that, in general, consensus does not point to "total agreement" (Ibid).

---

[2] Emphasis added.

One question that might arise then is that if the consensus does not do so, what then could be the means that could be used to "make" people attain consensus? Indeed, it is reasonable to argue that consensus can be legitimately talked of as an outcome of prior "diversity" (Wiredu 1997: 304; Ani 2013: 207). I take the term "diversity", as Wiredu uses it, as pointing at differences of positions and opinions on issues that concern a given group of people. As I see it, Wiredu does not seem to come clear on how, in the context of such diversity, consensus can be attained. In this connection, even if it may be granted that consensus, at least as it is described by Wiredu (1997: 304), is attainable, it would appear impressionistic to think that "all" will be agreeable to a certain position especially on matters of state functions in present times. Perhaps, at a very small scale and in cases where many, in principle, share fundamental commonalities in perspectives and aspirations, it is possible to envisage a scenario where "all" people might agree. However, such cases are rare and in the complex state of affairs such as that of a country where there is diversity and difference not only in terms of opinion but also more importantly in terms of, for instance, ethnicity and race, it might turn out to be illusory to envisage such consensual unanimity. In this light, it appears reasonable to argue that Wiredu (1997: 303-311) did not sufficiently explore the potential of consensus in contemporary Africa even though it appears quite promising to "traditional" political conditions.

Wiredu is aware of the reality that, at times, issues can polarise opinion to the extent that there are fundamental differences between and among people. As it were, consensual living might not translate to absence of difference (*see* Nkrumah, 1964: 45). In this light, Wiredu argues, "...where there is the will to consensus, dialogue can lead to a *willing suspension of disagreement, making possible agreed actions without necessarily agreed notions.*[3] This is important because certain situations do, indeed, precipitate exhaustive disjunctions which no dialogic accommodations can mediate" (1997: 304) In this light, in a situation where "no dialogic accommodations can mediate", it is considered possible to suspend disagreements so that "agreed actions" can be performed without necessarily changing people's ideas and perceptions about a certain issue.

In my view, consensus so conceived is somewhat deceptive because parties to the contention choose to suspend their opinions in favour of "agreed actions", which by this reasoning, clearly negates their considered views on the given issue or position. In addition, the operational aspects leading to such a consensual position appear to be contentious and suspect. How

---

[3] Emphasis added.

disagreements may end up being suspended, raise fundamental questions pertaining to the democratic nature of such a process. The issue here is that there are disagreements that may not be mediated by dialogue. In this light, whose position then would become the outcome of consensus given that parties or individuals involved hold divergent positions that might be irreconcilable? As Wiredu (1997: 304) notes:

> the problem then is how a group without unanimity may settle on one option rather than the other without alienating anyone. This is the severest challenge of consensus, and it can only be met by the willing suspension of disbelief in the prevailing option on the part of the residual minority. The feasibility of this depends not only on the patience and persuasiveness of the *right people*,[4] but also on the fact that African traditional systems of the consensual type were not such as to place any one group of persons consistently in the position of a minority.

These claims about rule by consensus invite critical comments, especially when they are considered in the light of the alien paradigm of democracy that Wiredu (1997: 303-311) considers inappropriate for Africa.

While Wiredu (1997: 304) rightly notes that the situation whereby groups substantially differ on issues under consideration provides a formidable challenge to the rule by consensus, the proposal that he suggests as a corrective to this situation seems to credit it with similar faults of the alien model of democracy which, as he proposes, ought to be dropped in favour of a return to consensus. In other words, if the said consensus is to be attained by ensuring that the "residual minority" somehow "willingly" suspend "disbelief in the prevailing option", then it might be plausible to say that rule by consensus promotes what has been called "tyranny of the majority" (Locke, 1823: 193; Mill, 1859, 2001: 8-9). I understand that the problem of the "tyranny of the majority" is the reason behind Wiredu's (1997: 303-311) rejection of majoritarian democracy and the quest for a return to rule by consensus.

Arguing that the minority is mandated to drop their reservations to the option that has the backing of the majority contradicts Wiredu's (1997: 304) main rationale for rejecting majoritarian democracy, which is the plight of minorities. The terms "majority" and "minority" here are understood numerically. What it would then mean is that even if the position of the minority were to be valid and more convincing, it does not stand a chance against the option that is held by the majority. By this reasoning, the majority

---

[4] Emphasis added.

will always prevail upon the minority by virtue of their numerical advantage and not necessarily because of the inherent strength and quality of the position that they hold. I will pursue this position further when I undertake to make a comparison between consensual democracy and majoritarian democracy with the objective of showing that consensual democracy is preferable to majoritarian democracy. Even though consensual democracy may have its fair share of problems, I insist that it remains a preferred democracy paradigm that could be improved by ensuring that it answers to the present complexities of countries in Africa.

With respect to the obligation of the minority to drop their disapproval of the option or position that the majority support, Wiredu (1997: 304) argues that this task hinges on two critical conditions namely (1) "the patience and persuasiveness of the right people" and (2) "the fact that African traditional systems of the consensual type were not such as to place any one group of persons consistently in the position of a minority." It is not spelt out who the "right people" are (or what attributes they might have that renders them to be viewed as such) who have to employ patience and persuasive power to convince the "residual minority" to drop their rejection of the option that is supported by the majority. By designating some people as the "right people", Wiredu appears to be separating them from the rest. I will show later that once Wiredu (1997: 311) falls into the trap of numbers, that is, by comparing the decisional influence of the majority and the minority; his position will therefore share significant commonalities with the majoritarian system of governance that he somehow vehemently opposes.

However, Wiredu's (1997: 304) consensual democracy seems to evade this criticism because consensual democracy does not keep certain minorities permanently out of power and certain majorities permanently in power. This means that the consensual systems of governance do not forever place some people under the banner of minority. Perhaps following this line of reasoning, some people may be minorities on a certain issue under contestation and may turn out not to be so in another. Whichever way, the admission that there are "minorities" and "majorities" in African consensual democracy might mean that at some point, there are some groups of people who have overriding decision-making powers while others are out of power.

Wiredu (1997: 304-308) proceeds by way of an example of the Ashanti system of governance in order to elucidate and defend the functionality of consensual democracy in "traditional" African societies. I will briefly focus on aspects of the Ashanti traditional system of governance, as presented by Wiredu (1997: 304-308), that I consider important for my purposes in the present chapter. Wiredu (1997: 307) argues that decisions among the Ashantis were by consensus. Even the choice of leaders or representatives in councils of leadership was conducted by consensus (Wiredu, 1997: 306). In this connection, "…this adherence to the principle of consensus was a premeditated option. It was based on the belief that *ultimately* the interests of all members of society are the same, although their immediate perceptions of those interests may be different" (Wiredu 1997: 306). However, the belief that sustains such a claim may be contentious and could be challenged. The reason is in "real-life situations", people may not operate on such an objectionable assumption. This is not to deny that the Ashantis may have had such a belief.

My cause of disagreement with Wiredu here is that if a belief is premeditated, there might be a tendency for people or groups to act in ways that are simply meant to confirm or conform to its dictates. This would then render such "negotiations" leading to consensual outcomes illusory because the deliberate desire for consensus compels parties to find grounds for agreement, even if it means manufacturing grounds in the absence of any. That being the case, Wiredu (1997: 306) feels that the immediate perceptions of people, however, may point to a lack of unanimity in characterising and conceiving human interests. Yet, through dialogue, people may endeavour to overcome their differences and reach consensual positions. In arguing thus, Wiredu (1997: 311) is making a case for consensual democracy as an ideal paradigm for present-day Africa while faulting the majoritarian democracy that has been imposed on Africa for creating the crisis of governance that has characterised some African governments in Africa. Below, I seek to show that Wiredu's idea of consensual democracy could be transformed into a more promising and relevant paradigm to the present circumstances in countries in Africa if it incorporates multi-party politics in its scope.

Towards a "Multi-party" Consensual Democracy Model

In this section, I argue that Wiredu's defense of a consensual polity may need some bit of refreshing in order to render it more suited to the prevailing circumstances in countries in Africa. The idea of consensual democracy might appear to be a promising one when, at some point, one elects to divert from Wiredu's descriptions and move towards improving it. However, this is not to say that Wiredu's account ought to be totally abandoned. As I see it, where Wiredu's account appears to be out of line with the prevailing circumstances in countries in Africa, it might be necessary to suggest possible correctives that could strengthen it. In this connection, I defend the "multi-party consensual democracy model" as a plausible option for countries in Africa. One can argue that the idea of a multi-party consensual democracy shares similar problems with majoritarian democracy.

However, as has been noted above, the problem of "majorities" and "minorities" is not something that we can completely avoid in any social or political theory, and what matters is how much respect is at least shown to minority views. This applies to a consensual polity as well. Even though the "majority" and "minority" are part of a consensual democracy's decisional processes, these are not fixated designations that permanently mark certain individuals as such. What is important is to consider how the "minority" on a particular issue in a consensual polity are treated compared to the situation in a majoritarian democracy. In the case of Wiredu's idea of consensual democracy, the minority on a particular issue under consideration are not treated as outcasts as such who have no say altogether since those in the majority try to show them the merit of a certain preferred position and why it is in their best interest to accept it. In the end, an agreed position on any issue under consideration is a product of consensual deliberations (Wiredu 1997: 304). Even though it is unavoidable to talk of the minority and the majority in a consensual polity, the decisional contributions of the minority are recognised and respected.

The situation is different with majoritarian democracy whereby the minority or the losers in a given issue, say elections, are completely shut out of decision-making processes of the political party in power (Venter 2003: 1-2). As a result, there is not much difference, if at all there is, that is extended to the minority or the losing parties in terms of their decisional contributions to governance issues in the state. It is a matter of life and death (Wiredu 2007: 160). This means that these political parties are not given the requisite respect concerning their decisional influence and contribution in matters of the state. Though it appears impossible to eliminate the problem of minorities completely in any social or political theory, it is plausible to conclude that the decisional contributions of the minorities in a consensual polity are recognised and respected. This renders the consensual polity more suited to circumstances of countries in Africa often characterised by ethnic and regional tensions since the minorities are involved in the decisional processes and outcomes within the framework of consensus.

In proposing a consensual multiparty democracy, I have in mind a consensual polity where the minorities or losing political parties are recongnised, respected and accepted as co-contributors to decision-making in the governance affairs of the state. In other words, rendering respect and acceptance of minorities or loosing political parties as vital in contributing to the decisional processes and development of the state within the framework of a consensual paradigm will help to transform them from solely power-seeking entities for its own sake to political formations that are bestowed responsibilities to contribute significantly to consensual decisional processes. In this sense, some consensual element is needed in such a democracy model as opposed to the brute superiority of the majority in a simple majoritarian model.

The difference between the political party in a consensual multiparty democracy and a political party in a simple majoritarian democracy would then reside in the respect that is extended to minorities concerning the decisional matters in the state. If the minorities, in a consensual multiparty democracy, were granted respect and acceptance as co-contributors in the decisional processes of the state in the spirit of consensus, such a model would be a more suited corrective to challenges facing countries in Africa such as ethnic and regional tensions. As Wiredu avers, "…one of the most persistent causes of political instability in (contemporary) Africa is that majoritarian democracy has placed certain ethnic minorities consistently outside the corridors of power" (Wiredu 1996: 189, cited in Ani 2014: 344). The element of inclusiveness in the consensual polity would then render a multi-party consensual polity more suited to the problems of ethnic and regional divisions that face the majority of countries in Africa in present times.

However, one may argue that multiparty politics breeds confrontations and adversarial political engagements that may not bode well with Wiredu's idea of a consensual democracy. In fact, Wiredu's (1997: 308) idea of "parties" is that of entities that participate in consensual processes leading to consensual positions. He differentiates these "parties" from those found in majoritarian democracy that have an obsession with competing against each other in order to win electoral processes and contestations with the sole objective of ascending to power and leaving other parties out of power.

However, the element of competition subsists even in parties that participate in consensual processes, so is some form of confrontation. In this connection, Wiredu accepts that, in a consensual polity, there are certain situations that might "…precipitate exhaustive disjunctions which no dialogic accommodations can mediate" (1997: 304). Such levels of confrontations and contestations could also manifest among political parties. What might be of interest is the degree and gravity of such confrontations and how they could be resolved in a manner that does not create further unnecessary and irresolvable animosity among parties. More importantly, if in their diversity and difference, political parties and what they hold are respected and accommodated in the consensual polity, then the degree and gravity of confrontation could be lessened, leading to chances of amicable resolution and attainments of consensual outcomes.

Perhaps, what matters is the realisation that the adversarial confrontations that often characterises the political activities of political parties ought not to lead them to lose sight of the fact that they are competing to serve the electorate and not necessarily to serves themselves. Such a realisation might spur them to resolve their differences and pursue consensual deliberations leading to possible consensual outcomes that are beneficial to the governed. I think that even in a majoritarian democracy, consensual deliberations are not altogether absent, especially when one considers that the winners of political contestations often engage in negotiations with losers to address certain national questions. Here, I have in mind governments of national unity that could often be evoked to resolve political contestations among adversarial political parties.

I consider such governments as outcomes of consensual deliberations within the framework of multi-party politics where declared winners and losers in electoral contexts realise that electoral processes on their own are insufficient to resolve economic and socio-political questions. A case in point is that of the negotiated settlement between political parties in Zimbabwe in 1999 aimed at ending the country's economic and socio-political crises. I take this example as important in defending my thesis that multiparty consensual democracy might be possible as a corrective to problems that simple majoritarian democracy has created in Africa.

Conclusion

In this essay, I have engaged Wiredu's (1997: 303-311) thesis that consensual democracy is a realistic possibility in solving the political crises in Africa that have been blamed on the use of an alien majoritarian democracy paradigm. While I agree with Wiredu (1997: 308-310) that majoritarian democracy paradigm has led to some significant problems in Africa, thereby justifying the clarion call for a return to the African consensual democracy model, I argued that a multi-party consensual democracy appears more suited for the present complexities of countries in Africa.

However, in the light of the confrontational nature of multi-party politics when understood in the context of majoritarian democracy, it would appear anomalous to suggest that it could be invoked in order to make consensual democracy more suited to the prevailing circumstances in present-day Africa. This concern seems justified, especially when one considers that political parties under majoritarian democracy are generally conceived as obsessed with power-seeking and retention antics, thereby causing animosity between winners and losers within countries. The losers in electoral contests would feel left out of the decisional processes of their respective countries, thereby creating animosity between the winners or the majority and the losers or the minority.

The result of such politics has been high levels of tensions and instability within countries in Africa mainly because the losers in electoral contests are excluded from participating meaningfully in governance issues (Mukandala 2001: 3; Rodrik 2016: 51). However, as I have noted in this chapter, the problem of minorities cannot be eliminated in any political theory. In this light, I have argued that a "multi-party consensual democracy" might be a viable and plausible democracy paradigm for countries in Africa if it is granted that such a paradigm seriously respects and accommodates the minorities in decisional and governance issues. As I see it, this could prove to be a worthy corrective to the problem of politics of exclusion that often characterises simple majoritarian democracy.

References

Ani, E. I. 2013. Africa and the Prospects of Deliberative Democracy. *South African Journal of Philosophy* 32(3): 207-219.

Ani, E. I. 2014. On Traditional African Consensual Rationality. *The Journal of Political Philosophy* 22(3): 342–365.

Eze, E. C. 1997. Democracy or Consensus? A Response to Wiredu. In E. C. Eze (ed.) *Postcolonial African Philosophy: A Critical Reader*. Cambridge, Massachusetts: Blackwell Publishers, Inc, 313-323.

Fatton, Jr., R. 1990. Liberal Democracy in Africa. *Political Science Quarterly* 105(3): 455-473.

Gross, D. 1992. *The Past in Ruins: Tradition and the Critique of Modernity*. The University of Massachusetts Press: Amherst.

Gyekye, K. 1996. *African Cultural Values: An Introduction*. Accra: Sankofa Publishing Company.

Gyekye, K. 2010. *Philosophy, Culture and Vision: African Perspectives, Selected Essays*. Accra: Sub-Saharan Publishers.

Hountondji, P. J. 2009. Knowledge of Africa, Knowledge by Africans: Two Perspectives on African Studies. *RCCS Annual Review* 1: 1-11.

Locke, J. 1823/2001. *Two Treatises of Government*. London: Thomas Tegg.

Mazrui, A. A. 1975. Africa and Cultural Dependency: The Case of the African University. In R. R. Laremont & F. Kalouche (eds.) *Africa and Other Civilizations: The Collected Essays of Ali. A. Mazrui, Vol-2*. Trenton, N. J: Africa World Press, 57-93.

Metz, T. 2012. Developing African Political Philosophy: Moral-Theoretic Strategies. *Philosophia Africana* 14(1): 61-83.

Mill, J. S. 1859. *On Liberty*. Kitchener: Batoche Books.

Mukandala, R. 2001. The State of African Democracy: Status, Prospects, Challenges. *African Journal of Political Science* 6(2): 1-10.

Nkrumah, K. 1964. *Consciencism: Philosophy for De-Colonisation*. London: Panaf Book Ltd.

Oladipo, O. 1995. Reason, Identity, and the African Quest: The Problems of Self-Definition in African Philosophy. *Africa Today* 42(3): 26-38.

Ramose, M. B. 1992. African Democratic Tradition: Oneness, Consensus and Openness: A Reply to Wamba-dia-Wamba. *Quest: Philosophical Discussions-An International African Journal of Philosophy* VI(1): 63-83.

Ramose, M. B. 1999. *African Philosophy through Ubuntu.* Harare: Mond Books.

Ramose, M. B. 2009. Towards Emancipative Politics in Modern Africa. In M. F. Murove (ed.) *African Ethics: An Anthology of Comparative and Applied Ethics.* Scottsville: University of KwaZulu-Natal Press, 412-426.

Rodrik, D. 2016. Is Liberal Democracy Feasible in Developing Countries? *Studies in Comparative International Development* 51(1): 50–59.

Sklar, R. L. 1983. Democracy in Africa. *African Studies Review* 26(3/4): 11-24.

Tar, U. A. 2010. The Challenges of Democracy and Democratisation in Africa and Middle East. *Information, Society and Justice* 3(2): 81-94.

Uwizeyimana, D. E. 2012. Democracy and Pretend Democracies in Africa: Myths of African democracies. *Law, Democracy & Development* 16: 139-161.

Venter, D. 2003. Democracy and Multiparty Politics in Africa: Recent Elections in Zambia, Zimbabwe, and Lesotho. *EASSRR* XIX(1): 1-39.

Wamba-dia-Wamba, E. 1992. Beyond Elite Politics of Democracy in Africa. *Quest: Philosophical Discussions-An International African Journal of Philosophy* VI(1): 29-42.

Wiredu, K. 1996. *Cultural Universals and Particulars: An African Perspective.* Bloomington and Indianapolis: Indiana University Press.

Wiredu, K. 1997. Democracy and Consensus in African Traditional Politics: A Plea for a Non-party Polity. In E. C. Eze (ed.) *Postcolonial African Philosophy: A Critical Reader.* Cambridge, Massachusetts: Blackwell Publishers, Inc., 303-312.

Chapter 5

Conceptualizing Traditional Consensus in Modern Africa

Bernard Matolino

University of Kwazulu-Natal

Introduction

This chapter seeks to achieve three aims. Firstly, I seek to show that Martin Odei Ajei's (2016) attempts at making traditional consensus conceptually relevant and viable for a modern African polity, does not succeed in diffusing the tension between a traditional mode and its possible transference to the modern era as a conceptually attractive polity. Secondly, I dispute Ajei's narrow interpretation of my objection to Kwasi Wiredu's notion of party as represented in subscripts $_{1,2,3}$ and $_{1,3}$. I will rehash the conceptual shortcomings in Wiredu's depiction of party as signified by the subscripts and show that Ajei's intervention in favour of Wiredu does not rescue Wiredu's notion of party from its inherent meaninglessness. Thirdly, I seek to show the difficulties attendant to attempts at conceptualising consensus for a modern African polity, particularly when that modern concept is drawn from a traditional communalistic orientation. The significance of what I seek to do here is to point out those stubborn areas around the viability of consensus that its supporters really need to think through and either concede to (as posing a danger to their advocated system), or begin to find adequate responses to.

Ajei's Intervention on the Consensus Debate

Ajei's intervention in the debate is to support the viability of consensus. His support is marshalled via three avenues. He starts by offering a presentation of Wiredu's well-known claims on the attractions of consensus, from which Ajei accepts that indeed consensus is viable and superior to majoritarian democracy. He then proceeds to provide answers to some critics of consensus, mainly being Emmanuel Ifeanyi Ani (2014) and myself. In some place, Ajei erroneously claims that Ani and I share the same objection to the possibility of rationality working in a traditional communal society. This is despite the fact that I (Matolino 2016) have excoriated Ani for his ungenerous suspicions against the possibility of a pure rational framework of deliberation in traditional consensual democracies. Finally, Ajei proposes to strengthen Wiredu's notion of consensus by supplementing it with Nyerere's view of community, which is inseparable from self-reliance.

This move is ostensibly made in response to Ani's complaint that Wiredu's traditional society is too remote and cannot be verified for our present purposes. Instead of answering this serious suspicion raised by Ani, Ajei chooses to fortify Wiredu's traditionally motivated account by adding yet another layer of appeal to traditionalism. The justification of this move is found much earlier in Ajei's article, where he outlines *the* aims behind Wiredu's position to lie in the conceptual decolonization of both African thought and practice. For Ajei, Wiredu achieves this by showing the relevance of traditional concepts to modern society and by demonstrating the appropriateness of jettisoning unsuitable inherited colonial practices.

Additionally, Ajei also considers Wiredu's project to be a crucial factor in the campaign against decolonizing African systems of thought. Clearly aware of the problem that this presentation may create for our understanding and appreciation of the role that tradition might be expected to play in our modern world, Ajei attempts to pre-empt such worries by insisting that Wiredu's use and understanding of tradition is not resistant to change or modernity.

He amplifies this claim by citing Humeira Iqtidar's (2016) interpretation of tradition as a structure of knowledge that has a method that organizes how knowledge is produced and consumed. This structure then places either implicit or explicit constraints on the tradition itself. Ajei's view, proceeding from this, is that "such constraints neither preclude methodological continuity after discontinuities, nor imply limits on theoretical alternatives or the ambit of debate. Its inspirational role includes license to develop the ideas and practices consisting the tradition by criticizing them. Such a view of tradition aptly describes Wiredu's understanding of it. It also represents the understanding of it that this paper will defend" (Ajei 2016: 447). However, and quite disappointingly, the promise contained in the immediately preceding sentence is not defended in the paper. What occupies Ajei in the rest of his paper are two major concerns; his specific fight against Ani and my objection to Wiredu, as well as a presentation of Wiredu's main reasons for supporting consensus (the naturalness and plausibility of its traditional antecedence to present-day Africa and opposition to liberal majoritarian democracy). The third and minor part is concerned with an attempt at revamping Wiredu's traditional consensus by supplementing it with Nyerere, as already indicated.

If we follow the sequence of the presentation of the support of consensus and its attempted re-modelling, we easily see that there are serious problems that immediately present themselves as a foil to Ajei's attempts at painting a plausible picture of consensus. The first challenge relates to how Ajei presents Wiredu's project as a contribution to decolonial engagement as well as an opposition to the imposition of alien political systems that are not well suited for Africa. The problem that Ajei creates is not so much his support for what Wiredu intends doing with the notion of consensus but the gaps that exist in Ajei's rushed approval of Wiredu's intention with his project. It is not unjust or unfair to expect or anticipate that Ajei would, at least, offer an explanation of what this project of decoloniality is. While it might appear obvious to Ajei what the sense of decolonialism is, for Wiredu, and what the markers of its success are going to be, it doesn't follow that such an understanding holds for all who come across both this word and the concept it represents. Not only is the burden on Ajei to delineate the word beyond common use, but he has to show where the conceptual marker and success of such a term has to lie. Is it to be understood in the same manner as Ngugi wa Thiongo's use of the vernacular, or in Tsenay Serequerberhan's politics of hermeneutics or Frantz Fanon's decolonial project? It appears as if Ajei has assumed that the term has a shared conceptual significance, which is not only desirable but represents a certain form of success and representation of the path that Africa must/has to take. While I may sound as merely quibbling on terminology and its notation, I think I have a more serious point operating behind this query. The point has to do with questions of how we think of the relationship amongst the pre-colonial, colonial, and post-colonial vis-à-vis the decolonial project. What does it mean to advocate the decolonial project in relation to all these epochs of our reality and what do we hope our conceptions of decoloniality to achieve? If, for instance, the decolonial project is to be successful, it has to be able to speak meaningfully and in a continuous and unifying way to our three epochs just pointed. It has to outline the form of relations that exist, whether in succession or in effect amongst these epochs and how those relations have an effect on us, the fauna.

The story, as presented by Wiredu, and Ajei's attempts to help him, do very badly. The failure is to be found in the very quick manner that Ajei, in particular, moves to recommend consensus' decolonial prowess by virtue of advocating the relevance of indigenous modes on modern life. It is here that he explains Wiredu's orientation towards tradition as one that is not stagnant but open to critique and is sensitive to extant experiences. However, the very paper that Ajei has written is an antithesis of this proposition. For a start, Ajei extols, in a very uncritical, if not altogether a dogmatic manner, the virtues of consensus. Much like Wiredu, he is rather too satisfied with what he thinks will be the guaranteed inferiority of majoritarian democracy when compared to the consensual variant. The shared assumption, in this instance, is that the repetition of the conditions that enabled consensus to work or the very presentation of the details of its workability in traditional communal societies and the accompanying claim that we should think of ways of animating it in modern-day independent Africa, is enough. The detail that is particularly lacking is in how the correspondence between traditional communalistic mores and a modernising Africa can be easily attained. In this specific instance, I am not denying the possibility of such a correspondence but am merely pointing that it is not forthcoming. We are simply requested to accept that it is possible without accompanying indicators of what would make that possibility a fact to be reckoned with. The transfer of the conceptual supports of traditional consensus to our present-day ideals and aspirations of democracy may prove to present special challenges to supporters of consensus. These challenges will have to do with what the justificatory tool of consensus could be in modern society. For example, Wiredu maintains that at the rock bottom, there is an identity of interests. Of course, in a small undifferentiated traditional, same ethnic society such a rock bottom is not only possible but highly desirable. If such a fact is used as an informant of the conceptual tool that is deployed in support of a democratic dispensation in the modern era, we expect that there be a description of the facts of this society that are responsible for the security of the concept.

This brings me to my next point; where do we get our concepts from? To be more precise, what is the source of our political theorization? I think that two plausible roots of sourcing our political conceptualization can be stated as either proceeding from our experiences or from what we think as an ideal to be aspired towards. With the former, our experiences could be either good or bad and we could draw from them information/lessons/practices that we think totally desirable or best avoided. With the latter, we could both think about our current situation and seek ways to improve the current details, or we could start from nowhere and imagine what the best society for us would be. I doubt that the last possibility obtains in its entirety. I suggest that all our thinking has to start from somewhere, has to be grounded in some fact and whatever we theorize about has to return to either improving that fact or discarding it or simply thinking about it further. No matter how we want to make a concept pure and simply one that is devoid of constraints of colouring of its specific point of origin that is not possible. As Bruce Janz (2009) argues, no concept is completely covered by nothing, it has to come from somewhere. This is why supporters of consensus always start from somewhere; the traditional communalistic life. It is this description of traditional communal life that gives consensus its conceptual impetus. It is from this continuity from practice to conceptualization that supporters of consensus find themselves in a very discomforting situation. They have to give an account of the all-time attractiveness of the concept yet, at the same time, are painfully aware that its grounding is located within a time frame whose way of life has been significantly lost. For Ajei the solution to this problem is to insist that Wiredu's use of tradition or traditional sources is open to critique, correction and a progressive understanding. He distinguishes Wiredu's sense and usage of the traditional and what is tradition from that of Horton and Lévy-Bruhl, which can be called traditionalism. I don't think we should allow Ajei to get away so cheaply. For a start, his reading of Wiredu seems oblivious to the crucial tension that is found in Wiredu. On one hand, Wiredu (1980) advocates that anachronistic traditional practices must be discarded and also, on the other hand, Wiredu (1997) invokes practices with all the appearances and sounds of being anachronistic as a fitting model of re-invigorating the African polity. The problem with Wiredu's drawing on consensus, from its traditional resources, to guide the modern polity lies in that he fails to explicate the level of relevance of that traditional resource to other resources that inform present-day political formation and reality. Thus he, probably unwittingly, glosses over the tension that exists between his irreconcilable commitments. However, and most worrying, is that there is no evidence in both Wiredu and Ajei that demonstrates any willingness or actual commitment to the usage of tradition that is open and willing to self-critique. Starting with Wiredu's anthropological presentation of the Akan traditional practice right up to Ajei's approval of it, one finds no self-reflective criticism. On the contrary, what one finds is stubborn insistence on the conceptual correctness of consensus in the face of criticism, including Ajei's project. But what is even worse from Ajei is his attempt at showing that Wiredu's version of tradition is superior to the one advocated for by Robin Horton and Lucien Lévy-Bruhl. One can only hope that Ajei's appreciation of critiques of tradition did not stagnate with the narrow traditionalism of the now widely discredited Horton and Lévy-Bruhl. It is worrisome and suspicious why Ajei does not deal with serious criticisms of tradition, such as found in E.C. Eze, M.O. Eze, and J.O Famakinwa. While the distinction between traditionalism and tradition holds, I do not think that there is any serious thinker who would rely on traditionalism to express reservations about the viability of consensus. On the contrary, those who question the use of tradition, to support consensus, are genuinely seeking to inquire into the conceptual and practical devices that can enable the transfer of consensus from traditional societies such as the Akan into modern-day West Africa. Such worries do not proceed from a traditionalistic orientation but from wanting to know the suitability of traditional practices for non-traditional set-ups.

Even if it were to be maintained that there is a timeless and conceptually defensible continuity of consensus from traditional communal societies to the here and now, it still has to be specified what precise aspect or aspects of consensus enable it to be so appealing in a timeless and noncontextualist fashion. My supposition is that such an argument is not forthcoming for the simple reason that there is a continuation between the social facts from which consensus emerged and the subsequent theoretical presentation of its viability. Such a close connection between social facts and the theorization that follows, presents a difficulty to supporters of consensus. The challenge is that their desire to cast consensus as evidently superior and preferable can only be true if accompanied by specifications that pick out the context in which consensus' superiority could be guaranteed. Without such a specification that natural superiority is open to questioning both practically and conceptually. Besides repeating what Wiredu has already indicated as the natural superiority that consensus has over majoritarianism and how consensus was made real in traditional Akan society, Ajei fails to take the matter any further.

The real problem, then, is not the comparison between the hapless versions of traditionalism and an appropriate use of tradition, as Ajei suggests. Rather, the real problem has to do with how tradition can ever be said to be capable of the very self-reflective process that Ajei thinks certain to consensus. What those who object to consensus are after, are the details of the enduring universal and African nature of consensus. What we are asking for is the spelling out of the characteristics that make consensus both viable in traditional Akan and fragmented West African post-colonial African societies. The challenge for supporters of consensus is how to transfer a purely traditionally rooted concept to a modern articulation of its usability when all the scaffolding pillars that made it work have all but disappeared. If the conceptual mapping of consensus is to succeed, I would suggest, that mapping has to be equally sensitive to the historical cum traditional underpinnings of the attraction of consensus as well as the realities that have shaped and continue to shape present-day Africa. These post traditional factors, for better or worse, have become a part of the political outlook that Africa presents and represents. Any responsible and hopeful conceptualization will have to take into account the effects of colonialism and its after-effects, as seen in the various complications presented in the agonies of the postcolonial state of Africa. That is why a comprehensive and fruitful analysis of the postcolony is necessary as opposed to a smug condemnation of foreign-imposed systems accompanied by demands for the need to return to the successes of democratic traditions as found in consensus. If supporters of consensus were truly advocates of an open tradition, they would be dealing with issues such as the challenges that traditions that sponsored consensus would present to a modern African polity. Such challenges, to my mind, would include the limited sources of political identity in traditional set ups. What cannot be disputed is that ethnicity/the clan and aligned notions of close kinship and reciprocal duties found in such a set-up, were the key elements of all political organization and subsequently consensus. Without the ethnic alliance and the natural ease with which members of a group understood themselves to be a holistic unit, including their religious beliefs and commitments, political expectations and duties, interpersonal relations and individual and state relations, legitimate authority and factors legitimizing that authority; one is left to wonder as to what exactly would make consensus work in the modern era where these necessary supporting elements are absent. It is here that the supporters of consensus are rather not very forthcoming in presenting detail that points to what approximates, in modern-day Africa, to the key elements that made consensus work and that will also make consensus work. If we stick to Ajei's demand for conceptualization when dealing with the issue at hand, we find that it is he who is failing at the requirement. He is unable to think of Africa as a shifting conceptual image that is in need of constant engagement to work out how its affecting forces are shaping it.

Yet besides all this, another intriguing failure on the part of Ajei has to do with his closed assumption that the failure of multi-party liberal democracy has to do with its foreign status and forced imposition. This approach betrays the dogmatic approach that supporters of consensus have become rather too comfortable with. What they do not seem to recognise is that there are many things on the continent, both practically and conceptually, that have been forcibly imposed that we have either come to support or think as justifiable. One of these things is the way we have come to think of African philosophy and what we now commonly accept African philosophy to be. Actually, Wiredu (1980) is at the forefront of transforming African philosophy from the hocus pocus of ancestral authoritarianism and unverifiable supernaturalistic claims to a more rigorous and conceptually sound endeavor. This rigour and conceptual soundness is not born out of our ancestors' love for the philosophical method that Wiredu strongly prefers, that he has led a large part of the continent into believing, and which he is remembered for both originating and excelling at. Rather, that method was learnt, first at the University of Ghana, and then perfected at Oxford. Wiredu's fame as an African philosopher, or even a pioneering and compelling figure in African philosophy, is not based on any project of decoloniality that shows a distinct flair in philosophizing on the African continent. Rather his fame is due to a debunking of an unworkable traditionalistic approach in favour of a well-known Anglo-Saxon approach. There are a good number of African philosophers who find this method not only acceptable but the only mode of philosophizing in Africa that is free of incoherencies and limitations of some or other traditional mode of philosophizing. As this is the case, supporters of consensus have to think carefully about their general conceptual commitment to their own art of philosophizing and how it relates to their conceptual commitment to consensus.

Ajei on Wiredu's Party Politics

In this section, I do not wish to give a detailed objection to Wiredu's attempt at showing how the notion of consensus as a non-party works. What is well known is that Wiredu's consensus is one that abhors and condemns multi-party politics. In the place of majoritarian multi-party democracy, Wiredu proposes and argues for what he calls a non-party polity. He provides a detailed outline only in his 2001 article where, through his use of subscripts attached to party, ranging from one to three, he attempts to show both the desirability and workability of a non-party polity. Throughout his argument, he makes it clear that his non-party version is different from a one-party polity, which he abhors as much as a multi-party system. However, as I have pointed (Matolino 2016a) there are some problems with this characterization.

Ajei, then, seeks to respond to some of the objections I have raised against Wiredu, and it is Ajei's response that I will address in this section. The first objection that Ajei addresses is wherein I accuse Wiredu's depiction of the various senses of party through the subscripts as quite intolerant of opposition. My problem, which Ajei does not point out in his paper, was the manner in which $party_1$ was initially characterised, by Wiredu, as an association of like-minded people but who ultimately seek to be $party_2$ to the final decision. By virtue, according to Wiredu, of those in $party_1$ seeking to be $party_2$ to a decision, then $party_3$ (which is an oppositional organisation/party) is ruled out. My difficulty with Wiredu was that his instance of $party_1$ was necessarily geared towards attaining $party_2$, and by his own account $party_3$ was the evil opposition that was to be avoided and whose occurrence was to be condemned. My second, and perhaps more significant problem, is how these subscripts are actually meant to do some hidden conceptual work. $Party_1$, $party_2$, and $party_3$ are actually representations of a desirable assemblage of political preference, how that political preference morphs itself into an acceptable interaction with other assemblages of political preference, and what is to be avoided, respectively. In the work that Ajei is responding to, I argue at length in an attempt to show that Wiredu's notion of $party_{1,3}$, which he brands the most evil instance of sectional appropriation of power, does not make sense on account of the subscripts $_1$ and $_3$ as stand-alone concepts. Their combination does not inherently or independently lead to the evil envisaged by Wiredu. Due to this incoherence, which is not insignificant since this was supposed to be Wiredu's demonstration of the irrelevance/evil of political parties, I concluded that Wiredu is intolerant of opposition parties and his polity could be seen as closely aligned to a one-party state. It was my argument that the reason for this view would naturally emanate from Wiredu's failure to offer compelling reasons either genuinely showing the conceptual evils of the party system, as he had hoped the subscripts to achieve, or to show the conceptual distinction, through the subscripts again, between his non-party polity and the one-party variant.

Ajei's response to the foregoing is presented as follows: Firstly, Ajei states that I ignore that Wiredu actually claims that consensus does not presuppose cognitive or moral identity of opinions, rather, even though there is a diversity of opinion what is required is that this diversity is reconciled so that the decision undertaken is acceptable to all, not obnoxious to anyone (Ajei 2016: 457). Even though this is taken as a response to my concerns, Ajei fails to address Ani's paper aptly titled *On agreed actions without agreed notions*, published in 2014. In that paper, Ani (2014a) contests the very idea proposed by Wiredu that all his idea of consensus is concerned about is the possibility of various parties coming to agree on a course of action without necessarily going through a cognitive or moral conversion. Ajei's ingenious contribution to this aspect of the debate is doubly to ignore Ani's serious reservations and merely insist that this is Wiredu's position.

Secondly, Ajei accuses me of having a misapprehension of the distinction between the analysis of an idea, at a theoretical level, and the misapplication of that idea in practice. As these considerations belong to different realms, the condemnation of the ideal should not be implicated in the abuse of its practice (Ajei 2016). I take Ajei's point to be that my objection condemns consensus for its practice as opposed to its idealistic formulation. I hold that even if it is the case that there is a distinction between the ideal and its practice, there is one slight problem with the version of consensus as presented by Wiredu. Wiredu's ideal of consensus is not drawn from a source of ideas but from a source of practices that Akans adhered to for the harmonious co-ordination of their political life. Take, for example, Ajei's citation of Wiredu's commitment to the idea that consensus was about the right action as opposed to the cognitive or moral agreement. What this, inadvertently, points to is the importance of the relationship between a certain practice and the so-called concept that comes from such reality. In this case, the conceptualization of consensus as a political ideal is a product of a particularized practice (in Wiredu's case the traditional Akans), which tends to downplay the significance of ideological difference. The continuation between the practice and the concept is so tightly formed, in this instance, that it cannot be ignored as if it did not exist. My objection, then, is to this formulation, which gives rise to a concept (supposedly of universal applicability) while the facts are of a very specific social and political setting. It surely can't be the case that the idealistic formulation of this sort will survive its social conditions. My argument has been that once the social conditions that served as an enabler of the ideal go, then the appropriate fit of that ideal disappears. While Ajei might wish to object to this clarification by pointing out that there are certain ideals that are attractive beyond the specificities of their time, such an objection needs to be cognisant of two important factors. The first is that philosophical ideals will always be found to be inadequate, in need of improvement or further clarification. That is what makes both moral and political philosophy (and indeed most of philosophizing) possible. It is also this very ability of philosophy that makes it a reflective exercise and worthy of its title. I am not convinced that Ajei is particularly interested in this sort of exercise. On the contrary, he is narrowly focused on offering die-hard defenses of the validity and viability of consensus at all times. He is unwilling to even consider Ani's (2014) suggestion that consensus must initiate a conversation with other systems in its neighborhood, such as deliberative democracy. Ani's (2014) belief is that the particularization of consensus to Africa will not add to its conceptual soundness. Secondly, Ajei must be prepared to come up with an account of the seamless transfer of consensus from its traditional Akan setting into its generalisability to the whole continent. Such conceptual continuity must be able to show the line of stability in consensus that makes it resilient in the face of vicissitudes and discontinuities that have marred the political topography of the continent, both ideologically and practically.

Ajei then swiftly moves to locate the real difference between Wiredu and myself in respect of parties and it is worthy to quote him fully in this respect.

> In my view, the substantive difference between Matolino and Wiredu on the nature of parties and status of parties$_3$ boils down to assumptions about the underlying values of a social and political philosophy: of different visions of what constitutes human ends, and of different conceptions of the conditions and ends of social cohesion. In Wiredu's view, the decisions that parties$_1$ endorse are conditioned by the principles of communalist ethics. A social system built in accord with such ethics is unlikely to produce parties$_1$ that consider their own interests to be diametrically opposed to other parties$_1$. In such a social setting, the institutions and processes of political practice, as vehicles to human good, are unlikely to be designed to encourage mutual exclusion of substantive positions but seek to reconcile them. Therefore, in such a setting it is conceivable, despite Matolino's belief, that parties$_1$ can work with the aim of seeking consensus and cooperation, and to carry on the business of policy making without a need for parties$_3$. What is required to be able to imagine the possibility, or even likelihood, of this happening is to be able to envision a political system built on the ethic of cooperation, and to admit that a cultural tradition can condition a people to build a social system that encourages parties$_1$ to adjust their aims to this ethic (Ajei 2016: 457).

This passage epitomises Ajei's approach to reading Wiredu; a committed and unquestioning endorsement of even troublesome facets of the pioneer. If we take the first two sentences of the quote, we might be led to think that the matter is simply of choice. That Wiredu and I have different choices in visions of what human ends are and what underlies social and political philosophy. But I hardly think that is the case. The differences are informed by serious disputes, not mere assumptions, about what our commitments are, in dealing with human differences. I take it to be the case, pretty much like Eze, that there will always be differences amongst human beings clustered together in any grouping, including political groups. Such differences can be trivial or serious, but they can't be reducible to some rock-bottom identity of interests. It is from this belief that I carry the conviction that an instance of party$_3$ is a legitimate expression of difference and must be protected. With Wiredu not sharing this thought, the issue, then, is no longer about the assumptions we have about the nature of political values, but of the nature of humanity and how humans relate to their interests. Even though Wiredu knows and acknowledges that deadly conflict could occur in traditional societies, as a result of different interests, we must remember that he maintains that consensus could be mostly had and he goes to some length to show that indeed it could be had (Wiredu 1997: 306-307). Thus, in the third sentence of the quote above, Ajei inadvertently succeeds in accurately outlining the very specific circumstances that enabled consensus to be had. The communalistic ethos of traditional African societies underpinned by a set of lifestyles that did not promote distinctiveness in what was seen as value and what is worthwhile, enabled all instances of differences captured in parties$_1$ to seek each other out and to be self-reconciling. That is how polities in a communalistic societies are, both by practical reckoning and theoretical postulation. It therefore follows, within this communalistic logic, that frowning on and resenting the possibility of party$_3$ is totally acceptable if not encouraged. Conceptually, even, the possibility of party$_3$ obtaining or serving any function of expressing distinct interests is rendered futile. The difficulty with Wiredu's position is its particularized, in both place and time, social and institutional ability to rule out interests of a nature that can legitimately coalesce to form equally legitimate party$_3$ interests and associations. It is its inability to talk to all ages and social circumstances that force Ajei to make a call, in the last sentence of the quote above, to come up with an imagination of the possibility of an ethic and polity that encourages its subjects to adhere to a limited sense of party$_1$. As a supporter of consensus, Ajei fails to realise that the onus is on him to provide us with that possible imagination.

As the issue stands, Ajei fails to provide conceptual frames that would rule out the desirability or demonstrate the alleged innate evil attendant to party$_3$, other than the claim that it never did and never will suite the traditional Akan understanding of the formulation of, and shifting of political preferences. My point must not be taken as a rejection of the appeal of something that is founded on traditional experience or traditional thought systems, rather what I am asking for is a presentation of as clear and as conceptually compelling demonstration of how any instance of a party$_3$ was undesirable in communalistic societies and how that remains so in non-communalistic societies. If this argument can be presented, even in sketchy detail, we might begin to see the reasons that Ajei has against any instance of party$_3$. But as things stand, and in the absence of such detail, Ajei can only resort to calls for the possibilities that consensus presents and our duty towards resuscitating those possibilites.

Conceptualising Traditional Consensus

In the last section of this essay, I wish to outline what I consider to be pertinent hindrances to the successful conceptualization of consensus. I suggest that three factors have to be reckoned with if consensus is to stand a chance. The first has to do with conceptualizing within changing social frameworks. The second has to do with what we could understand the role of a concept to be in political philosophy. And the third has to do with what we should imagine the political future of Africa to be.

With regard to the first factor, I consider myself to be under some obligation to explain with precision in what ways it is a hindrance to the supporter of consensus. And my explanation is as follows: Supporters and opponents of consensus share the same knowledge and acceptance of both historical and social facts that have shaped the past and current reality of this continent. Both camps accept the changed circumstances in which consensus operated, and that whatever its resuscitation would have to operate in remarkably different circumstances from its traditional antecedent. In the face of these bare facts, what supporters of consensus would need to produce, is a theory that is reflective of these changes or in keeping with the shifting grounds of the facts of society, the relations among people, and the ordering of important facets of life such as economic structures and entailed life opportunities. Such considerations, I suggest, cannot allow any responsible thinker to simply rehash the communalistic appeal and ethos of consensus as a plausible political theory. While certain facts are true, for example, the tense relationship between Africa and its former colonial powers (and the Northern hemisphere in general), what is not so obvious is how we should relate to these facts in as far as our thought processes are concerned. Capturing them as they are, thinking through them as they are, and protesting against them as they are, may perpetuate their historical toxicity and turn it into an intellectual toxicity. A toxicity which traps us to fail to see beyond its fumes. I suggest this is what has happened with supporters of consensus on the continent. Their continued and almost unrelenting comparison of a traditional mode of politics, and what disrupted it, with an eye on showing the superiority of consensus, is the trap of fumes I speak of. Why cannot supporters of consensus think of consensus in comparable deliberative theory, as Ani demands? Why can they not think of consensus in comparatively friendly political systems such as the Swiss? And I do not mean passing acknowledgement, but a meaningful conceptual conversation of how such systems (with or without rich traditional origins) are promising avenues of conceptualizing a polity that is relevant and workable to our present circumstances. I think the inability to transcend the trap of the fumes and develop newer frameworks has everything to do with how we choose to relate with our colonial experiences and what we think are the best ways of overcoming their humiliation. I suspect that since our conquest was largely carried through humiliating us, we seek not only to assert our pride but to also conceptually counter all misrepresentations about us. We fight to show, through a direct comparison, how woefully shortcoming the Western democratic mode is, and how our traditional polity fares better. We seek to show this traditional polity to be authentically ours, in its superiority, and hence for this reason alone worthy of immediate revival and application. While it is understandable that our pride is at stake and that its defense is not inappropriate, we have to ask ourselves at what cost does this exercise come. The very obvious cost from the foregoing is that it limits our possibilities of developing as many conceptual frameworks as possible to be of service to ourselves. In the quest to retrieve admirable aspects of our glorious and uninterrupted past, we turn a blind eye to our own complicities to our present and we fail to see an effective way out of the current morass. We neglect engaging useful concepts from the regions we accuse of brutality.

If Wiredu's project is conceived as steeped in the decolonial project, one can't help but notice the limitation of that decoloniality. Essentially by relying on communalistic and traditional spectrums to advance an account of decoloniality, the project is limited to a comparative exercise between an idyllic past and liberal Western majoritarian democracy. This invites the question of whether this is all that there could possibly be to decolonial endeavours. Why would we not think beyond both frameworks to envisage a state of affairs that is open to the possibility of encountering and processing other ideas beyond the traditions of our colonisers and our ancestors? While decoloniality presupposes engaging the colonial experience, the most important part of that engagement has to lie in finding ways of transcending that colonial experience. When it comes to thinking of ways of transcending the colonial experience, and all its negative effects, the process of working this possibility is limitless. Unlike Ajei, I would call for a more expansive imagination of possibilities of what our polity could look like, including acceptance of certain aspects of majoritarianism that might prove valuable. We do not have to always think, as a matter of necessity, that there is a need to offer an account that easily shows Western majoritarianism and traditional African consensus as naturally irreconcilable opposites. While I do not wish to venture into a proposal about the exact detail of what a helpful conceptualization of the polity has to be, I strongly caution against Ajei's defensive approach. I see such an approach as conservative in its unwillingness to go beyond the ethos of communalistic influences on our thinking of the shape and nature of a workable polity.

With respect to the second factor or hindrance, I wish to approach it by discussing the core nature of political philosophy and what concepts are supposed to do in that field. Political philosophy, like any branch of philosophy, is a reflection of human nature and existence. In particular, it reflects on a broad range of topics such as the nature of humans, their inter-relations, their relations with authority such as the state or governing authority, the legitimation and termination of political authority, institutions that govern all these relations and legitimate decision-making processes. This list is, of course, not exhaustive but is meant to give an indication of what we think as falling under political philosophy. However, these topics, and others we think appropriate to political philosophy, can be thought of and processed just about by anyone who might have an interest in politics. What distinguishes political philosophy from any other discussion, I suggest, is how philosophical conceptualization comes into play. It is when conceptualization occurs that we can say we have a political theory. But as to what a political theory does, David Archard answers the question as follows: "I do not mean by this the question of whether a theory should be about justice, the state, the class struggle, or whatever. I mean what is a theory taken to be doing when it answers a self-chosen question such as 'What is justice?'" (Archard 2003: 277). And a little later, he adds; "Analogously the task of political philosophy may be to reveal what our shared meanings do not and cannot say about our political world. The function of critique is to display these gaps and thus the distance between actuality and the moral pretensions generated by that actuality" (Ibid 278). What is worth considering is how we pursue the investigation into our chosen questions. The point is that a theory is not so much about what its contents are but how it exposes the inter-relations of the multiple layers of some truths we have accepted about ourselves. It is even incumbent upon the theory to show the shortcomings and contradictions of our certainty. We should, probably, in keeping with Karl Popper's falsification, not seek to be too trusting of our own theories but be prepared to open them to as much philosophical introspection as possible. This call is not weird or totally at odds with what supporters of consensus are intent on achieving. On the contrary, it is totally in keeping with Wiredu's identification of three evils that keep African conceptual systems from developing. The evils, according to Wiredu (1980), are anachronism, authoritarianism and supernaturalism.

Conceptual work, then, must be freed up from ideological defences of what is thought to be authentic modes of being African in the face of colonial mischief. Political concepts must be permitted to operate in pretty the same way they do when exposed to the rigorous demands of ordinary philosophical conceptual analysis, which is pervasive in and characteristic of all philosophy (including what Wiredu is famed for). An apologetic defense of, or abrasive advocacy for consensus is a limited usage of both conceptual tools and effectively narrows the field of political philosophy. This is reminiscent of the objections raised against ethnophilosophers. Remember that their conceptual scheme was geared towards the defense of a particular version of authentic African systems, ironically in opposition and as an alternative to Western systems of thought. It was that commitment that made their conceptual fashioning odd and not of any service in advancing the gains of African philosophy as a discipline that is worthy of respect as philosophy. While I am not presently claiming that supporters of consensus are moulded on the same principles as ethnophilosophy, it is incumbent upon them to guard against their conceptual framework developing essentialistic traces of the conceptual failures of ethnophilosophy. This is not a misguided hunch or call from my random thoughts, on the contrary, it is a well-considered reservation I have about consensus. Elsewhere I (Matolino 2017) have expressed some serious misgivings I have about consensus sharing the same features as theories of negritude and ujamaa, which are calls for the return to the source. In those places, I have sought to show the problems of the return to the source accounts. I maintain that supporters of consensus need to guard against a conceptual narrowing of their political philosophy.

Regarding the third hindrance, I suggest that it is incumbent not only on supporters of consensus but all involved in the field of political philosophy on the continent to imagine what polity would best represent an Africa we want in the immediate future. The two dominant theories that have been tried and that have failed on the continent being African socialism and majoritarian democracy, what can we say to transcend these failed and failing systems? What sort of future do we wish to develop that would avoid or completely rule out military take-overs, petty dictatorships, violation of citizens' political rights and suppression and murder of political opponents by those who hold state power? I think it is fairly easy to come up with a detailed description of what that future must look like. We will find it very easy to list all demands that will be representative of sanitized political spaces and conduct. However, what will prove a little more difficult is to establish a conceptual framework that will be responsible for establishing and overseeing the sanitization of political spaces and conduct. What will make this attempt even more difficult will be a willful insensitivity to realities that constitute the political landscape of the continent. An obdurate search for a communalistic inspiration for our modern polity, will miss the key characteristics that are supposed to be taken seriously in our theorization. I cite three such factors that the advocates of consensus appear to be not so cognisant of. Firstly, our nations are born out of an arbitrary assemblage of different ethnic groups. There is nothing wrong with this formation, however, at times, tribally generated conflict has led to the loss of life. As Wiredu correctly points out, this conflict is exacerbated when political activity and membership is tribally aligned and there is a lot to gain from the political spoils. If this reality prominently marks the African political scene, then we have reason to doubt the communalistic ethos and polity. What we then need is not so much of a consensus-seeking, or a reconciliation of values but the development of a system that will be sensitive and responsive to the problems occasioned by ethnic conflicts. Secondly, there are developments on the continent both at a material and conceptual level that are at odds with realities of communalistic arrangements responsible for the plausibility of consensus both as an ideal and political arrangement. At the material level, we live in societies that are characterised by radical differences in the economic standing amongst political citizens. Our economic arrangements have become predatory against the majority of citizens, they have become exploitative and are not run along ethos of commonness and co-operation. Many citizens lead materially debasing lives and struggle to make ends meet on less than one US dollar a day. We have witnessed many man-made disasters such as wars, thieving and looting, incompetencies and endemic corruption. At the conceptual level, a significant number of citizens have come to associate their political identity and understanding of political organisation as based on their successful agitation and defence of their rights. And the individual rights are conceived in a liberal way! Many citizens have multiple sources of identity, which transcend the immediate boundaries of their communities. It would be beneficial for consensus, as a theory, to speak meaningfully to these aspects and how its communalistic mores will be generated to a level where it is able to profitably align itself to all these realities. Thirdly, we as a people of this continent, are now connected to the rest of the world in more meaningful ways since the end of colonialism. Although we are a disadvantaged, exploited, and almost insignificant global player, we are still a player. In our multiple engagements with the rest of the world, we need to be highly assertive in establishing our respectable place in the order of international standing. We have to think of creative ways of asserting our political identity that is going to work for us at the international stage. Excessive reliance on traditional communalism as a source of such a polity is doubtful as an effective tool in improving our lot.

Conclusion

Consensus needs clarification at various levels. While there is an initial appeal and attraction of its possibility, that promise disappears when we start peeling off the layers that inform its sustainability. Once we start asking serious questions around the conceptual viability and possibility of consensus in the modern African space, we find that consensus does not have the capacity to provide readily convincing explanations of that viability. While my argument does not seek to debunk the usefulness of traditional sources in, possibly, inspiring the future, I maintain that such usefulness and promise cannot be assumed offhand. What is needed is detail in response to the worries that opponents or critics raise as worries around consensus' suitability in a modern African polity. What Ajei has provided is short of that detail. On the contrary, he has simply repeated the basics of what consensus is, in Wiredu's view, and brushed off criticisms as merely unpleasant interjections.

References

Ajei, M.O. 2016. Kwasi Wiredu's Consensual Democracy: Prospects for Practice in Africa. *European Journal of Political Theory* 15(4): 445-466.

Ani, E.I. 2014. On Traditional African Consensual Rationality. *Journal of Political Philosophy* 22(3): 342-365.

Ani, E.I. 2014a. On Agreed Actions without Agreed Notions. *South African Journal of Philosophy* 33(3): 311-320.

Archard, D. 2003. Political and Social Philosophy. In N. Bunnin and E. P. Tsui-James (eds.) *The Blackwell Companion to Philosophy*. Hoboken: John Wiley and Sons.

Iqtidar, H. 2016. Tradition and Islamic Revivalist Thought. *European Journal of Political Theory* 15(4): 424-444.

Janz, B. 2009. *Philosophy in an African Place*. Lanham: Rowmann Littlefield.

Matolino, B. 2016. Rationality and Consensus in Kwasi Wiredu's Traditional African Polities. *Theoria* 63(146): 36-55.

Matolino, B. 2016a. Ending Party Cleavage for a Better Polity: Is Kwasi Wiredu's Non-party Polity a Viable Alternative to a Party Polity? *Acta Academica* 48(2): 91-107.

Matolino, B. 2017. Return to the Source? Challenges and Prospects. in P. Ngulube (ed.) *Handbook of Research on Social, Cultural, and Educational Considerations of Indigenous Knowledge in Developing Countries*. Hershey PA: IGI Global 2017.

Wiredu, K. 1980. *Philosophy and an African Culture*. Cambridge: Cambridge University Press.

Wiredu, K. 1997. Democracy and Consensus in African Traditional Politics: A Plea for a Non-party Polity. In Eze, E.C. (ed.) *Postcolonial African Philosophy: A Critical Reader*. Oxford: Blackwell.

Wiredu, K. 2001. Democracy by Consensus: Some Conceptual Considerations. *Philosophical Papers* 30(3): 227-244.

Chapter 6

The Problem of Elections in Wiredu's Consensus Democracy

Vitumbiko Nyirenda

University of the Witwatersrand

Introduction

Kwasi Wiredu, in his paper, "Democracy by Consensus: Some Conceptual Considerations" (2001) offers an alternative system of governance, different from the modern-day majoritarian democracy.[1] He claims that this alternative offers a better solution in dealing with most of the problems of governance in Africa, which he associates with the majoritarian system of governance, problems that arise as a result of the need for parties to retain power and lack of substantial representation of the electorate (Wiredu 2001). I choose to contextualize my discussion within a modern African society where the proposed system is meant to be applied. I argue that as long as consensus democracy involves elections, it will present the same problems as majoritarian democracy. A successful conclusion of this view means that Wiredu does not offer a better system of governance to that of majoritarian democracy. I specifically discuss voting by looking at a clash between self-regarding values and other-regarding values within the context of consensus democracy in modern Africa. Thus, I look at the challenge of how a particular dominant value may feature in what/who people vote for, and the value they ought to promote through their vote in a particular political system. As a critique of Wiredu's consensus democracy, this chapter aligns itself with other prominent critiques of Wiredu such as those of Kazeem Fayemi (2010), Bernard Matolino (2013), Emmanuel Eze (1997), Emmanuel Ani (2014), just to

---

[1] By majoritarian democracy Wiredu refers to the kind of democracy based on the majority principle. That is, where decisions are taken based on the interests of the majority (see Wiredu 2001: 232).

mention a few, which seek to show that Wiredu's consensus democracy may not be a better alternative to majoritarian democracy.

This chapter is structured in the following way, in section one, I will provide some general views of Wiredu's consensual democracy. In this section, I will only discuss ideas I believe would help the reader to have a general overview of Wiredu's consensus democracy. In section two, I will provide an exposition on how Wiredu argues for elections in the consensual democracy he proposes. I will discuss Wiredu's views on elections and more especially, how he proposes that representatives will be chosen. In section three, I will offer a discussion of the problem(s) of elections based on the assumptions and arguments made in section one. Lastly, I offer a conclusion to the chapter.

Wiredu's Consensus Democracy

Wiredu's discussion of consensus democracy starts by defining the term "democracy." According to him, democracy is a political system in which the executive and legislative powers are assumed and exercised only by groups. These institutions are not necessarily identical. Furthermore, representatives are periodically chosen by the people in free elections, provided there is an independent judiciary and a free press (Wiredu 2001: 227-228).

Central to the above characterization is the need for representation. That is, choosing a particular group of people after a set period of time who are given the power or authority to govern. Nonetheless, what is important is that the decisions of the members of the society are made by or deliberated upon by these elected individuals on behalf of the society. Furthermore, the presupposition is that these members are chosen as representatives in a free and fair election. In this chapter, I take it that the choice of the particular representative, given that the election was free and fair, corresponds to the kind of changes people need or goal they seek to promote in a particular system. That is, people choose representatives who represent the goals of a particular system they want and the changes they need in their society. Whether this is usually a success or achievable is a different question. Ideally, it is reasonable to accept that the election itself and the representatives chosen in a free and fair election are those that support a particular goal or system.

In any case, Wiredu's main task is to provide an account of consensus democracy by critiquing its rival, majoritarian democracy. Consensus democracy as an alternative is borne out of the major problems associated with majoritarian democracy. These problems include the strong need to acquire and retain power as well as lack of substantial representation

(Wiredu 2001). Wiredu is unequivocal is stating that in most African countries, especially those practicing multiparty democracy, there is always fierce competition for power among individuals belonging to different parties. Parties that manage to acquire power continue to hold on to it to the extent that taking away power from such parties may result in bloodshed. I believe that part of the reason for this is that most of the parties that had acquired power become corrupt and maintaining power gives them some kind of immunity from prosecution. This may be because with their power, they can influence or control structures that may demand accountability and prosecution. Therefore, it is not surprising that those in power would take advantage of the election with the hope of holding on to power. By taking advantage here, I mean being able to utilize resources to participate in all such evils common during elections (whatever these might be). Furthermore, in discussing lack of substantial representation, Wiredu has in mind some groups within a society, mostly the minority, whose voices are not considered or heard because the majority's decision tends to carry the day whenever there is deliberation. This is not problematic if the minority agrees with the majority, but it is a problem if the majority disagrees with the minority and it becomes obvious that it is the majority's decision that would carry more weight. Thus, individuals or groups who might always find themselves at the side of the minority will never have their voice carry much weight. According to Wiredu, the problem with this is that it violates one of the moral principles that every individual or person has the moral right to consent to actions or forbearances that affect their interests and concerns (Wiredu 2001: 231). It is in line with these and other problems I have not mentioned that Wiredu proposes consensus democracy. He considers consensus democracy as a better alternative to majoritarian democracy (Wiredu 2001).

In presenting a structure of consensual democracy, Wiredu presents one which is different from the majoritarian. A kind of structure that could be described as a "non-party type of government" and this should not be understood as a "non-party state" (Wiredu 2001: 239). It would help to unpack what Wiredu means by these two phrases. In general, the distinction rests on the different meanings of the word "party," a move that has not been happily accepted by other philosophers (Matolino 2013; Wiredu 2011). Wiredu expresses the word party by different subscripts, which I will explore below.

Wiredu discusses three notions of party; Party$_1$, Party$_2$ and Party$_3$.[2] Party$_1$, represents an association of individuals or group of individuals with an issue or concern. Thus, it is about members who share ideas and come together to discuss them. More importantly, it is a platform where members of the society exercise their right to free expression (Wiredu 2001: 238). Party$_2$, means being a participant to "a consensual decision reached" (Wiredu 2001: 238). It can be understood as the moment of being part of an agreement (decision) between individuals. Party$_3$, represents formal or ordinary "political parties" which, according to Wiredu, aim at winning governmental power. He seems to consider them as opposition parties. One question that still needs to be answered at this stage is regarding what Wiredu means by non-party polity. Reference is here made to party$_3$, hence a non-opposition party system of government. Two reasons can be provided for this view. First, his account of consensus democracy is modelled on the Akan traditional political system, which did not have opposition political parties, hence influencing the kind of consensus democracy he comes up with. Second, Wiredu locates most of the problems of majoritarian democracy to the idea of having opposition political parties who are always fighting for power. Thus, majoritarian democracies work under a multiparty system through which representatives are chosen. Competition for power becomes a competition between various parties (the opposition and the ruling parties). In Wiredu's consensus democracy, instead of having these political parties who fight for power, there will be associations which would be a platform for citizens to discuss issues that affect them (Wiredu 2001). He states that "if all parties$_1$ are party$_2$ to the decision, there is nothing to oppose and no need of a party$_3$ to do the opposing" (Wiredu 2001: 238). Thus, central to consensual democracy is reaching consensus, party$_2$, rather than basing decisions on majority or unnecessary opposition aimed at bringing down the government as commonly attributed to party$_3$. According

---

[2] Bernard Matolino has objected to using the word "party" in these three senses. He argues that it is incoherent to consider party$_2$ as the same as party$_1$ and party$_3$. This should not be the case because the method and content of agreement of parties$_1$ does not make it the agreement of party$_2$. Party$_1$ is made of association of individuals who come together to share and discuss their ideas. This is not the same as party$_2$, of deliberating on an issue and arriving at a consensual decision. Party$_3$ being political parties, institutions. Thus, inconsistences are rooted in the idea that party$_2$ is a moment, party$_3$, an institution, and party$_1$, an association (See Matolino 2013). However, there would be charitable reading of Wiredu. One would argue that Wiredu does not dispute the different meanings of the word "party." It is what he endorses. The use of the word party in all senses would be because of the underlying theme, and that is, "being part of something" which is found in all the three senses. The actual differences and meanings have been captured by the subscripts.

to Wiredu, there will be no "sectional appropriation of power," which is a characteristic of governments having party₃(s) (Wiredu 2001: 239). In this kind of democracy, power will be shared among party₁ through party₂. However, Wiredu is quick to point out that the denial of party₃ need not be taken to imply the absence of having opposing views. Having party₂ and many party₁(s), is in some sense an indication that there are different opposing views. In other words, talking about consensus, party₂, would be irrelevant if there are no opposing views among different party₁(s) (Gyekye & Wiredu 1992). Having many party₁(s) partly presupposes different groups having different ideas.

Given this structure of democracy, Wiredu moves on to discuss his ideas on election or how representatives will be chosen. Since his presentation of consensus democracy is based on the African traditional model of the Akan it would be helpful to consider that a discussion of issues or problems of elections in consensus democracy should also refer back to the traditional political system to explore its distinctiveness from the modern system within the proposed consensus democracy. There are things that I believe can be said about elections in modern-day democracy as well as in the traditional past. This is in line with answering two questions, firstly, whether in the Akan political system people were voting for representatives to the council of elders as it is done in modern democracies or it was by appointment.[3] Secondly, whether the choice of representatives in the traditional past, say the Akan elders present a similar criteria (requirements) as in modern democracies.[4] Unravelling these questions can help one understand the changes that have occurred in modern political system and whether modelling a political system from the traditional African past responds to these changes or turns a blind eye. Without paying attention to changes, one is likely to have the same political problems there are in any other new political system. I will return to these views later, but for now, I will consider Wiredu's presentation of elections in the proposed consensus democracy.

---

[3] The first question presupposes that the process of voting would be a questionable idea for some cultures. This is because the concept of voting seems to be new to them. I argue that it might be new on the basis that one would not find the local word for voting. For instance, in one of the Malawian languages, Chewa, there is no local word for "voting." What one finds is the word *"kuvota"* which is a combination of the local prefix *"ku-"* and the English word "vote" translated as *"-vota."* The same seems to hold true for Zulu, a south African language.

[4] I have in mind such requirements as one's ideas in standing for something shared by the people or what may be called a clear manifesto, one's character, knowledge or wisdom and age.

Consensual Democracy and Elections

In the proposed consensus democracy, Wiredu provides an account of elections. According to him, free elections do not mean an electoral competition of duly registered parties. Rather, it means a process in which individuals as well as associations can exert themselves in the persuasion of the electorate. In this process, associations will not be contestants, but only individuals will contest in general elections. And at the very least, civil organizations, for him, may be assigned some agreed number of representatives in the governing body (Wiredu 2001: 243).

One interesting feature is the nature of elections Wiredu provides. Wiredu argues that elections will not be a competition of party$_1$(s) (associations). Part of the reasoning would be the evils and worries he associates with registered political parties as found in majoritarian democracies. Parties in a majoritarian democracy are usually associated with competition for power. This goes back to the view that parties would do anything to make sure that they get the power. Part of what is meant by "doing anything" includes evils such as bribing of the electorate, laying out false accusations against other competing parties, starting riots and manipulation of votes (Wiredu 2001). Even though these problems have been linked to party systems in majoritarian democracies, they can also be linked to associations and that could be a good reason for not letting associations contest in the general elections. Instead, Wiredu argues that it is individuals who will have to contest in the general election (Wiredu 2001). However, my understanding of Wiredu shows that there is nothing in consensus that would stop individuals from doing the very same evils that are associated with majoritarian political parties or associations. If one looks closely at problems in the majoritarian system, some of the evils are attributed to particular individuals despite operating under the banner of their parties. Therefore, it is not clear to me what feature in consensus democracy would prevent individuals competing in an election, rigging votes or being involved in violent campaigns. It seems to me that the problem can easily shift from being attributed to registered parties to being attributed to individuals.

Furthermore, Wiredu claims that the associations will be given an agreed number of representatives in the governing body. This plan, Wiredu notes, "should raise the probability of any given individual being in at least one large voting group" (Wiredu 2001: 244). Although Wiredu does not unpack what he means by this view, I believe the idea here is that associations do not just represent one voting group, they may represent a number of voting groups hence an individual who belongs to an association is likely to have a wider representation than an independent candidate. In any case, belonging to more than one voting group seems to be compatible with the whole idea of consensus democracy, where this particular type of democracy offers better representation than majoritarian democracy. I will not go into details here because this view is not part of the concerns of this chapter. My general worry, however, is that there is less information regarding elections in Wiredu's paper raising questions whether he took them seriously or he was concerned about proposing a general account of consensus democracy. However, a new polity would not be viable if one does not pay attention to important features that make that system work, and elections are that one feature.

Nonetheless, Wiredu also looks into some of the problems that can be associated with elections. He seems to acknowledge problems such as bias in allocating development projects, and elections being majoritarian. Elections, he says, in their customary conception are a highly majoritarian procedure. In such elections, voters who vote for the triumphant candidate belonging to the triumphant party take on or assume some sort of ascendancy over those of the minority that did not vote for the triumphant candidate(Wiredu 2001: 243). For Wiredu, we see this in some parts of Africa, where democratically elected governments do mark areas that failed to vote for them so as to skip them when it is time for the apportionment or allocation of development projects (Wiredu 2001: 243).

The above view highlights something common about how the decision of the winner of the election is taken. Usually, the winner of the election is the individual or the party that got more votes than other candidates or parties. This makes elections to be inherently majoritarian. This seems to be the rule for most of the electoral systems. It is here that Wiredu also raises an important issue that has to be taken seriously. This is the view that when people are told to vote, and the outcome of the election is to be announced, the winner is determined by looking at the number of votes against the losing candidate. The one who has been voted by the majority (having the greater number of votes) is declared the winner of the election. The winner is here seen as the majority against other individual political parties. Those belonging to the winning party now tend to consider themselves as controlling the powers of the state. For instance, in Malawi, when the Democratic Progressive Party (DPP) was declared the winner of the 2019 election, the other opposition parties such as the Malawi Congress Party (MCP) and United Transformation Movement (UTM) did not accept the results, citing irregularities in the way the election was handled. MCP and UTM mobilized their supporters to protests in the streets. But the protests met opposition from the ruling party members, known as the "DPP cadets" who started beating the protesters. The opposition complained citing infringement on their rights (Muheya 2019). The point here is that winners of the election tend to consider themselves as exceptional and having control over other party members even when they all have the same rights and freedoms.

Furthermore, there is another specific problem that Wiredu provides. Some candidates take note of areas that did not vote for them and such areas are sidelined for development projects. The problem here is that it goes against the common expectation that everyone who has agreed to be part of the state (or a citizen) of the state, ought to enjoy some level of benefits (goods and services) the state offers. The assumption being that the state is a social contract and individual members belonging to that state are part of the contract (Hobbes 1651; Locke 2003). Any individual person who is part of the contract ought to share (enjoy) what the contract offers, both benefits and burdens (Rawls 1971; Gauthier 1986). Failure to take part or share benefits and burdens of the state is partially equivalent to not being in the contract.

Nonetheless, Wiredu argues that in a consensus democracy, this will be avoided (Wiredu 2001). Part of the suggestion is that making decisions by consensus would allow considering that everyone, more especially the minorities benefit as well (Wiredu 2001). That is, it will not only be the majority who enjoy various development projects offered by the state, but deliberations and final decision on who gets to benefit from development projects will require the minority's consent. Thus, in a consensual setting, the decision of the minority is equally as valuable as that of the majority.

In sum, this section was meant to provide a brief account of elections provided by Wiredu. This was meant to lay a ground for the critique that I offer in the next section. I started by providing an account of consensus democracy, according to Wiredu. I then presented what he takes to be a method of elections that will provide for wider representation of the electorate. In what follows, I will discuss what I take to be a more fundamental problem to any elections, that of decision making and more specifically, the problem of self-interests.

How Election is a Problem in Consensual Democracy

The idea that consensus democracy may involve elections is not problematic in itself. The assumption supporting this claim is that there is a need for elections in a modern democratic polity. The need here comes after considering the complexity of the political society in the modern era than in the traditional past. In the past, the communities were small and most of them were made up of people related by blood. For instance, among the Akan, each village or Akan town was made of clans, which were, in turn, made up of individuals having blood relations. At the village level, they had a chief who was the ruler and was assisted by a council of elders who were representatives of the various clans (Wiredu and Gyekye 1992). One should not take for granted the role of blood relations among individuals within the clans and how this develops a deeper sense of community. This is different from modern complex communities where individuals live together but there is no blood relationship among them.

It is here that one would see a distinction in the sense of community people might have.[5] Nonetheless, what I find important here is the issue of governance, specifically, choice of elders to the council. Since these were small groups of people belonging to the same clan, it would seem unproblematic if one were to consider how elders were chosen to the council. Part of the criterion includes eldership, wisdom and character (Rempong 2000). That is, they would choose a person who is the eldest in the community and believed to be wise and of good moral standing. At the same time, the person ought to have good character. I will not go into details explaining these three, but the general idea is that leadership in the African setting goes along with one's wisdom and character and these two are also linked to age (Menkiti 1984). The choice of leaders to the council who was fitting that criterion was by appointment rather than voting by ballot (Rempong 2000). In small societies, it is easy to identify individuals belonging to clans who would fit the requirements and through consultations or succession, an individual takes up the role. In this day and age, one does not go around looking for an eldest individual who has moral standing and wisdom, considering the kind of large and complex societies that are available now. In modern societies, there are also problems in determining the character of the individual and so the general requirement for many seems to be the absence of a criminal record. But the absence of criminal record is not an indication of good character. Some of these problems suggest that there has to be a different criterion in selecting leaders. However, this seems to be a trivial suggestion since there is a new method of selecting leaders, voting by ballot. But this new method can also be called into question given Africa's history. This is partly to answer questions on why Africans suddenly changed to new methods of choosing leaders. One obvious reason seems that choosing leaders by appointment seems implausible. But this may not be enough if one has to acknowledge the influence of colonialism on the African continent. For instance, Khabele Matlosa argues that the majority of the African countries, especially those that were under British colonial rule, adopted the Westminster constitution and its subsequent electoral system. The problem here being that the electoral system most of these nations are not born out of "public debate and internal political consensus" but are merely inherited from the colonial masters (Matlosa 2004: 26). This means that colonialism not only impacted on

---

[5] This might sound like an empirical question but it is also clear that there is a distinction between a communalist society common in African setting which may be defined by blood relations and an individualistic one common in the West which does not define itself in terms of blood relations. The underlying point here is that most post-colonial African societies exhibit individualistic tendencies and the sense of community defined in terms of blood relations has been undermined.

the social life of the African but also on the political life too. The idea here is that any proposed new political system like the one Wiredu proposes ought to pay attention to how elections feature in that new system. Wiredu, no doubt, proposes a model that seeks to speak to the traditional culture(s) of the African by modeling it on the Akan, but one question one may ask is whether his views on elections also speak to the African traditional past.

This now brings me to the main issue of whether having elections in a consensual democracy avoids the problems of majoritarian democracy. This is the question I seek to explore in this section. As highlighted before, the major draw-back is that Wiredu has not provided sufficient information regarding elections.[6] As such, I will be highlighting what I take to be a fundamental problem for elections, more importantly, for consensus democracy in modern Africa. I seek to discuss the problem of "self-interests" in decision making during elections, and specifically, when voting. The main argument here is that as long as consensus democracy involves elections, where elections would require voting as Wiredu proposes, then consensus democracy will have the same problems as majoritarian. I do this by pointing to one problematic feature of voting, that of self-interests. I have adopted the same approach Wiredu uses by going back to the traditional past. Thus, I look at a value that supported the consensus political system in the traditional past and how that value ought to feature in the Wiredu's proposed consensus democracy if voting is involved. In other words, my focus is on conflicting values present when making a decision about what to vote for and what I take to be a requirement for consensus democracy. The values I consider to be important in this paper are "self-regarding" values (I will use synonymously with self-interest) and "other-regarding" values. I seek to show how these values influence what people decide to vote for (self-interests or common good) and how this may be compatible or would conflict with what is required to be promoted by their vote based on the kind of political system within which elections are conducted (modern African consensus democracy).[7]

It is perhaps more important to put forward certain assumptions before discussing my argument. Consensus democracy in traditional Africa operated

---

[6] I have framed this argument in a way that it tackles the issues Wiredu presents, so that the argument does not become a straw man.

[7] I will not advance a particular conception of common good. What I take to be a common good here is just a function of individual good. Furthermore, when I argue that voting for common good is the virtue for democracy, I have placed myself already in a camp that takes the common good as more important, thus, the public-spirited view. See Jason Brennan for a discussion on this view, (Brennan 2011).

within communities that were "deeply" communal.[8] One common feature of communalistic societies important to this paper is that they are "other regarding." By other-regarding, I refer to the idea of putting (or promoting) the interest of others (the community) above one's own or individual interest.[9] This has to be distinguished from self-regarding, which in this paper, is used synonymously with "self-interest." I consider "self-regarding" as putting one's (individual, personal) interests above or without regarding community's or other people's interests. That said, the assumption here is that consensus democracy worked well in traditional African communities, which were communalistic and whose dominant value was the "other regarding." Thus, conceding to a decision in a consensual setting was not only the result of being persuaded by the argument the other person presents, rather, it was also grounded in an understanding that the interests of others are as important as my own and should be taken seriously.[10] One might ask whether this kind of attitude could be applicable in modern-day democracy. One way to do this is to look at how Africa has changed on the African continent and whether such changes would still support the promotion of other regarding values. Therefore, given the African history of colonialism, it is not easy to simply argue that the values that were practiced in the traditional African community are still alive and functional in the modern-day African community. The reason is that during colonialism, most structures of the community in Africa were destroyed, a new economy and political life was imposed on these communities by colonialists (Mudimbe 1988). This led to culture shock with new values replacing or challenging on old ones in precolonial societies.

A more specific example to the above view is that most of the African countries were colonized by the West, and most Western countries are individualistic.[11] Unlike communalism, individualism is more self-regarding. Individualism here is seen as the opposite of communalism. Thus, it puts the interest of the individual first above or without regarding the community's interest (Brennan 2011; Schwab and Pollis 1979). This means that individualism is more self-regarding. It is undeniable that much of what may

---

[8] Communalism here refers to "social formation founded on kinship relations" (see Wiredu 2008, p. 335).

[9] The idea of community interest here refers to the common good.

[10] I will not go into details defending this claim. For the sake of argument, I take it as an assumption. For a discussion, refer to Wiredu's discussion of social formation and obligations and his discussion of other regarding value (See Wiredu, 2008).

[11] Individualism puts the interest of the individual first before the community (See Brennan, 2011; Schwab and Pollis, 1979).

be taken as African (seen as that which is commonly practiced on the African continent) was affected by the imposition of Western values on the Africans. Thus, most African societies have adopted values associated with individualism. A self-regarding value has become the dominating value. There is no longer a deeper sense of community as one would find in the pre-colonial traditional societies where community members were made up of clans having blood relations. Therefore, I take it that the way of life and more particularly, the way people make decisions is self-regarding value. It should be noted that I do not make a stronger claim that this is the reality of the African now, rather I make a weaker claim that for the most part of the African life, this is the reality. In any case, such an environment, where the dominant value is now self-regarding, is a challenge for consensus democracy, which works better with other-regarding values.

The above discussion raises an interesting question about change of values, where the adopted value is not compatible with consensus democracy (as per assumption made above) and how this is a challenge for elections in general and voting in particular. The assumptions put forward should help one to understand how voting based on self-interests is problematic for consensus democracy and how it is also related to some problems discussed in section one. As I would argue, the very idea or concept of voting seems to be new in some African languages, with reference to the lack of the local word for voting in these languages (Chewa, a Malawian language, for example). Here one would prima facie question the whole idea of voting, a view that is supported by an argument made on electoral systems being an inheritance from the colonizers. The absence of the concept in some cultures and the adoption of the colonial heritage explains why voting remains central among most African countries. Nonetheless, one point to note is that to every voting process, whether in majoritarian or consensual democracy, decision making is unavoidable. As long as representatives are required to be voted into power, the voters will have to decide who to vote for, more importantly, what to vote for (the common good).[12] In this chapter, I consider voting as a way in which a political community seeks to promote a particular idea (being whatever it is people are voting for) more than merely putting someone in a position of power. The reason being that I consider the latter reason to be trivial since each person who presents him/herself as a candidate stands for some particular idea. It is this idea that people vote for when choosing who they have to vote for. For instance, if one takes the common good as something to

---

[12] I take the question of "what to vote for" as more fundamental than "who to vote for". The former is what underlies most decisions and the latter stands to represent the former.

promote in a consensual community, then voting for the common good by choosing an individual who represents it is one way of promoting it.

However, as pointed out, one problem that I have identified for elections in consensus democracy for modern African societies is making decisions based on self-interests. When members of the society are voting, it is not clear what interests are considered to be at play. Similarly, it is also not clear whether the candidate to be chosen wishes to advance his/her self-interests or the common good. Nonetheless, it is plausible to claim that decisions would be based on the internalized or dominant values of the society, while acknowledging that it needs not to be a strong claim of necessity.[13] In any case, based on the argument that in most modern African states, individualism (self-regarding) is the dominant value, it would follow that one's decisions during voting are likely to be guided by the promotion of one's self-interests. In other words, people may be considered as voting for their self-interests. The reason this is problematic for consensus democracy is that a consensual polity is one in which people ought to vote for or where people's decisions are guided by other-regarding values and not self-interests. Thus, it would occur within a context that does not require putting one's self-interest first. I take this as a clash between the requirement of both the individual *as a voter* and a candidate *to become a representative (potential representative)* in consensus democracy. Here the phrases "as a voter" and "potential representative" represent political roles that require something of the individual who has taken that role at that particular time. For the sake of argument, I assume that one requirement of the role of the voter or the electorate, is to vote for the common good.[14] Similarly, a potential representative understands his or her role as that of the promotion of the common good.[15] When a person registers to vote, the person takes up a political role where decisions and responsibilities for this role affect the society as a whole (Brennan 2011). As such, it would be more congenial to put community interests first than those of the individual. But as I argued before, this is already a value within communalistic societies whose members are other-regarding and promote the common good.

---

[13] This looks at how what people take as a value and something that has defined their lives is likely to influence how they live or make decisions over what they should vote for.

[14] In the traditional African community, members of that community were taught ways in which they would become persons (borrowed from Menkiti 1984) who put the interest of the community at heart (for a discussion see Mbiti 1970, Menkiti 1984, Etieyibo 2018, Metz 2007, Wiredu 2008).

[15] This argument is made with reference to African communalism where the common good is the highest good.

To express the point differently, it was pointed out that decisions are influenced by the values people have internalized about their societies. Therefore, voting in an individualistic society may be different. This is not to say that an individual in such a society always votes based on self-interests and votes for self-interests or that voting for self-interest is bad.[16] Nonetheless, the important point is that internalized values may manifest in the way people act and make decisions. Therefore, when it comes to voting, it can be said that a person who has internalized self-regarding values in an individualistic society is likely to base one's voting decisions on self-interests (in such a society, it would not be surprising if individuals promote self-interests by voting for them). This points to how voting would be conducted in consensus democracy within an African society that has been individualized. Thus, consensus democracy in modern-day Africa would not have the same effect it had in the past. The value to be promoted during elections will not be the same value that grounded the traditional model. Hence there will be conflicting values between what is promoted (self-interests) and a value that is required, that supports consensus democracy (common good); a value that is more profound in a society that has a deeper sense of community than an individualistic one.

There is a way to connect all these ideas about decision making, choice of representatives and the problems of majoritarian democracy that were presented in section one. This provides an explanation to the view that as long as consensus democracy involves elections, it will not be different from majoritarian democracy. Part of the argument is that the problems listed in section one are linked not just to the political system (structural) but also connected to individuals' self-interests. In other words, much as there is a structural problem in which majoritarian system allows for various political parties which are problematic, as presented by Wiredu, the problems that manifest during elections in majoritarian democracy can be linked to self-interest. These problems come because individuals seek to advance their interests above those of the community. Voting for self-interests opens the door to many electoral problems in which people are willing to indulge in immoral actions to make sure their interests are met. In other words, if self-interests are at the center of decision making, violence, corruption, bribery or

---

[16] Brennan has a discussion of voting for self-interest not being bad in itself. He has an analogy of the market economy where the invisible hand is central. Thus, promoting self-interests promotes the common good but central to it is the invisible hand. he argues that there is no reason to think voting for self-interest would promote the common good, as if by such invisible hand (for a discussion see Brennan 2011, p. 124-133).

manipulation of results would be inevitable. All these evils are against the idea of promoting the common good or general welfare of one's community. Individuals are likely to indulge in such behaviors, which, for the most part, only benefit certain individuals and have nothing to do with the common good or the society as a whole. Note that this is not to presuppose that promotion of self-interests is bad in itself. Self-interests and common good can coincide and this becomes less of a problem. The point I seek to draw attention to is that common good ought to be the center of decision making for voting and representation especially for consensus democracy, for reasons given in this paper but if self-interest is the dominant value in the modern society, it means that consensus democracy as long as it involves elections where people are voting for self-interests, still has the same problems as majoritarian democracy.

Conclusion

In summary, this essay has argued that if consensus democracy in modern Africa is to become a success, elections have to be taken seriously. I have argued that as long as consensus democracy involves elections, it is likely to be affected by the problems of majoritarian democracy in one way or another. I pointed out that elections involve voting and the main challenge to voting is decision making. I argued that in modern Africa, a dominant attitude now for most people is fulfillment of self-interest. Self-interests or self-regarding values result from an individualistic ethic, one that is dominant in a post-colonial Africa due to the influence of colonialism. I have argued that this is a challenge for consensus democracy, which Wiredu has proposed. A kind of democracy which was based on traditional African model whose dominant value was putting interests of the community first than individual interests (other-regarding). It is a challenge because people vote not guided by other regarding values so that they can promote the common good, important for consensus democracy, but people vote guided by self-interests raising questions towards the promotion of the common good.

References

Ani, E. I. 2014. On Agreed Actions without Agreed Notions. *South African Journal of Philosophy* 33(3): 311-320.

Brennan, J. 2011 *The Ethics of Voting*. Princeton University Press.

Etieyibo, E. 2018. Moral Force and the "it-it" in Menkiti's Normative Conception of Personhood," *Filosofia Theoretica: Journal of African Philosophy, Culture and Religions* 7(2): 47-60.

Eze, E. C. 1997. Democracy or Consensus? A Response to Wiredu. In C Eze (ed.) *Postcolonial African Philosophy: a Critical Reader*. Cambridge: Blackwell, 313-323.

Fayemi, A. K. 2010. A Critique of Consensual Democracy and Human Rights in Kwasi Wiredu's Philosophy. *Lumina: An Interdisciplinary Research and Scholarly Journal* 21(1): 1-13.

Gauthier, D. 1986. *Morals by Agreement.* Oxford: Oxford University Press.

Hobbes, 1651a. *Leviathan.* C.B Macpherson (Ed), 1985. London: Penguin Books.

Locke, J 2003, *Two Treatises of Government and a Letter Concerning Toleration,* Yale University Press.

Matlosa, K. 2004. Electoral System, Constitutionalism and Conflict Management in Southern Africa. *Africa Journal on Conflict Resolution* 4(2): 11-54.

Matolino, B. 2013. The Nature of Opposition in Kwasi Wiredu's Democracy by Consensus. *African Studies* 72(1): 138-152.

Mbiti, J. 1970. *African Religions and Philosophies.* New York, Doubleday and Company.

Menkiti, I. A. 1984. Person and Community in African Traditional Thought. *African Philosophy: An Introduction* 3: 171-182.

Metz, T. 2007. Toward an African Moral Theory. *The Journal of Political Philosophy* 15(3): 321–341.

Mudimbe, VY 1988. *The Invention of Africa.* Bloomington: Indiana University Press.

Muheya, G. 2019. DPP cadets beat marchers in Blantyre: Concerned citizen demanding Ansah to resign. *Nyasatimes,* 4 July. Available from: https://www.nyasatimes.com/dpp-cadets-beat-marchers-in-blantyre-concerned-citizens-demanding-ansah-to-resign/ [6 August 2019].

Rawls, J. 1971. *A Theory of Justice.* Cambridge, Massachusetts: Harvard University Press.

Rempong, N. A. 2000. Elite Succession among the Matrilineal Akan of Ghana. In *Elites: Choice, Leadership and Succession* [chapter 4], Lisboa, Etnográfica Press. Available on: http://books.openedition.org/etnograficapress/1338>. ISBN: 9791036516344. DOI: 10.4000/books.etnograficapress.1338 [6 August 2019].

Schwab, P. & Pollis, A 1979. *Human Rights: A Western Construct with Limited Applicability. Human Rights: Cultural and Ideological Perspectives.* New York: Praeger, pp.1-18.

Wiredu, K. and Gyekye, K. (eds.) 1992. *Person and Community: Ghanaian Philosophical Studies.* Washington DC: Council for Research in Values and Philosophy.

Wiredu, K. 2001. Democracy by Consensus: Some Conceptual Considerations. *Philosophical Papers* 30(3): 227-244.

Wiredu, K 2008, "Social Philosophy in Postcolonial Africa: Some Preliminaries Concerning Communalism and Communitarianism," *South African Journal of Philosophy* 27(4): 332-339.

Chapter 7

Consensus and Compromise

Emmanuel Ifeanyi Ani

University of Ghana

Introduction

The broad understanding regarding Wiredu's proposal for democracy by consensus is that we should aim more at achieving compromises than achieving unanimities. Along this line, this paper undertakes a taxonomy of compromising based on three broad categories of issues we normally try to compromise on. This exercise produces a categorization of compromises from the easiest and most common to the most difficult and rare. I then make some theoretical comparisons for insights arising from the categorization.

To do these, I have divided the chapter into five sections. The first section presents Wiredu's proposal for a consensual democracy, whilst the second section discusses Wiredu's vacillations between unanimity and a compromise understanding of consensus. In the third section, I explicate my three kinds of compromise: proportional, strategic, and normative compromise. In a proportional compromise, we compromise simply by adjusting our different intensities of the same principle, commodity or value. In a strategic compromise, we adjust our conflicting methods or strategies for achieving the same goals, but in a normative compromise, we could only compromise by letting go of our normative principles. In the fourth section, I summarize Lepora's three kinds of compromise: substitution, intersection, and conjunction compromise. She explains that in substitution compromise, conflicting agents abandon their original conflicting principles for a third alternative that partially satisfies their originally conflicting principles. In intersection compromise conflicting agents simply settle for those principles that overlap or are common between them, discarding those that are causing the conflict. And she explains that in conjunction compromise conflicting agents could only abandon their principles for concern for their opposites, making it the most difficult and morally implicating kind of compromise. In the fifth section, I compare our taxonomies of compromise and present intersections that offer insights for further research on compromising. This is, in turn, aimed to help practitioners of democracy by consensus make themselves abreast with strengths and loopholes of compromising, and to elucidate what a consensus polity has to deal with in the business of compromising.

Wiredu's Proposal for a Consensual Democracy

Kwasi Wiredu proposed a consensual form of democracy that borrows some principles of consensus from the consensual practices of some traditional African societies. He makes this proposal due to his dissatisfaction with the majoritarian arrangement of the modern multi-party system of democracy. His general observation is that majoritarian ways of deciding issues do not require much effort, is hardly inspiring, and that its cheapness comes with several costs, such as division and polarization (Wiredu 2011: 1060). Wiredu notes that for countries consisting of numerous ethnic groups, the majoritarian arrangement is a disaster, as it could keep certain ethnic minorities marginalized (2011: 1064).

As an alternative, Wiredu asks us to consider the method of consensus in decision making practised by some traditional societies such as his native Ashanti Kingdom. Lineage was the basic political structure of this system. Every lineage has a head, who is automatically a member of the town or village council. Consensus begins at the lineage level, where every lineage head is elected by a consensus of its members. Consensus is the method of decision making at the council, including the election of its representative to the divisional council, which in turn elects a representative to the national council presided by the Ashanti king. At all these levels, consensus is the method of decision making (Wiredu 1996: 184-185). The kinship system was therefore an enabling factor for the good operation of consensus in this kingdom. Wiredu admits that it would be anachronistic to suggest the kinship system as a model for contemporary African politics, given the ethnic diversity on the continent. But he argues that the history of inter-ethnic conflict is more reason why a consensual democracy should be considered (Ibid, 189).

Wiredu offered a few technical arguments for the viability of reaching consensus. First, he clarified that consensus does not entail total agreement; it, in fact, presupposes diversity. He admits that not all issues are straightforward, and because issues do not always polarize along the lines of strict contradictoriness, dialogue could serve to smoothen edges to produce compromises. And where there is a will to consensus, dialogue could lead to a willing suspension of disagreement (usually by the minority) making possible agreed actions without agreed notions, or agreement about what is to be done without necessarily agreement about our beliefs or our conceptions about what is true or false (Wiredu 1996: 183). This endeavour requires the patience and persuasiveness of the right people (Ibid).

Second, Wiredu argues that we may not always achieve consensus, but we can always aim at it. He writes, "In the rare case of an intractable division a majority vote might be used to break the impasse. But the success of the system must be judged by the rarity of such predicaments in the workings of the decision making bodies of the state" (Wiredu 1996: 190).

Unanimity or Compromise

In certain places, however, Wiredu gives the impression that by consensus, he means unanimity. He writes, "There was never an act of formal voting. Indeed, there is no long-standing word for voting in the language of the Ashantis" (1996: 184). The import is that voting is a Western influence. Wiredu also writes that any decision short of the agreement of 100% of participants is a loss of consensus (2011: 1065). He also writes that consensus is essential for securing the substantive or decisional representation of every participant in a deliberation in the decision of the deliberating group (Wiredu 1996: 189). These utterances have attracted some response from the literature. Kibujjo Kalumba writes that when Wiredu argues that consensus is essential for securing the will of every member in a group decision, it means unanimity, and Kalumba argues that a unanimity understanding of consensus is too high and unrealistic a moral requirement (Kalumba 2015: 106-108). Bernard Matolino suggests that consensus could be re-read not as unanimity but as mutual adjustment of the positions of two dissenting parties (2009: 40). This seems the realistic way out of Wiredu's unanimity understanding of a workable consensual democracy. However, the mutual adjustments that Matolino writes about are what we usually call *compromise*.

In spite of Wiredu's unanimity conceptions of consensus, he endorses the compromise understanding of consensus, Consensus, he notes, falls short of total unanimity; however, it is an affair of compromise, where compromise means the adjustment of the interests of individuals (in terms of incongruent convictions regarding what is to be done) to the common interest and necessity for something to be done (2011: 1057). So what we see from Wiredu is a vacillation between a unanimist and a compromise understanding of a consensus standard. There seems, therefore, a broad understanding that consensus as a project needs to be studied in terms of compromise. This paper is a project on our prospects of reaching a compromise and how these prospects vary across different categories of issues on which we seek compromise. I will then test this theory by comparing it to Chiara Lepora's three kinds of compromise, which explores different kinds of compromises based on what we give (or lose) to a compromise. The overlaps and intersections between my theory and that of Lepora provide a few insights for further research on studying the concept and business of compromising.

Compromise and What we Normally Compromise on

Compromise is the basic instrument for getting participants in a deliberation to adjust their positions towards a consensual or common ground. This makes compromise an important phenomenon for study. But our ability to compromise seems affected by the kinds or categories of issues or problems on which we seek compromise. It is this categorization of issues and the varying prospects of the different categories for a compromise project that I wish to outline. My outline is that the first category of issues permits only a *proportional* compromise, the second a *strategic* compromise, and the third a *normative* compromise.

Proportional Compromise

We engage in proportional compromise when we compromise in terms of proportions, degrees, scales, quantities, and/or quality. Technically, we talk of *proportion*, degree, scale, magnitude, intensity, or indeed *measurement*, when we reference quantity (and/or sometimes quality) *of the same item*. This is the commonest kind of compromise. A typical example of this is price bargaining. When we bargain the price of a tin of milk or a business conglomerate, the compromise would likely involve losing part of the original profit envisaged by the seller, and the loss of more money than the buyer wished to spend. This is a financial compromise: what is lost in different ways to both parties is money, not principles of concern.

Compromising over what we do with our time is also proportional compromise: it is similar to compromising about money and other material goods. This is because we spend our time making money. We also spend our time doing other things that are not profit-oriented but likewise valuable.

Due to their common, easy, and straightforward nature, there is a tendency to think that compromising over quantities (such as financial and other material compromises) is not compromise. There is, for instance, a common tendency in the literature to deny price bargains the qualification of compromise, probably due to their frequent and non-consequential nature (see Benditt 1979; Coons 1979: 191-192; Lister 2007: 17-18; Lepora 2012: 4; Jones and O'Flynn 2012: 120). Lepora, for instance, writes, "We ought to reserve the term 'compromise' in the inter-personal context, too, to refer to compromises over matters that are of principled concern to the parties to the compromise. A resolution of a dispute over some matter that is of no *principled* concern to anyone—like the price of a used car—might better be described as merely a 'deal' or a 'bargain'" (2012: 4). But this is a conflation of concepts because the terms 'bargain' and 'compromise' are operationally inseparable. We compromise *in order to* reach a bargain, and the later is not possible without the former. Also, any product of compromise is strictly a *bargain,* no matter whether the items of compromise are moral principles or prices of commodities.

These scholars are focused on the pettiness or non-consequential nature of the prices of commodities as items of compromise. But not all examples of proportional compromise are that simple. For example, two political parties (A and B) are represented in a parliament. These parties have radically different visions of how to generate and allocate revenue in the wellbeing of their constituencies. Party A is controlled by the wealthy and favours tax breaks for the upper class as well as fiscal allocations that make business easy for the rich but provide no advantages for the less privileged. Party B is a party of the 'masses' and favours the opposite principles (heavy taxes on the rich to provide amenities for the less privileged). In the event that a reconstitution of tax laws needs bi-partisan agreement, both parties must adjust their different visions of taxes on the rich until they meet at a mean. This is a proportional compromise, but it could take months.

Strategic Compromise

This is when we need to compromise to resolve a conflict over *method,* strategy, approach, tactic, interests, and so on. For clarity, I will discuss two broad sub-categories of conflict whose resolutions entail making strategic compromises. They are (1) conflict over strategies for achieving common goals, and (2) conflicting strategic interests.

Let me begin with a compromise over conflicting strategies for achieving common goals. Suppose that a minority demographic unit (such as a minority race in a multi-racial setting or an ethnic minority in a multi-ethnic setting) feels completely marginalized and ignored by the majority. The vexation of this demographic unit crystallizes over time in the formation of two groups with radically different methods of expressing self-determination. Group A favours the method of making supplications or appealing benignly to the national government to pay more attention to the needs of its demographic unit or region, whilst group B prefers to use armed conflict, threats and intimidation in sending the same message home to the national government. Let us assume that officials of the national government clarify that they cannot reach any workable agreement with any representative of this unit or region unless the unit or region speaks with one voice, since they would not reach an agreement with group A and continue to suffer attacks from group B. If both groups agree to form a single group for the purpose of speaking with one voice and tone for the region, some obvious compromises in method are inevitable. Suppose that group B decides to abandon armed insurrection whilst group A agrees to toughen its advocacy tone a little. This compromise ensures that none of the groups could continue with its original method for advocating the needs of its people, but it is better than nothing if both groups must unite to achieve their common goal.

I have mentioned that we could conflict over strategies for achieving common goals. Goals include human wellbeing or collective self-preservation (as seen in the above example) or implementing a normative value. An explication of the latter is that we could conflict in how to fight corruption. We may both believe that corruption needs to be reduced (a normative position) but I may prefer to chase after and prosecute corrupt past government officials whilst you prefer to focus on setting up online systems of collecting revenue that ensures revenues and taxes go directly from the citizenry into the government treasury controlled by the three arms of government. Your preference for this method may be premised on the argument that it is a huge waste of time prosecuting corrupt past government officials, and that a better strategy is simply preventing more public money from getting lost.

Let me now talk about the second broad category of strategic compromise: compromising over strategic interests. Strategic interests are *all* of those interests concerned with attaining material wellbeing. Strategic interests are *strategic* because, on the broadest interpretation, they are all *strategies* for attaining material and psychological human wellbeing. I contrast these interests with normative interests, that is, interests that arise from normative principles. All material (economic, career, political, demographic) interests are strategic *to the extent* that they are not intertwined with normative or metaphysical principles or beliefs. An otherwise economic interest ceases to be strategic if it is also motivated by a religious principle or belief.

For a good example of a conflict of strategic interests, consider a community at loggerheads with an oil company for degrading their environment with pollutants arising from oil drilling. Executives of this oil company argue that they have a license to drill oil in the vicinity and therefore owe the community no explanations. But members of this community threaten to commence lobbying of government officials to cause a withdrawing of this company's oil drilling license. Such an eventuality would be quite disastrous for the company's fortunes. The community is interested in its environmental wellbeing whilst the company is interested in its financial wellbeing, but both these interests happen to clash. Importantly, none of these (the company losing its license and the community losing its ecosystem) needs to happen if representatives of both parties could put heads together and fashion a compromise. Suppose that both sides agree to negotiation, and arrive at a deal in which the company greatly reduces its polluting activities and allocates some of its wealth to improving the living standards of the community by building a hospital and forming a scholarship scheme for funding the education of bright students from the community up to the university or tertiary level. This is a compromise because neither of the two sides ended with just exactly what it wanted. But both have arrived at a common position that makes life with the other side a bit tolerable.

The compromise above is possible because the interests of both parties are only strategic. Suppose that any of the sides believed that it has *divine mandate* to maintain its position. Let us assume, for example, that members of the community believe that their gods disapprove of the pollution of their environment. This makes a compromise quite impossible since agreeing to a compromise would be *wrongdoing* in the eyes of members of the community. This bleak picture of the prospects of normative compromise takes me into its fuller discussion.

Normative Compromise

Here I refer to reaching compromise in order to resolve conflicts involving differences in normative principles, such as differences in moral principles, religious beliefs, metaphysical conceptions of the universe, views about the nature of man, and so on. Elsewhere I discussed the most common example of normative conflict, the abortion debate (see Ani 2019). I think that conflicts over decriminalizing abortion arise from conflict over the normative status of abortion, and this normative conflict arises from conflicting metaphysical notions about the universe and man's place in it. Those who believe abortion should remain criminalized are likely to view the world as God's creation, to view man as made of body and soul, and to view every life (including the life of any foetus) as representing a divine mission on earth. It is normatively self-extinguishing for a holder of such a metaphysic to permit a decriminalization of abortion. A person holding such a metaphysical set of beliefs would see any compromise permitting abortion as wrongdoing in her own eyes. Such a perception of wrongdoing is absent in proportional and strategic compromise.

There are other examples of the challenge of reaching a normative compromise. I had discussed the example of a community that believes that its gods are angry with the pollution of its land. Permitting an oil company to continue to pollute the land is not likely, even in the face of the economic and social provisions offered by the company. Any material benefits promised by the other party to a proposed compromise is often rendered useless if it is up against the upholding of a religious belief and, sometimes, a consistently or jealously held moral principle.

More conflicts actually may be arising from conflicting normative positions than we may imagine. A few examples are disagreements over gay marriage, welfare packages for the poor and destitute, providing a very widely affordable health insurance, favouring a stronger military at the expense of a stronger economy or vice versa, even tackling climate change. There are indeed normative differences regarding economic distribution, such as the entire range of socio-economic ideologies from extreme socialism to extreme capitalism (far-right, centre right, centre left, and far-left). Adopting any of these ideologies is often a product of one's entire upbringing. And the perennial conflict arising from these ideological differences continue to fuel disputes regarding legislative and even daily economic decisions. More conflicts also arise from deep-seated differences in personally held moral principles. An example would be whether we should go to war or not: some interpret restraint as maturity, whilst others interpret it as naivety and setting a precedence of cowardice. It is not impossible for differences in religious principles to have a hand in many of these normative conflicts.

Let me take the liberty to add to the normative category certain other aspects of human living that may not exactly be described as 'normative' but manifest the stubbornness seen in normative conflict. These aspects of life include the desire to dominate, nationalism, and ethnic allegiance. Conflicts arising from differences along these tendencies could endure as much as normative conflicts, and compromising may be difficult except if an appeal is made to strategic compromise of one sort or the other. For example, it may be difficult to convince a person to stop desiring to dominate others, but it may be easier to convince such a person to dominate in more healthy ways (through superiority in academic, sport, entrepreneurial, and so on) performance than through bullying, intimidation or violence. It is also difficult to reconcile a lot of disputes in multi-ethnic societies except by convincing all parties that certain strategic compromises or agreements benefit all parties. In such a scenario, the ethnicity-motivated differences remain whilst strategic initiatives serve to smoothen colliding rough edges, or at least prevent them from getting too rough in perpetual collision. Just like ethnicity is probably the biggest threat to unity in many countries, nationalism has been the biggest threat to international harmony over the last two centuries. We could only continue to keep these aspects of life from going out of control by employing strategic compromises wherever we could to secure mutually beneficial initiatives. To be sure, strategic compromises do not eliminate differences in nationalism, ethnicity, nor does it even *reduce* these tendencies; strategic compromises only serve to produce piece-meal broad-based mutual compensations that make life a bit tolerable in pluralistic settings. It used to be hoped that tendencies such as ethnicity and nationalism would gradually diminish with more education and exposure.[1] But time is showing that this hope is probably exaggerated.

---

[1] See the findings of Roberta Mapp on the correlations between education and ethnicity as far back as 1972 (86-95).

In summary of this section, then, normative compromises are the most difficult to achieve because many metaphysical views are, in fact, products of upbringing. And when normative differences find their way into ordinary differences such as political or economic differences, such ordinary differences seem to take on an extraordinary stature. Apart from normative differences, ethnicities and nationalisms are also difficult human tendencies that affect our positions on a lot of issues, and we could at best employ strategic compromises to enable culturally diverse humans to live a harmonious life together.

Let me now turn my attention to Lepora's taxonomy of compromises in order to do some comparison of our theories and obtain a few additional insights for further research.

Lepora's Taxonomy of Compromise

Lepora had undertaken a different taxonomy of compromise that I find useful in testing the plausibility of my kinds of compromise. But her taxonomy was centred on finding out different kinds of compromises in terms of what we give and get in a compromise, how we give and get, and how the compromise is similar or different from our original positions before the compromise. Along these lines, she categorized compromises into substitution, intersection and conjunction compromises.

Substitution Compromise

The first kind of compromise is the substitution compromise. This is the compromise in which two conflicting parties abandon their original positions for a third position that partially satisfies their original positions. Lepora (2012: 8) gives an example with two doctors caring for a terminally ill patient who is unaware of her terminal diagnosis. Whilst one doctor believes that the patient should not know about the terminal illness because of her frail psychological state, the other doctor believes the patient has the right to know and that this supersedes the worry about her frail psychological state. So the principle of the first doctor is that we should not jeopardize people's wellbeing whilst the second doctor believes in the principle that we should be completely open and honest to patients. If the two doctors have the obligation to arrive at a joint position, then they need to arrive at a compromise. One such compromise might be to disclose the information to the patient's family. This decision only partially satisfies each doctor's principle: they have avoided hurting the patient psychologically with terrible news, but they have been honest at least to the patient's family. It satisfies neither doctor's position, but it at least partially caters for it. Lepora summarizes it by saying that doctor A abandons principles A, B, C and D whilst doctor B abandons principles E, F, G, and H; and both settle instead for principle X.

There is an insight that Lepora's substitution compromise provides in the light of my distinction between normative and strategic values. Both doctors share the same normative value (in this case valuing the wellbeing of the patient) but prefer quite opposing strategies (or strategic values) that service this normative value (one valuing the patient's psychological ease more and the other valuing the patient's cognitive consent more). It could suffice for both parties if they found a third and more embracing strategy that cater at least partially for their original strategic values.

Intersection Compromise

There are conflicting positions that *overlap*, and this makes for the easiest kind of compromise, since all the compromise needs to do is simply adopt the overlaps. In Lepora's example, doctor A holds principles I, J, K, L, whilst doctor B holds principles K, L, M, N. One notices that each of them holds principles K, L. It may also be the case that the other two principles held by each doctor oppose or are incompatible to those of the other doctor (I, J in doctor A opposing or are incompatible to M, N in doctor B). They may therefore agree to jointly pursue K, L (their overlapping principles) and drop the principles causing the opposition and incompatibility (doctor A drops I, J and doctor B drops M, N).

As a practical example, Lepora asks us to imagine two doctors working in an area with overwhelming health needs. One of them adopts the principle of treating as many patients as possible each day, but the other adopts the principle of giving as much time as possible to each patient. If, for example, both doctors must work together (one a surgeon and the other an anaesthetist, and each must examine patients prior to each surgery), then both must agree on a common pace of work. This would mean that each must decrease the degree of her own valued goal: doctor A must decrease the speed with which she sees patients whilst doctor B would need to increase her speed by decreasing the time with which she sees each patient. These mutual adjustments are simply continued until the two doctors achieve the same pace.

I am not convinced that this is a good example of an intersection compromise, at least as Lepora explained it in theory. Going by my earlier treatment of compromise, one could easily recognize this as a proportional compromise. On the other hand, an intersection compromise is one made by selecting the values that conflicting parties share (or the overlapping values) and building on them to the exclusion of the values that bring conflict. We see intersection compromise on a daily basis when two friends understand that they would both avoid issues that hurt any of them and take an interest in only those things that promote each of them. We see it when business partners eliminate aspects of doing business that could ultimately harm the interest or value of any partner, and instead stick to aspects that benefit all the parties. Indeed, common interest is by itself a product of intersection compromise. In politics, we see intersection compromise play out in the kinds of laws being enacted when rival parties are fairly represented. Proposals that suit one party to the exclusion of others do not succeed, and only those bills that all or majority wants to some degree or the other get passage. Next to my proportional compromise, then, Lepora's intersection compromise is the commonest form of compromise.

Conjunction Compromise

Lepora speaks of a third kind of compromise, that between parties that have *nothing* in common, either before or after negotiation. Their principled positions directly conflict, but they have a reason to resolve the conflict. However, this kind of compromise means abandoning one's principled position for its opposite, such as abandoning O for not-O (Lepora 2012: 10).

Lepora considers that parties may later come to realize that what initially seemed incompatible principles were actually somehow reconcilable, and that some subset of both parties were the same (in which case we are talking about an intersection compromise) or that the initially incompatible principles could be modified to produce a more compatible principle (which would be substitution compromise). But conjunction compromise is quite different from these because it takes place when parties' entire sets of principles are completely opposing. For example, agent A has principles O, P, Q, and R; whilst agent B has principles not-O, not-P, not-Q, and not-R. If these agents must really reach a compromise, then they may share half of the principles of each for both agents to adopt. For example, both may adopt O and P from agent A and not-Q and not-R from agent B, and thereby arrive at a compromised common position of O, P, not-Q and not-R. There is no intersection and no mutually agreed substitution from outside the initial sets of conflicting principles. Instead, the principles of compromise are drawn from opposing sets, to be pursed by each with the forbearance of the other or jointly by both (Ibid).

Lepora argues that this kind of compromise, in which parties compromise by abandoning principles of concern for their very opposites, makes conjunction compromise a wholly different ball game in terms of the responsibility felt by compromising parties for compromising. This is because anyone nursing a particular principle of concern sees a party believing in the opposite principle of concern as *doing something wrong.* Therefore someone who adopts a principle that is opposite her principle of concern also sees herself as doing something wrong, or at least allowing something wrong. It therefore follows that parties to a conjunction compromise, in which parties adopt wholly opposing sets of principles, would see themselves as contributing to wrongdoing from each party's perspective (Ibid., 11).

For an example of conjunction compromise, Lepora asks us to consider a humanitarian convoy carrying medical supplies that needs to cross a militarised zone in order to reach a hospital. According to the Geneva Convention, those carrying medical aid need to be unarmed, white flagged, and neutral with respect to any fighting force. This convention is to enable them to be respected by all sides. But disgracefully, there are wars where some fighters attack medical supplies and workers. So, contrary to the Geneva Conventions, some medical supplies might accept armed escort. This compromise is needed to deliver medical aid in dangerous wars. So humanitarians would accept armed escort, whilst armed forces would provide armed escort to humanitarians, which is contrary to their own rules of engagement. Both parties have compromised their principles of concern for their very opposites, and therefore, certain uneasiness is inevitable attached to the arrangement (Ibid, 11-12).

Even the very idea of forming a *joint agency* with a party holding sets of principles completely opposite to one's sets of principles of concern is repelling. This is a quite different matter from *whatever* the joint agency is meant to achieve. A compelling example given by Lepora is that the International Committee of the Red Cross (ICRC) had agreed to provide health care in concentration camps during World War II, and this entailed "some sort of connection with the Nazi camp managers, talking to them and shaking their hands regardless of any crime they were and were known by the ICRC to be responsible for. It is precisely this 'joint agency' rather than anything (and despite everything) that they did through it, that still haunts the ICRC today" (Ibid, 14).

I think that another example of a conjunction compromise is the abortion compromise I cited in normative compromise, a compromise that is expected in decriminalizing abortion, in which a person who originally believes that abortion is killing is expected to abandon that belief for its opposition, since this is the only way she could consent to decriminalizing abortion. This applies even if the abortion is to be decriminalized only for cases of rape. Abandoning moral principles for their opposites fit into this category of compromise, making it the most difficult kind of compromise. Indeed, Lepora tells us that conjunction compromise is the only kind of compromise where compromising feels like *self-compromise,* or the compromising agent compromising herself (Lepora 2012: 19; also see Jones and O'Flynn 2012: 118). This kind of compromise increases rather than decreases the responsibility a compromiser feels for causing, permitting or omitting wrongdoing from her perspective (Lepora 2012: 15-16). The fact that the compromise aims to achieve something that is not possible without the compromise does not reduce the guilt felt by the compromiser for compromising principles of concern (Ibid, 19-21). So, even in cases of rape, a pro-life who is a theistic believer might remind us that abortion is murder nonetheless, that God knows best why he allowed the rape, and that considering it as rape does not reduce the feeling of responsibility for decriminalizing abortion in the cases of rape (see Ani 2019: 311).

Theoretical Comparisons

Lepora's discussion of kinds of compromise is about what we give and get in a compromise, the different methods in which this is done, and different ways in which the compromise is similar or different from our original positions before the compromise. My taxonomy of compromises is about three broad categories of issues upon which we reach compromises (material, strategic, and normative issues) and the kinds of compromises we should expect to reasonably achieve when we try to compromise in these issue categories.

In spite of the fact that Lepora's taxonomy is about what we lose and gain, and mine is about the content or item upon which we wish to compromise, there are other interesting overlaps and intersections between Lepora's taxonomy of compromises and mine that could provide insights for reaching compromises. To begin, one notices that Lepora's kinds of compromises (substitution, intersection, and conjunction) apply only to my strategic and normative compromises. This is because Lepora's taxonomy of compromises applies only to matters of principled concern (Lepora 2012: 4). But my proportional compromise need not apply to any principle of concern, although it occasionally could (like we see in the conflict between the surgeon and the anaesthetic). Because proportional compromise only applies to adjusting different degrees of the same commodity, practice or principle shared by different parties to arrive at a common moderation, it is the easiest form of compromise. No party strictly *loses* a principle of concern, only a material loss or an adjustment of a principle.

The second most common kind of compromise is my strategic compromise. This is where we compromise over conflicting strategies and methods that are otherwise quite reconcilable because we can effectively compare these strategies and methods by explicating their consequences in the empirical world. It is only natural that human beings differ in their approaches to solving similar problems. The good aspect is that differing approaches could always be reconciled by comparing the implications and consequences of each approach. Mapping implications and consequences helps us see which approaches are better in which respects. Conflicting strategies are therefore quite amenable to easy resolution and compromises because there is something empirically calculable about them.

Indeed, most substitution and intersection compromises are strategic compromises. This is because principles and interests could be adjusted to a version that could accommodate the principles and interests of other parties (in the case of substitution compromise) or contain elements that overlap with the principles, interests and methods of others (in the case of intersection compromise). In any case, most strategic compromises are products of elements of *both* substitution and intersection compromises: those elements that do not overlap may be modified or replaced with more accommodating elements if parties do not wish to abandon them simply because they conflict.

Normative compromises are the most vivid examples of conjunctive compromises. This is because a conjunctive compromise is quite likely to be a normative compromise. It is in the nature of normative principles that they are disjunctive: either they hold or they do not. Either I believe that abortion is murder or I do not, either I believe that taking a human life is wrong or I believe it is right. Middle grounds are not easy to find in many moral and metaphysical disagreements, as we see in strategic or proportional disagreements. I would allow that it is quite possible for some normative disagreements to possess the malleability of strategic disagreements, but I do not have examples of these. Due, however, to such a possibility, I would distinguish a compromise involving an abandonment of one's principles of concerns for their very opposites as a *conjunctive* normative compromise. Clearly, this is the most difficult (and, some may say, treacherous) kind of compromise. It would be too ambitious to expect this kind of compromise in our daily attempts to reconcile people's conflicting positions.

Conclusion

In this chapter, I have attempted to provide insights into our ability to reach compromises by examining three broad categories of issues upon which we usually compromise. This taxonomy of issues for compromise was intended to show the varying ease with which we could achieve compromise in different areas of life. This exploration is, in turn, intended to provide more clarity for further research on Wiredu's proposed democracy by consensus, which is now re-read as a democracy by compromise due to the failure of a unanimity interpretation of his proposal. I included a discussion of Lepora's taxonomy of compromise, a different taxonomy based on what we give and take in compromising, in order to shed more light on my kinds of compromise, and map out in a little more detail how we gain what we gain and how we lose what we lose in a compromise, and the situations and issues where such losses and gains are technically plausible. Scholars exploring the prospects and challenges of a democracy by compromise would need to take in stock these kinds and sheds of compromise to figure what practitioners in such a democracy are up against, as well as how, in what ways, and in which situations they could maximize the material and psychological benefits of compromising, as well as reduce its psychological costs to compromisers.

References

Ani, E. I. 2019. The Consensus Project and Three Levels of Deliberation. *Dialogue: Canadian Philosophical Review* 54: 299-322.

Benditt T. M. 1979. Compromising Interests and Principles. In J. R. Pennock and J. Chapman (eds.) *Compromise in Ethics, Law, and Politics.* Nomos XXI. New York: New York University Press, 26–37.

Coons, J. E. 1979. Compromise as Precise Justice. In: J. R. Pennock and J. Chapman (eds.) *Compromise in Ethics, Law, and Politics.* Nomos XXI. New York: New York University Press, 190–204.

Jones, P. and I. O'Flynn. 2012 Can a Compromise be Fair? *Philosophy, Politics, and Economics* 12(2): 115-135.

Kalumba, K. M. 2015. Consensus and Federalism in Contemporary African Political Philosophy. *Philosophical Papers* 44(1): 103-119.

Lepora, C. 2012. On Compromise and Being Compromised. *Journal of Political Philosophy* 20(1): 1-22.

Lister, A. 2007. Public Reason and Moral Compromise. *Canadian Journal of Philosophy* 37(1): 1–34.

Mapp, R. 1972. Cross-National Dimensions of Ethnocentrism. *Canadian Journal of African Studies* 6(1): 73-96.

Matolino, B. 2009. A Response to Eze's Critique of Wiredu's Consensual Democracy *South African Journal of Philosophy* 28 (1): 34-42.

Wiredu, K. 1996. *Cultural Universals and Particulars.* Bloomington and Indianapolis: Indiana University Press.

Wiredu, K. 2011. The State, Civil Society and Democracy in Africa. In H. Lauer and K. Anyidoho (eds.) *Reclaiming the Human Sciences Vol II.* Legon-Accra: Sub-Saharan Publishers, 1055-1066.

Chapter 8

Afro-consensual Democracy for Twenty-first Century Africa: In Pursuit of an Indigenous Maximalist African Democratic Paradigm

Great Zimbabwe University

Introduction

Current debates on the normative principle of democracy in Africa seem to hover around the ways in which African nation states could be made to conform to Western styles of liberal and constitutional democratic principles. Such liberal democratic principles are mostly informed and guided by regular free and fair elections, majoritarianism, election competition and above all, multi-party liberal democracy. As I will attempt to establish here, these principles of Western liberal democracy could be seen as part of what Dismas Aloys Masolo looks at as "the colonist epistemological imperialism" (Masolo 2010: 18). Confirmatory to this view, Ademola Kazeem Fayemi notes that, "for many African political scholars and politicians, it is absurd to think of [the possibility of an African theory of democracy] because their thoughts have been patterned towards aping alien theoretical models and practices of democracy" (Fayemi 2009: 101). While I am convinced that non-African models of democracy remain unpersuasive in Africa, at the same time, I must admit it is difficult to conceptualise an African indigenous political democratic framework without courting the fallacy of anachronism.[1] As

---

[1] This is the mistake of unshakably 'remaining' in the past by holding on to ideas and concepts that no longer appeal to current circumstances.

Masolo sees it, "the problem with doing things merely because 'tradition says so' is that such reasoning often fails to produce universal principles as a justification for moral action" (Masolo 2010: 106). In most cases, universal moral principles are taken on the basis on which they appeal here and now instead of just following tradition.

Notwithstanding these fears concerning both non-indigenous African models of democracy and the quest for an African indigenous model of democracy, I present strong arguments to accept a social and political relativist framework rooted in indigenous Afro-consensual form of democracy as the basis for sound social, political and economic accountability in Africa today. (*See also* Chemhuru 2010: 180-191; Chemhuru 2013: 32-42). As I depart from the inherently Western-centric conceptions of looking at social and political organisation in Africa, I seek to establish the way in which Afro-consensual democracy could be acceptable as more appealing than the multi-party style of liberal democracy as it is currently being understood and practiced in post-colonial Africa.

In addressing the question of whether Afro-consensual democracy could be taken seriously in Africa's twenty-first century, I appeal to the African indigenous democratic heritage by comparing it with the current scenario in post-colonial Africa where conflict, adversity, aggression and division are the order of the day among different individuals, politicians and political parties. I argue that the African traditional social and political reality was mainly characterised by consensual democracy (*See also* Wiredu 1996:176-185; 1997: 303-313 and 2001: 227-244). Yet, today, much of post-independent African nation states are characteristic of, and aspire for a multi-party political culture. Ultimately, I argue here that this is a system of governance that is alien to, and incompatible with an African democratic history, culture and heritage. As Emmanuel Ifeanyi Ani sees it, the problem of the post-colonial African state is that it has "inherited the aggregative democracy of the colonial masters" that is based on "the aggregation of preferences that occurs in voting". (Ani 2013: 207 and 210). This is why I propose for a serious consideration of Kwasi Wiredu's Afro-consensual democracy which Ani also prefers to call "deliberative democracy" (Ani 2013: 207). Reasons for my preference for this model will mainly be motivated by appealing to the African traditional democratic frameworks.

In reality, the African traditional political culture of consensus or deliberation remains lacking in much of post-colonial African systems of democracy and governance owing to various factors like the controversies and workability of consensus itself (*See also*, Ani 2013: 207). At the same time, although recently there has been a considerable body of literature on the role of traditional systems of governance in Africa, the notion of consensus remains elusive and underexplored in much of African social and political writings. I therefore take a comparativist approach to the normative principles of democracy and consensus in Africa and provide strong reasons why an appeal to Afro-consensual democracy sounds appealing as opposed to non-indigenous forms of governance and political organisation.

Overall, I seek to flesh out the idea of consensus as the basis for inclusive democratic political practice in post-colonial Africa. As I situate democracy and consensus in traditional Africa, I first take stork of the prospects and problems of multi-party system of democracy. As I espouse what I refer to as an Afro-consensual democracy as the basis for grounding a reasonable inclusive democratic political practice in post-colonial Africa, I proceed in the last section to provide various reasons why consensual democracy guarantees participation, inclusivity and freedom because of its appeal to the maximalist model of democracy. Ultimately, while "a number of scholars have in recent times seen the need for the utilisation of Africa's democratic heritage and values, rooted in her traditional past, in resolving her peculiar problems" (Fayemi 2009: 102) this is a deliberate effort to examine the extent to which Africa's post-colonial challenges could be solved by an appeal to such an African indigenous democratic heritage.

Understanding Democracy in Africa

Democracy is a political concept that has generally been taken as the buzzword for sound political organisation in the world in general. Yet broadly conceptualised, democracy is broader and means more than majority rule, election competition, multi-partyism, liberalism or constitutionalism. (*See also,* Wamba-dia-Wamba 1992: 29). For Emmanuel Chukwudi Eze, democracy in postcolonial Africa is mostly "understood and articulated in the multiparty language of the political traditions of the West, a democracy that the West also sometimes requires of African states as a precondition for economic and military aid" (Eze 1997: 314). However, very few people can doubt that democracy is not synonymous with multi-partyism, liberalism, electioneering, liberalism or constitutionalism as prescribed by the Western world. Democracy can actually entail and accommodate any of these aspects, while it is not sufficient to substitute one of these aspects for democracy per se.

Understood from its Western perspective, democracy, Wiredu points out, is a political system according to which the "executive and legislative powers are assumed and exercised only by groups, not necessarily identical, periodically chosen by the people in free and fair elections, provided that there is an independent judiciary and a free press" (Wiredu 2001: 227-8). This conventionally accepted view of democracy shows that there are many ingredients for democracy, such as majority participation, free and fair elections, independence, freedom and free press, among others. However, in recent times, the guarantee of these democratic ingredients has always been a source of controversy for contemporary African democracies considering the human rights abuses, repression, and intimidation of civil society, partisan politics, polarised media and the history of disputed elections in post-colonial Africa. (See Ihonvbere 1992: 88).

The generally acceptable view of democracy "… implies, as it must, that the standard by which to judge the democratic nature of a political system is the degree of adequacy allowed for the expression of the will of the people, the extent to which the people are involved or included in the decision-making processes that affect their lives" (Gyekye 2013: 240-1). However, democracy is generally characterised by various ingredients such as majoritarianism, representation, constitutionalism, liberalism and multi-party elections. On the other hand, in most post-colonial African democratic states, it has not been clear whether all these aspects of democracy are sufficient as nation states tend to rely on any of the above forms of democracy when it is convenient for them to do so. At the same time, the role that consensus plays in ensuring best representation, high participation and attaining social justice has been downplayed as democracy itself has been mainly understood from the elitist conceptions of minimalist and medium conceptions of democracy.

Accordingly, in order to arrive at my working understanding of maximalist democracy, which is what I think consensus satisfies, I appeal to Abraham Lincoln's maximalist conception of democracy. Following Abraham Lincoln's Gettysburg definition of democracy, "the elitist type based on a minimalist conception of democracy can be seen as *government of the people*; the participatory type relies on a mid-range concept of democracy and aims at *government of, and by the people*; and the social type of democracy stands on a *maximalist* understanding and could be best described as *government of, by and for the people*" (Bühlmann et al. 2008: 5).

The paradox of democracy in the world in general has been the presence of purportedly democratic governments that run their affairs contrary to the wishes of the majority of their populations and maximalist expectations such as best representation, high participation, inclusivity and social justice. This is why Gyekye argues, "it would be correct to say that quite a number of the policies and actions of democratic governments in the world often run counter to the wishes and desires of a great majority of the people of the nation" (Gyekye 2013: 238). Yet maximalist democracy is not something that is new to Africa. It is only in its liberal and minimalist form that democracy is having problems with the post-colonial African condition. This is why some analysts have come to the conclusion that Africa is experiencing the global democratic recession (Mattes and Bratton 2016: 2).

Although democracy and consensus are two different concepts that also mean different things altogether, within the African traditional political heritage, consensus plays a very crucial role towards the promotion of democracy (Wiredu 1997: 303). While the word democracy is broader than consensus, it does not mean that consensus is not compatible with democracy. Consensus has always been, and continues to be an important component of democracy itself. According to Wiredu, democracy entails government by consensus (Wiredu 2001: 227). This is what makes it reasonable to argue that it is possible for post-colonial Africa to do away with Western-style forms of democracy and re-think Afro-consensual democracy. According to Wiredu, there is an explanation for the propensity to identify government by the consent of the people, i.e., "democracy, with government by the consent of the majority" (Wiredu 2001: 23). This tendency, he says, is "obviously born of excessive fixation on Anglo-American models of democracy. Once liberated from the hold of those majoritarian models, it becomes possible to explore the possibility of a polity even more radically consensual than that of, say, Switzerland" (Wiredu 2001: 23).

Although it may not be taken as implying that African traditional life was a 'bed of roses', governance in African traditional life was mainly a rule by consensus. According to Wiredu, "there is considerable evidence that decision by consensus was often the order of the day in African deliberations, and on principle" (Wiredu 1997: 305). Some of the products or results of consensus include but are not limited to agreement, joint action and reconciliation as Gyekye notes in the following:

> Consensus allows for everyone an opportunity to speak his or her mind and to contribute to a debate on the issue at hand; it promotes patience, mutual tolerance, and an attitude of compromise – all of which are necessary for inclusive democratic practice in which everyone is expected to appreciate the need to change or even abandon their position in the face of more convincing arguments by others (Gyekye 2013: 244).

In Afro-consensual democracy, however, the emphasis is mainly on decision making that primarily comes from, and based on the consent of the people, and that such consent is for the good of the people. This is contrary to what the majority says over the minority as a result of flawed multiparty election processes in Africa that continue to generate and guarantee what I would look at as the "government of the people" and "government of, and by the people" as implied in the minimalist and medium views of democracy respectively (*See*, Bühlmann et al. 2008: 5). Except for the problems associated with flawed elections in minimalist and medium conceptions of democracy, there are other problems associated with the multiparty system of democracy, which are what I now proceed to examine in the next section.

The Dilemma of Multiparty Constitutional Democracy in Post-colonial Africa

Constitutional democracy in Africa's post-colonial era has generally been synonymous with the multi-party system, periodic elections and majority rule. Although I do not wish to totally dismiss these key aspects of democracy as unappealing to Africa, I wish to maintain that these aspects are the definiens of democracy in the minimalist perspective of democracy that is currently at play in Africa. According to this minimalist view, democracy is only understood in so far as it protects individuals from arbitrary rule while it remains elitist because it is mainly based on skilled personnel and representatives who are thought as "capable of making public decisions and protecting individual liberty" (Bühlmann et al. 2008: 5). Also, notwithstanding the role of some of the key tenets towards promoting and upholding democracy in the Western world, the understanding of democracy from the multi-party system, electioneering and majoritarian perspectives is also a "language of the political traditions of the West" (Eze 1997: 314). This is why I argue that such a political framework should not be prescribed on African political traditions like what has been the tradition in post-colonial Africa.

After the independence of most African countries, the first generation of political leaders like Kwame Nkrumah, Julius Nyerere, Kenneth Kaunda, Hastings Kamuzu Banda and Robert Mugabe initially wanted to establish the one-party political system in their respective countries. Perhaps their initial scepticism with regard to the multi-party political system could be attributed to their quest for African traditional systems of governance, such as those based on kingship and consensual democracy. Surprisingly, however, most of these political leaders later adopted and settled for the multi-party political system in Africa as one of the major pillars of democracy in Africa. As a result, the multi-party political system in Africa has been seen as one of the cornerstones of democracy in post-colonial Africa.

At the same time, the party system of governance which post-colonial Africa has adopted cannot be spared because of its natural emphasis on the existence of the party and belonging to it as well as upholding its ideology. As a result, this approach to politics has prompted the emergence of what Wamba-dia-Wamba describes as the *elite politics of democracy* (1992). According to this view, politics is only understood with reference to belonging to a party. Otherwise, it is worth taking Wamba-dia-Wamba's argument that "people outside the Party *do not exist politically*" (Wamba-dia-Wamba 1992: 31). For this reason, the party system of governance in most elitist and minimalist rules such as monarchs, military governments and dictatorships cannot therefore be considered to be the best forms of governments of the people who naturally are not part of the system in government, which is the ruling party or party in government. However, with Afro-consensual democracy, this kind of political elitism is non-existent because all the parties are involved in fundamental decisions that concern them.

Apart from the political elitism that is propagated by the minimalist applications of democracy, the emergence of pseudo-political parties under the pretext of multi-partyism has also been, and continues to be the major characteristic of much of African democracies. Although the idea behind the formation of multi-parties could be to combat this kind of political elitism, in reality, the multi-party system has failed to meet its objectives owing to the emergence of these pseudo multi-parties. These pseudo-political parties are actually *de facto* political parties that are sponsored by the one-party system in order to give the world the impression that all is well in terms of the multi-party condition of democracy. Yet on the ground, the elitist one-party political system continues unabated. Eze confirms this view when he notes that;

> . . . we know that African dictators have invented 'tricks' to resist such external pressures: they put up mock multiparty elections that deceive the Western governments (who, we all know, need a lot of convincing!) into continuing the supply of military weapons, while keeping intact and untransformed the mechanisms of autocratic, dictatorial, and terroristic exercise of state power (Eze 1997: 315).

This explains why it has been very *difficult*[2] for the *various* multi-party political parties in different African nations to dislodge these *strong* political parties such as FRELIMO in Mozambique, MPLA in Angola, Chama cha Mapinduzi in Tanzania, ANC in South Africa and ZANU PF in Zimbabwe. Accordingly, Wamba-dia-Wamba comes to the conclusion that "the multi-party parliamentary mode of politics is characterised by its state-centredness, oppressiveness and tendency to freeze creativity and imagination" (Wamba-dia-Waba 1992: 31).

Two cases in point are that of Kenya in 2017 and Zimbabwe in 2018. In August 2017, Kenya held its elections where there were more than one

---

[2] I have italicised the words 'different' and 'various' in order to make emphasis on the deceptive nature of the strong political leaders of traditional political parties who create pseudo opposition parties that pretend to be opposing the main political party, yet they are simply there to give an impression to the outside world.

thousand presidential candidates, and several political parties registered for the elections, which have also been disputed by the main opposition movements led by Raila Odinga[3]. The same scenario applies to Zimbabwe, which on 30 July 2018 also held its harmonised elections in which there were twenty-three presidential candidates and one hundred and thirty-three political parties. In addition to this kind of political grand-standing by the main political players in Kenya and Zimbabwe respectively, the political violence that ensured in both Kenya and Zimbabwe as well as the continued dispute of the two respective election results even to date cannot be justified. This demonstrates the failure of the multi-party system and the dangers that it poses for the post-colonial African state. Governments under a multi-party system purport to be democratic yet in actuality, they represent the interests of the major political party and its interests. For this reason, it is worth taking Wamba-dia-Wamba's view that the multi-party system fails to "incorporate a process of human and social emancipation at this time" (Wamba-dia-Wamba 1992: 30).

Also, the problem with the multi-party democratic system in Africa is when Western nations demand it as a pre-condition or condition for some aid. In the post-colonial African context, periodic multi-party elections continue to be looked at as an incentive for foreign aid and good international relations. Otherwise, failure to conform to the multi-party political system in Africa is as good as an invitation for political and economic sanctions. According to Julius Ihonvbere, "prescriptions of democratic forms and models by Western nations, and the forced adoption of orthodox structural adjustment packages will not create the required changes that will move Africa from its current pathetic conditions on to the path of development and democracy" (Ihonvbere 1992: 87). This is why the condition for multi-party politics in Africa could be looked at as a tool for Africa's neo-colonialism. As Ramose looks at Jonathan Moyo's (1992) argument for the need for multi-party politics in Zimbabwe, he contends that the pursuit for multi-party democracy is mainly based on the epistemological paradigm of the European conqueror (Ramose 1992: 72). This kind of a political paradigm is mainly based on the politics of conquering through certain conditions like food aid, military aid and economic sanctions, among others.

---

[3] Of course, at the time of writing this chapter, there are current overtures for consensus between Raila Odinga and Uhuru Kenyatta. Whether these succeed or not, that remains to be seen, but what is important is the quest for consensus which is in sync with the argument of this chapter.

A key feature of post-colonial African democracy is the holding of periodic elections in order to choose political leaders based on whom, and which political party wins the majority of votes. As a result, majoritarianism, through periodic elections, has been seen as a yardstick for Africa's multi-party democracy. However, the history of elections in post-colonial African states like Kenya (2007 and 2017), Gambia (2016) and Zimbabwe (2000; 2005; 2008 and 2013) could be looked at as the history of disputed elections and election violence. To confirm this point, Ajei also observes that "since 2000 until October 2015, the outcomes of 26 of the 103 presidential elections held on the continent have been disputed. Eleven of these disputed elections have provoked atrocious violence and the loss of life, property and human security" (Ajei 2016: 453). This is contrary to traditional African societies in which ethnic conflicts, tribal conflicts and violence were not as pronounced as they are now despite being invented and psychologically orchestrated (Ani 2013: 214-5).

In addition to these problems associated with elections in Africa, the concept of majority vote is fundamentally flawed in itself because of its implications on the suppression of fundamental human rights of the minority whom the majority always outplays. The implications of this system of governance are far-reaching considering the way tribalism, xenophobia and genocide have mostly been experienced by minority populations in various post-colonial African democracies like in South Africa, Zimbabwe and Rwanda respectively.

> Majoritarian democracy involves a multi-party system of politics, in which the party that wins the most seats at the election forms the government. In such a political set-up, the losing party or parties become the opposition, singly or jointly. In this system, the minority representatives' votes are overridden by the votes of the majority. The implication of this is that the right of the minority representatives and their constituencies to meaningfully participate in the actual making of decisions is rendered nugatory. In many contemporary African states, certain ethnic groups and political parties have found themselves perpetually in the minority, consistently staged outside the corridor of power. Not only this, their fundamental human rights of decisional representation are permanently denied with impunity (Fayemi 2009: 115).

Overall, from the foregoing, that the multi political party system, elections and majority rule are alien to African social and political heritage is plain to see. In the African traditional democratic heritage, democracy is largely at play through the frameworks of consensus. Yet these traditional political frameworks have not received much attention by African political leaders.

Afro-consensual Democracy: Towards an African Indigenous Maximalist Model of Democracy

It is a fallacy that is mainly propagated by the Western colonial system that indigenous African societies were primitive and not democratic (see, for example, Ajei 2016: 447). The same fallacy can also be used to uncharitably hold the view that African indigenous models of governance are no longer appealing presently. This is what I seek to dispel as I flesh out an African indigenous model of democracy that is based on consensus.

A sympathetic reading of traditional African systems of governance will reveal that, despite some inherent monarchical structures in the African indigenous systems of governance, decision making was mainly arrived at by consensus among the different members of the community or *body politic*. According to Wiredu, "it is more interesting to observe that the habit of decision by consensus in politics was studiously cultivated in some of the most centralised and, if it comes to it, warlike ethnic groups of Africa such as the Zulu and the Ashantis" (Wiredu 1997: 305). Despite considerable indifferences to consensus by other communities in some parts of traditional African societies, one can state, with emphatic conviction, that consensus could be taken as one of the most appealing forms of political governance in traditional Africa.

In Afro-consensual democracy, the system of governance is arranged in a similar way that a family is composed and how it functions. While a typical indigenous African society is headed by the King, the family unit is also headed by the Family Head. Just like the Family Head, the King is simply there to make sure that all the contributions, opinions, suggestions and even points of contrast of each and every member of the community are heard and considered in matters to do with decision-making (Fayemi 2009: 111). Understood this way, Afro-consensual community is therefore a family *writ large* in so far as the functions, unity, and purpose of the family resemble that of the community (Wiredu 1996: 185).

Perchance what might be a challenge in contemporary African society is the structure for such an Afro-consensual democracy. Traditional frameworks of governance, such as kinship structures, no longer exist and function as they used to do in traditional African communities because of the extinction of institutions like the family. (see Wiredu 1996). However, even in the current systems of governance individuals elect other members to represent them in various assemblies such as in councils, parliament or cabinet, as well as in various institutions like universities and civil society where Afro-consensual democracy can still be appealed to. Wiredu sees the possibility of this kind of framework in a non-party system of democracy in the following:

A non-party and consensual democratic system is one in which parties are not the basis of power. People can form political associations to propagate their political ideas and help to elect representatives to parliament. But an association having the most elected members will not therefore be the governing group. Every representative will be of the government in his personal, rather than associational capacity (Wiredu 1996: 179).

Although he settles for a non-party polity, which might be difficult to conceptualise in contemporary political realities, Wiredu's view is worth taking because of its emphasis on the need to guarantee participation, autonomy, independence and freedom to the individual and not necessarily the political party in terms of decision making. According to Wiredu, "Politically speaking, consensus is democratic, since all to be affected by decision-making must participate in it, physically or through substantial and decisional representations" (Ani 2014: 344) (Wiredu 1996: 7-8 and 186). This is why Wiredu concludes, "this dual sort of representation made traditional African democracy genuinely participatory and inclusive of minorities, unlike the Western-style democracy of political parties" (Wiredu 2011: 1059; cited in Ani 2014: 344).

Having envisaged a non-party system of democracy, Wiredu espouses a view of consensus as a reasonable premise for decision making in contemporary Africa, although he is cautious about whether to take the notion of consensus wholesome. This explains why he observes that;

It is often remarked that decision making in traditional African life and governance was, as a rule, by consensus. Like all generalizations about complex subjects, it may be legitimate to take this with a pinch of prudence. But there is considerable evidence that decision by consensus was often the order of the day in African deliberations, and on principle (Wiredu 1997: 303).

From the above view, while Wiredu seems to be somewhat sceptical about the role that consensus could play as a complex system of governance in contemporary African political reality, I will take his understanding of consensus as the basis of what could be considered as an Afro-consensual democracy. This is an African model of democracy that is rooted in consensus as the basis for social organisation, interactions, decision-making and solving various social and political conflicts. Despite his scepticism about the role of consensus towards contemporary African governance, Wiredu himself admits that "where consensus characterises political decision making in Africa, it is a manifestation of an immanent approach to social interaction. Generally, in interpersonal relations among adults, consensus as a basis for joint action was taken as axiomatic" (Wiredu 1997: 303).

It is also a fallacy to think that where there is no multi-party system and majority rule, there is no democracy, peace, stability, cohesion and opposing views from individuals in society at large. According to Ramose, "traditional African political culture embodied and invited opposition in the very principle of consensus" (Ramose 1992: 76). In actual fact, the very principle of consensus itself pre-supposes conflict in the first place. Otherwise, it is not possible to have consensus without first having some form of conflict of ideas and opinions among individuals. Also, the appeal to consensus in African traditional society cannot be taken to imply that such traditional societies were free from conflict. This is why Wiredu himself admits that ". . . conflicts (including mortal ones) among lineages and ethnic groups and within them were not infrequent" (Wiredu 1997: 303). However, the quest for constitutional multi-party democracy is mainly premised on the false promise of stability, cohesion, peace and tranquillity all of which consensus democracy strives to achieve. Consensus democracy aims to achieve these because it is underpinned by a maximalist conception of democracy where every part and individuals are involved in decision-making processes as well as the safeguard for fundamental ingredients of democracy such as plurality, diversity of views, justice, equality and freedom among others.

Traditional African consensual democracy is for the community or that it is communitarian oriented and not individualistic or partisan. For this reason, it ensures best representation, high participation and social justice. In a multi-party system, eventually, power and everything else boils down to one political party and the individuals who are in control as opposed to consensual system that is all inclusive. This is why the other virtue of Afro-consensual democracy is its quest for the common good, that is, the good of all. It recognises all human interests, which are ultimately the same (Wiredu 1996: 185-6). Afro-consensual democracy can therefore be conceived as a coalition of individuals pursuing their common good and not of political parties that seek to further the interests of their party or individual ideologies. In this way, Afro-consensual democracy becomes a welfarist view of political organisation in so far as it "appeals to considerations of both human welfare and human dignity" (Metz 2012: 61). In Southern Africa, for example, an important aspect of this kind of consensual democracy is encapsulated in *ubuntu* or *hunhu*. As Samkange and Samkange see it, "*hunhuism* dictates that the main task of the victor at the next election should be reconciliation" (Samkange and Samkange 1980: 44). Contrary to the tyranny of the minority by the majority as in majoritarian democracy, Afro-consensual democracy through *ubuntu* demands that the *minority* who would have *lost* in reaching the consented decision should be reconciled with first, and also be considered in terms of their welfare and dignity.

Although I espouse consensual democracy as satisfying the maximalist conditions for democracy, one objection that may be raised against Afro-consensual democracy is the question of whether the attainment of consensus is as competitive as in a minimalist model of democracy espoused by Joseph Schumpeter, Karl Popper and Russel Hardin where "positions of power are filled through a competitive struggle for the people's vote" (Diamond 2002: 21). On the other hand, it may also be hard to imagine whether this Afro-consensual model of democracy satisfies certain maximal conditions of democracy such as competition, participation and civil and political liberties like those that enable individual human beings to freely express themselves in a community in which they exist with other human beings (Mill, 1859/2001: 52). According to Wiredu, a maximalist view of democracy involves "government constituted on the basis of explicit consent of all the people and operated by way of decisions enjoying the same quality and extent of consent" (Wiredu 2001: 227). Accordingly, one can therefore affirm that Afro-consensual democracy fulfills maximalist conditions of democracy. Because of its emphasis on promotion of unity, harmony, respect for human and people's rights and agreement/consensus, Afro-consensual democracy is therefore based on the promotion of the things that human beings value as opposed to adversarial politics that is characteristic of election competition in multiparty democracies under current forms of constitutional democracies in Africa. (Ramose 1992: 75). Although Ani thinks that "consensus and voting do overlap in practice and that voting is a basic human solution to group decisional intractability" (Ani 2014: 346); in Afro-consensual democracy, the way consensus is arrived at is as good as the competition for the people's vote in majoritarian democracies, except that with consensus, there is no competition to out-do one another. Overall, following Afro-consensual democracy and its emphasis on equality, dialogue, inclusivity, participation and freedom, it becomes apparent that the maximalist conditions of competition, participation and the guaranteeing of civil and political liberties are also guaranteed (Wiredu 2001: 227).

Conclusion

That the traditional African political and democratic heritage should be revisited cannot be overemphasised. Presently, the dilemma that multi-party constitutional democracies face in post-colonial Africa is that of whether they should continue to be espoused and practiced through multi-party majoritarian elections. Yet there is no consensual democracy on the ground, especially among different individuals, political parties with diverse opinions on fundamental issues and different social and political ideologies. This is what makes the appeal to Afro-consensual democracy relevant and worthy of considering in Africa's post-colonial era. In defending my position, I do not wish to pretend that the Afro-consensual system of governance is so perfect that it can be easily taken as a ready replacement for current systems of governance in Africa. However, I have tried to strongly argue why an appeal to an African indigenous model of democracy proves worthwhile by appealing to Afro-consensual democracy.

References

Ajei, M. O. 2016. Kwasi Wiredu's Consensual Democracy: Prospects for Practice in Africa. *European Journal of Political Theory* 15(4): 445-466.

Ani, E. I. 2013. Africa and the Prospects of Deliberative Democracy. *South African Journal of Philosophy* 32(3): 207-219.

Ani, E. I. 2014. On Traditional African Consensual Rationality. *The Journal of Political Philosophy* 22(3): 342-365.

Baromoter for Established Democracies. *National Center of Competence in Research*. Zurich: University of Zurich.

Bühlmann, M., Merkel, W., and Wessels, B. (2008). The Quality of Democracy: Democracy Baromoter for Established Democracies. *National Center of Competence in Research*. Zurich: University of Zurich.

Chemhuru, M. 2010. Democracy and the Paradox of Zimbabwe. *The Journal of Pan African Studies* 3(10): 180-191.

Chemhuru, M. 2013. Consensus and Conflict Resolution in Post-colonial Zimbabwe: Philosophical Reflections on an Indigenous Method of Conflict Resolution. *Journal on African Philosophy* 7: 32-41.

Diamond, L. 2002. Elections without Democracy: Thinking about Hybrid Regimes. *Journal of Democracy* 13(2): 21-35.

Eze, E. C. 1997. Democracy or Consensus? A Response to Wiredu. In Emmanuel Chukwudi Eze (Ed.) *Postcolonial African Philosophy*. Cambridge: Blackwell Publishers, 313-323.

Fayemi, A. K. 2009. Towards an African Theory of Democracy. *Thought and Practice: A Journal of the Philosophical Association of Kenya (PAK)* 1(1): 101-126.

Gyekye, K. 2013. *Philosophy, Culture and Vision*. Accra: Sub-Saharan Publishers.

Ihonvbere, J. O. 1992. Is Democracy Possible in Africa? Elites, the People and Civil Society. *Quest: An International Journal of Philosophy* VI(2): 84-108.

Masolo, D. A. 2010. *Self and Community in a Changing World*. Bloomington and Indianapolis: Indiana University Press.

Mattes, R. and Bratton, M. 2016. Do Africans still want Democracy? *Afrobarometer Policy Paper* 36: 1-26.

Metz, T. 2012. Developing African Political Philosophy: Moral-Theoretic Strategies. *Philosophia Africana* 14(1): 61-83.

Mill, J. S. 1859/2001. *On Liberty*. Kitchener, Ontarion: Batoche Books.

Moyo, J. N. 1992. State, Politics and Domination in Zimbabwe. *The Journal of Modern African Studies* 30(2): 305-330.

Ramose, M. B. 1992. African Democratic Tradition: Oneness, Consensus and Openness: A Reply to Wamba-dia-Wamba. *Quest: An International Journal of Philosophy*, VI (2): 62-83.

Samkange, S. and T. M. Samkange. 1980. *Hunhuism* or *Ubuntuism: A Zimbabwean Indigenous Political Philosophy*. Salisbury: Graham Publishing.

Wamba-dia-Wamba, E. 1992. Beyond the Elite Politics of Democracy in Africa. *Quest: An International Journal of Philosophy* VI(1): 28-43.

Wiredu, K. 1996. *Cultural Universals and Particulars*. New York: Indiana University Press.

Wiredu, K. 1997. Democracy and Consensus in African Traditional Politics: A Plea for a Non-party Polity. In, Emmanuel Chukwudi Eze (ed.) *Postcolonial African Philosophy*. Cambridge: Blackwell Publishers, 303-312.

Wiredu, K. 2001. Democracy by Consensus: Some Conceptual Considerations. *Philosophical Papers* 30 (3):227-244.

Chapter 9

African Consensual Democracy, Dissensus and Resistance

Edwin Etieyibo

University of the Witwatersrand

Introduction

The rigorous interrogation of beliefs, ideas and values that aims towards some deep understanding as well as showing their practical value in terms of certain norms of behaviour and actions seem to me to be some of the chief tasks of philosophy and philosophers. By making this point, I may be taken to be aligning myself with a certain kind of philosophy, the practical and transformative kind, whose chief proponent appears to be Karl Marx. One of Marx's famous quotes has to do with the point he made about practical philosophy, the idea that philosophers have hitherto interpreted the world but the point is to change it. In saying this, Marx is reminding us of what the philosopher should be doing and his or her role both in philosophizing and in the world.

Kwasi Wiredu may thus be taken to exemplify this idea of practical, applied and transformative philosophy in his presentation of an African consensual democracy insofar as his overarching aim is not only to interrogate and excavate consensual democracy from African indigenous or traditional societies but also to make the case that our current political realities ought to be influenced by these ideas. The point is that democracy by consensus is not some abstract and theoretical philosophy but applied and practical philosophy insofar as it is taken to have roots in traditional or indigenous African thought and meant to have application to real-life political spaces in Africa, as well as understood as an alternative that can and ought to be endorsed and embraced by the modern societies and nation-states of Africa. Wiredu takes consensual democracy to avoid some of the problems that bedevil multi-party or majoritarian democracy. Furthermore, he takes African traditional societies to be quintessentially democratic and consensual.

In this chapter, I discuss dissensus *qua* resistance in the context of Wiredu's presentation of an African consensual democracy. I understand resistance to be embedded in opposition. For if opposition embodies the idea of resistance, and dissent qualifies as a token of opposition, then opposition politics represents one form of political resistance insofar as it involves dissensus and actions that challenge or seek to undermine the status quo. In my discussion of opposition, I will examine the sense in which dissensus *qua* resistance is implicated in a majoritarian democracy. I do this as a way of teasing out the sense of how and why one might think that resistance is not fully accommodated in an African consensual democracy — the type advocated by Kwasi Wiredu. The conclusion that I gesture towards is that, although Wiredu's consensual democracy recognises dissensus as the starting point for consensus, and allows for suspension of disbelief by parties or representatives, the role and value of opposition seem to be lost by the very nature of consensus *qua* compromise, particularly in Wiredu's claim that consensus leads to genuine reconciliation and abstention from further disputation and recrimination.

Dissent, Opposition and Opposition Politics

In a general sense, resistance refers to opposition precisely, being in opposition to something. In this sense, we can say that opposition embodies the idea of resistance insofar as opposition is about taking a position or staking out an idea or view and distancing that position or view from another view or position. Three ideas can be isolated from this broad understanding of resistance.

The first idea is that resistance requires taking a position or view (of course, such position or view is directed at something, i.e., it is about something).[1] Second, the position that is taken is against something else (say, another position). Third, by taking a position, one is implicated in some form of performance.

On the first idea, the opposition can take various forms, but central to all of the forms is the notion of staking out a stance, that is taking of a particular stance that either one wishes to advance or to put others on notice about. So when person or institution X resists person or institution Y, what X does is to stake out and crystalize a position. In effect, X is saying this is what "I or we stand for".

The second idea, which is presupposed in the first idea, is that by staking out a position, X not only crystalizes that position but generally does contrast

---

[1] Henceforth, I will only talk about position and when I do so I should be taken to also mean a view.

it in the same breath with some other position. X, in effect, says mine or our position diverges from that of yours or Y. It is in this sense that one says that opposition is something about something else or a stance that is directed at something else.

The third idea is the performance element of the position that is taken. On this idea, one performs through one's words or deeds (behaviour or actions) what one is for and against. X may perform just by some utterance or locution. Alternatively, X may perform by outward bodily movements, i.e., specific actions such as demonstrations, protests, picketing, strikes, or even engaging in acts that may be termed "warlike."

This way of characterizing resistance as embedded in opposition makes resistance an act[2] of refusal directed against something that one disagrees with or a behaviour that attempts to prevent something that one is opposed to from manifesting or being realized, or efforts aimed at superimposing one's ideal over another. It also makes resistance an act that targets a particular object or state of affairs in order to bring about some other object or state of affairs, one that may be taken to be good or desirable. The aim of the opposition here becomes either of challenging certain state of affairs or undermining them with a view to bringing about a different and more desirable state of affairs.

If the discussion about resistance as opposition embedded in certain behaviour is right, and given that the opposition thus manifests in different forms, then there is something that can be said about the politics of dissent. Regarding dissent, it will qualify as a token of opposition since it involves the expression or holding of opinions that are different from or opposed to those expressed or held by others. As for opposition politics, it will represent one form of political resistance insofar as it involves dissensus and actions that challenge or seek to undermine the status quo. In a way, then to talk of the politics of dissent is to talk about the politics of opposition or opposition politics.

Resistance and Multiple-party System or Majoritarian Democracy

Most of the modern forms of democracy that we find practiced in many societies today are of the majoritarian type or are found in multiparty systems and politics. Some of the features that define majoritarian democracy include

---

[2] I'm using act here broadly to mark both acts of commission and omission. That is, in cases where one positively acts one does perform by doing something (commission) and in cases where one omits to act one also is performing and consequently doing something (omission).

the rule of the majority and the exclusion or marginalization of the minority. In other words, majoritarian democracy is a system of multi-party politics, which involves some opposition of various parties, usually the majority party against other minority parties. These features of majoritarian democracy or multi-party system have led to the criticism of majoritarian democracy as a "tyranny of the majority" in the sense that the majority in society could oppress or marginalize minority groups. That is, in many ways, the minority are oppressed via policies and decisions that either work in favour of the majority or broadly represent interests that subtly diverge from those of the minority.

Dissent or dissensus as a form of resistance shows up in majoritarian democracy when we focus on the nature of opposition politics at play. The very nature of the sorts of politics at play in opposition politics in terms of the majority having power leads itself to the idea of resistance since, by its nature, the majority seems to be perpetually pitched against the minority. This shows up in at least two ways.

First, in terms of political parties whereby the party that loses out in the election and which forms the minority is already an opposition by law. The minority opposes the majority and is generally expected to do so. Indeed, they may be construed to be failing morally and legally if there is no clear strategy from it that is directed to opposing the majority. The minority as the opposition not only simply opposes or resists as a way of fulfilling their legal or constitutional role and mandate as a minority/opposition party but as part of a way of providing some form of check on the majority.

The second is in public or citizens' participation whereby citizens are split into majority and minority depending on the parties that they support. Of course, those that did not vote for the majority party are likely to be classified as or to group themselves as some sort of opposition just in virtue of their disagreement with the majority party. And (ignoring intra-party differences) those that voted for the majority party may, in general, not be opposed to the majority party. For those that voted for the majority or ruling party may view themselves as part of the party or see the party as reflecting some of their values and interests.

Majoritarianism and Consensual Democracy

Partly owing to some of the problems of majoritarian democracy, some have suggested that we should look up to other forms of democracy such as deliberative or discursive democracy and consensual democracy, where deliberative democracy combines features of consensus decision-making and majority rule and where deliberation is central to decision-making.[3] These forms of democracy are generally touted to be better alternatives to majoritarian democracy. In the main, the worry of the tyranny of the majority for majoritarian democracy is one that dovetails into questions of marginalization. But beyond this, the very nature of the conflict between the majority and minority does have the potentials in some (perhaps many) democratic settings to snowball into further problems, such as those of resentment and constant antagonism between both groups. Indeed, the majority and minority divide may fragment society beyond repair and reconciliation such that the "us" vs. "them" mentality is exacerbated and entrenched.

I think that both the problem of the tyranny of the majority and that of antagonism are what Wiredu calls a form of injustice in which the views of citizens who belong to the minority or the defeated party (the party not in power) tend to be marginalized, excluded and ignored. This injustice manifests more visibly in the sense that the ideas and interests of the minority are affected by the decisions of the majority who may be said to in general have no interests in the interests of the minority. According to Wiredu, such is a violation of moral principle which says, "all persons have the moral right not to have their interest and concerns affected by actions or forbearance that do not enjoy their concern" (Wiredu 2001: 231).

Since majoritarian democracy is guilty as charged, i.e., of committing an injustice, Wiredu proposed consensual or consensus democracy or democracy by consensus. Unlike other advocates of consensual democracy, Wiredu's recommendation of this form of democracy is not solely because of the problems of majoritarian democracy. Consensus, he argues, is not a new phenomenon in Africa because it was used in African traditional political system (Wiredu 2001).

Consensual democracy avoids problems that come with competition for power in majoritarian democracy since the "party that wins the election gets to control the executive and legislative powers" (Wiredu 2001: 234-235). Given that such systems promote competition, parties always do want to control and retain power. This thus makes politics a struggle for power between the ruling party and opposition party. This is in contrast with consensual democracy, where power struggles are absent because power is shared. Because democracy by consensus promotes peace and rational dialogue, it,

---

[3] I do not discuss deliberative democracy in this essay since the focus is on consensual democracy.

according to Wiredu, can potentially dissolve some of the social, political and economic injustice faced by most minority ethnic groups (Wiredu 2001:235).

Outlining some of the aspects of consensus and why, in this context, democracy by consensus is a better alternative than majoritarian democracy, Wiredu says that "consensus, as a factor of decision-making in social action, does not entail unanimity or conformity in intellectual or ethical belief" (2011: 1058). For him, consensus implies the idea that "in spite of any diversity of such belief, a willingness to compromise in order to reach an understanding regarding what is to be done would facilitate harmony in group action. Beyond this, it is suggested that in the political sphere such a spirit of compromise can be expressed in institutions that are different from those familiar in some of the most glorified democracies in the world today" (Ibid). The point *simpliciter* is that compromising is a way of adjusting or calibrating one's interests so as to be aligned with the interests of society and to maintain social harmony.

An African Consensual Democracy

What I want to do in this section is to talk briefly about the African consensual democracy that is presented by Wiredu. The discussion here will stand me in a good stead in the next section to make a case that dissensus *qua* resistance may not be fully accommodated in an African consensual democracy. It should be noted that Wiredu's discussion of an African consensual democracy takes off from his discussion of the problematic of majoritarian democracy, foremost of which is, according to him, the exacerbation of political conflicts in ways that are divisive and fragmentary. In Wiredu's view, democracy by consensus can avoid the problematic of multi-party politics or majoritarian democracy. Speaking about the ills of majoritarian democracy Wiredu notes that multiparty majoritarianism has politicised and exacerbated pre-existing dissensions and created new ones with deadly consequences. He notes:

> On only a little reflection it should have been clear that, in view of the ethnic configurations and other divisions in many African countries, such a system [multiparty majoritarianism] bore nothing but danger for us. Frequently, small ethnic groups have been politically marginalised in the face of the dominance of larger ones. Sometimes, historical grounds of division, not necessarily ethnic, have operated to produce the same results. In either case disaffection has tended to find non-constitutional manifestations to the doom of peace and stability and loss of countless lives (2011: 1064).

And it is in this spirit of outlining this problematic of multi-party politics that he presents an African consensual democracy.

Wiredu's proposal of consensual democracy is informed by what he takes to be present in traditional consensual practices in Africa. By traditional consensual practices in Africa, Wiredu means that multi-party politics in Africa does not exist. He claims that the view that political conflict is foreign to Africa, is absurdly false, but rather that what is true is that conflicts that arise from the activities of some special forms of organization, namely, those of political parties are not indigenous to Africa (Ibid 1060).

Representative of the traditional consensual system in the context of traditional consensual practices for Wiredu is the consensual political system of the Ashanti of Ghana. According to Wiredu, in the Ashanti Kingdom, which is led by the national council and headed by the *Asantehene* or King of the Ashantis, decisions are arrived at not through some formal voting process but by consensual decision-making. This process and practice is made easy given the nature of the political structure of the kingdom where the most fundamental political unit is the lineage, which has a head and who is elected through consensus. The lineage head is chosen on the basis of certain qualifications such as "seniority in age, wisdom, a sense of civic responsibility, and logical persuasiveness" (Wiredu 1996: 184). The lineage is represented by the head in the village or town council, and the village or town council elects someone to represent it at the regional council. On its part, the regional council elects someone to represent it at the national council (Wiredu 1996: 185).

The representation of the traditional consensual system using the consensual political system of the Ashanti of Ghana presents for Wiredu elements for an African consensual democracy.[4] One such element is that discussions and decisions must aim toward consensus. As well, there is no place for party politics in such a political system. Furthermore, the choosing or election of representatives (the heads of lineages, village or town councils, regional councils) is guided by the idea that they meet important qualifications that are supposed to engender consensual decisions. One may worry, though, if the minimal aspect of choosing or electing representatives does not introduce its own problem for democracy by consensus: the problem of election that we find in majoritarian democracy.[5]

---

[4] For discussions and broad support for Wiredu's descriptions of traditional African consensual practices see Wamala (2004), Teffo (2004) and Gyekye (2013).

[5] For some discussion of this problem, see the essay (in this volume, chapter 6), "The Problem of "Elections in Wiredu's Consensus Democracy" by Vitumbiko Nyirenda.

An important element in Wiredu's consensual democracy is the idea of compromise, which could be said to be very fundamental in arriving at a common ground or getting participants that are involved in decision-making to modify their positions towards consensus. In his utilization of the concept of compromise, Wiredu seems to suggest that democracy by consensus is about achieving compromises rather than unanimities. This interpretation has been endorsed by scholars like Bernard Matolino (2009) and Kibujjo Kalumba (2015). This idea of compromise, as I will show in a moment, is connected to the idea that decision-makers do not change their beliefs in reaching consensus but compromise in order to achieve a particular outcome or achieve a common ground (with the ultimate goal of achieving social harmony).

Dissensus *Qua* Resistance and African Consensual Democracy

The argument that I advance in this section is that dissensus *qua* resistance may not be fully accommodated in an African consensual democracy — the type advocated by Wiredu. That is, the role and value of opposition seem to be lost by the very nature of consensus *qua* compromise, particularly in Wiredu's claim that consensus leads to genuine reconciliation and abstention from further disputation and recrimination. The objection is rooted in the idea that consensual democracy is about compromises, namely, the giving up of one's ideas (or suspension of one's beliefs not the changing of one's beliefs) to accommodate those of another and to achieve social harmony.

Consensual democracy, Wiredu notes, should be about compromises and not unanimities. This means that when individuals are called upon to make decisions they ought to aim more at making concessions rather than aligning their mental state with those of others. This is perhaps what Wiredu is getting out with the idea of agreed action without agreed notion.[6] I read Wiredu's proposal of aiming towards compromises and not unanimities to be suggesting that consensual democracy is about agreeing and compromising on what to do, and not about changing one's beliefs. The idea of compromise in consensual democracy is a clear recognition by Wiredu that disagreement or dissensus constitutes the starting point for consensus insofar as this allows for or opens up the space for the suspension of belief by parties or representatives. However, the striving towards compromise seems both to eliminate the possibility of opposition and to blunt an individual's resistance sensitivities. I will discuss these two issues in turn.

---

[6] For an in-depth discussion of this idea see Ani (2014: 311-320).

The elimination of opposition or its possibility seems problematic because enough weight appears not to be given to the value of dissensus *qua* resistance. For resistance, as I have discussed, is an act of refusal, which is directed against something that one disagrees with or a behaviour that attempts to prevent something that one is opposed to from manifesting or being realized or efforts aimed at superimposing one's ideal over another. Now, if consensus is about compromises, it is not clear what space there is for resistance. The moment one has compromised on one's position and agreed in action, namely, agreed to go with the others, there ceases to be any further role for the opposition. For one cannot still be in opposition or opposed to the others or some other ideas once one has compromised with them.

I now come to the second issue. Besides the problem posed for opposition by the notion of compromise, there is the further worry that the practice of compromise in consensual democracy blunts an individual's resistance sensitivities. This is because in compromising, individuals have and develop a particular disposition, a cooperative disposition one might say. But one is not only required to have and develop this disposition but maintain it throughout the life of the decision that has been taken or the action that has been agreed upon. As a decision-maker, one will be displaying bad faith if one were to show any contempt for the decision reached. One is, in fact, required to support the decision that has been made. But in doing this one pockets and shelves any propensity one has towards resistance. The point is that to be a good team or group player, a player that supports the decision reached one's disposition towards compromise has to be honed and in the honing process of the disposition, one loses a bit of the disposition that is directed towards resistance.

A possible retort to me here could be that I have not completely given enough weight to Wiredu's point that in compromising one does not change one's beliefs but agrees only in action. The idea here is that in changing one's beliefs, one's beliefs do not get dislodged but remain intact. And given that one's beliefs have not been dislodged the impact of cultivating the disposition to compromise will not negatively impact the disposition to resistance. In a sense, then, and as long as one's beliefs remain intact, the decision-maker leaves open the possibility of later confronting the decision reached.

I do think that the above riposte is problematic. Let me outline briefly two reasons why I hold this view. The first reason revolves around the issue of stability and the second is about the possibility of resistance. I begin with the issue of instability.

The retort claims that given that one's beliefs are not dislodged, the possibility to later confront the decision reached is always there. In principle, coming back to the decision is possible whether or not one has changed one's beliefs (but particularly so when one's beliefs remain intact). However, this is problematic for the whole process of compromise and for consensual democracy in general since instability is now introduced into it. The point is that when people have compromised and agreed on an action through a rigorous, deliberative and rational process, they expect that the decision will be followed through by everyone. However, their faith and confidence in the decision reached will be undermined, if the possibility of confronting the decision reached is left open and there is indeed the prospect that such a decision will be revisited. It is perhaps due to this and the worry of instability that John Rawls (1999) introduces the principle of finality to protect his two principles of justice. In Rawls' finality principle, parties or representatives are required to evaluate the system of principles of justice as the final court of appeal in practical reasoning, i.e. to take the principles chosen as having some finality in the sense that they are suitable to be the highest authority within society and supersede the demands of law and custom, and of social rules.

I now come to the question of the possibility of resistance. The kernel of this problematic is encapsulated in the question: If resistance is opposition, how then does one resist? The idea here is that even if we agree that the impact on the disposition to resistance by the cultivation of the disposition to compromise is not negative, the kind of resistance that is available to decision-makers will be a lame one, what might be called "lame duck opposition." In the regime of the disposition to compromise, one may be forbidden from protesting since that will undermine the fact that we have agreed with the decision. As well, one cannot remind others that one is unhappy with the decision or express the wish or desire to reverse one's view, as this suggests that one is distancing oneself from the decision. And protest (whether overt or covert, verbal or through actions) is essential for resistance. So, what we are left with is the possibility of resistance without any *real* or *actual* resistance, almost akin to the distinction between formal freedom and effective freedom. Where formal freedom refers to the absence of interference and effective freedom refers to the ability or having the power or capacity to act in a particular way. In this sense, there is the possibility of resistance, where resistance is available to decision-makers in principle (akin to formal freedom) and *real* or *actual* resistance, where the people have all the resources that are necessary for them to resist (akin to effective freedom). Although both the possibility of resistance (formal freedom) and *real* or *actual* resistance (effective freedom) are valued, the latter, i.e., *real* or *actual* resistance (effective freedom), is more valuable.

Conclusion

I now want to end by suggesting what seem to be two parallel worldviews that are capable of grounding the idea of compromise. The first is a purely market-oriented worldview, the sort of worldview that we find articulated by social contract theorists, particularly of the sort that is defended by a moral contractarian like David Gauthier. For this worldview, individuals make compromises as part of the bargain strategy of rational actors or the general bargaining process and because of prudential reasons — reasons that have to do with some overarching interests of individuals and society.[7] I think this seems to be part of what Wiredu had in mind when he said that one compromises knowing fully well that next time others may have to compromise and the need for the individual to adjust his or her interests to those of the community (Wiredu 1996; 2001: 227–244; 2011:1055–1066). To be clear, this process is rational. For people who do comprise because of prudential reasons act rationally since they are driven by what they take and understand to be worth pursuing, what speaks to overall interests and what is important for practical reason. This notion may have bearing on the debate about rationality in Wiredu's consensual democracy, logical persuasiveness of ideas and whether compromise or deliberation leading to consensus is a purely rational activity, and the place of non-rational factors such as mythological or nationalistic factors (e.g., the flag, motherland, common ancestry, etc.) in compromise or deliberation. [8]

The second worldview is a communitarian worldview, where people take the development and maintenance of relationships to be essential for personhood and the *summum bonum*. An Ubuntu morality undergirds this worldview. Desmond Tutu, the Nobel Peace Prize winner, seems to summarize the point about Ubuntu, relationship and the *summum bonum* in two separate passages. Firstly, "A person with Ubuntu is available and open to others, affirming of others, does not feel threatened that others are able or good, for he or she has a proper self-assurance that comes from knowing that he or she belongs in a greater whole and is diminished when others are humiliated or diminished, when others are tortured or oppressed (Tutu 1988), And secondly, "Harmony, friendliness, community are great goods. Social harmony is for us the *summum bonum*—the greatest good. Anything that subverts or undermines this sought-after good is to be avoided like the plague. Anger, resentment, lust for revenge, even success through aggressive

---

[7] For a discussion of the nature of bargaining in the context of prudential reason for Gauthier moral contractarianism see Etieyibo (2013: 221-233).
[8] For this debate see Emmanuel Ifeanyi Ani (2014a:311–320); Emmanuel Ifeanyi Ani (2014b:342-365); Emmanuel Ifeanyi Ani (2018:251-273) Emmanuel Chukwudi Eze (1997: 313-323); Emmanuel Chukwudi Eze (2000); Bernard Matolino (2009:34–42); Bernard Matolino (2013:138-152); Bernard Matolino (2016:36-55).

competitiveness, are corrosive of this good" (1988: 35). We can see how the idea of Ubuntu as a communitarian worldview could potentially undergird compromise given that for compromise, one does adjust or calibrates one's interests so as to be aligned with the interests of society and to maintain social harmony. Ubuntu is about a universal bond of sharing that connects all humanity, about human embeddedness in humanity. Because it emphasises the importance of humanity towards others and of humans existing with other humans it points to the relevance of non-rational factors such as communal membership or one's social embeddedness with others in driving compromises. Because one is part of the humanity of others, or because "I am because we are, and since we are, therefore, I am" (Mbiti 1970), there is the obligation imposed on one not to unsettle the "we", but to compromise and to adjust one's interests to those of the community.[9]

Although both worldviews that undergird the notion of compromise may seem parallel, there may be some way of reconciling them. One way perhaps is the sort of move that Anthony Oritsegbubemi Oyowe and Edwin Etieyibo have made in the article, "Ubuntu and Social Contract Theory," where they tried to draw some connections between Ubuntu and social contract theory in the area of mutual advantage, consent, agreement and negotiation (2018: 343-365). Another way is to endorse and embrace a much broader view of rationality, which takes rationality to be satisfied as long as the interests of the community can be said to collapse into the interests of the individual. On this understanding, acting rationally is to realize, at the same time, the interests of the community (the "we") and individual (the "I"). That is, the act of compromising is a rational act that brings the "I" closer to the "we" such that the realization of the interests of the community is the realization of the interests of the individual.

---

[9] For some of the literature on Ubuntu see N. Mkhize (2008:35-44); Mogobe Ramose (2002); Dirk J. Louw (2001:15-36); Wim Van Binsbergen (2001:53-89); Kgalushi K. Koka (1997); E.D. Prinsloo (1994); E. D. Prinsloo (1997); Johann Broodryk (1995:31-37); Johann Broodryk (1998); Edwin Etieyibo (2017a: 139-162); Edwin Etieyibo (2017b: 311-325); Edwin Etieyibo (2017c: 633-657); Lovemore Mbigi (1995); W.J. Ndaba (1994); Lesiba J. Teffo (1994a); Lesiba J. Teffo (1994b); Thaddeus Metz (2007 321–341).

References

Ani, E. I. 2014a. On Agreed Actions Without Agreed Notions. *South African Journal of Philosophy* 33 (3): 311–320.

Ani, E. I. 2014b. On Traditional African Consensual Rationality. *Journal of Political Philosophy* 22(3):342-365.

Ani, E. I. 2018. The Question of Rationality in Kwasi Wiredu's Consensual Democracy. In Edwin Etieyibo (ed.) *Method, Substance, and the Future of African Philosophy*. New York: Palgrave Macmillan, 251-273.

Broodryk, J. 1995. Is Ubutuism Unique? In J.G. Malherbe (ed.) *Decolonizing the Mind*. Pretoria, Research Unit for African Philosophy, UNISA, 31-37.

Broodryk, J. 1998. *Ubuntuism: Philosophy of the New South Africa*. Tshwane, Pretoria: Ubuntu School of Philosophy.

Etieyibo, E. 2013. Bargaining and Agreement in Gauthier's Moral Contractarianism. *South African Journal of Philosophy* 32(3): 221-233.

Etieyibo, E. 2017a. Ubuntu, Cosmopolitanism and Distribution of Natural Resources. *Philosophical Papers* 46(1):139-162.

Etieyibo, E. 2017b. Moral Education, Ubuntu and Ubuntu-inspired Communities. *South African Journal of Philosophy* 36(2): 311-325.

Etieyibo, E. 2017c. Ubuntu and the Environment. In A. Afolayan and T. Falola (eds.) *The Palgrave Handbook of African Philosophy*. New York: Palgrave Macmillan, 633-657.

Eze, E. C. 1997. Democracy or Consensus: A Response to Wiredu. In Emmanuel Chukwudi Eze (ed.) *Postcolonial African Philosophy: A Critical Reader*. Oxford: Blackwell, 313-323.

Eze, E. C. 2000. Democracy or Consensus? Response to Wiredu. *Polylog*. Available at http://them.polylog.org/2/fee-en.htm (accessed 21 August 2019).

Gyekye, K. 2013. *Philosophy, Culture and Vision*. Legon-Accra: Sub-Saharan Publishers.

Kalumba, K. M. 2015. Consensus and Federalism in Contemporary African Political Philosophy. *Philosophical Papers* 44(1): 103-119.

Koka, K. K. 1997. *Ubuntu: People's Humanness*. Tshwane, Pretoria: Ubuntu School of Philosophy.

Louw, J. D. 2001. Ubuntu and the Challenges of Multiculturalism in Post-Apartheid South Africa. *Quest: An African Journal of Philosophy* (African Renaissance and Ubuntu Philosophy Special Issue), P. Boele Van Hensbroek (ed.) 15(1-2):15-36.

Matolino, B. 2009. A Response to Eze's Critique of Wiredu's Consensual Democracy. *South African Journal of Philosophy* 28(1): 34-42.

Matolino, B. 2013. The Nature of Opposition in Kwasi Wiredu's Democracy by Consensus. *African Studies* 72(1):138-152.

Matolino, B. 2016. Rationality and Consensus in Kwasi Wiredu's Traditional African Polities. *Theoria* 146: 36-55.

Mbigi, L. 1995. *Ubuntu: A Rainbow Celebration of Cultural Diversity*. Tshwane, Pretoria: Ubuntu School of Philosophy.

Mbiti, J. 1970. *African Religions and Philosophies*. New York: Doubleday.

Metz, T. 2007. Toward an African Moral Theory. *Journal of Political Philosophy* 15(3): 321–341.

Mkhize, N. 2008. Ubuntu and Harmony: an African Approach to Morality and Ethics. In R. Nicolson (ed.) *Persons in Community: African Ethics in a Global Culture*. Scottsville: University of KwaZulu-Natal Press, 35-44.

Ndaba, W.J. 1994. *Ubuntu in Comparison to Western Philosophies*. Tshwane, Pretoria: Ubuntu School of Philosophy.

Nyirenda, V. 2019. The Problem of Elections in Wiredu's Consensus Democracy. Chapter 6 in this volume.

Oyowe, A.O. and Etieyibo, E. 2018. Ubuntu and Social Contract Theory. In Edwin Etieyibo (ed.) *Perspectives in Social Contract Theory*. Washington, D.C.: The Council for Research in Values and Philosophy, 343-365.

Prinsloo, E.D. 1994. *Ubuntu: In Search of a Definition*. Tshwane, Pretoria: Ubuntu School of Philosophy.

Prinsloo, E.D. 1997. *The Ubuntu Concept of Caring*. Tshwane, Pretoria: Ubuntu School of Philosophy.

Ramose, B. M. 2002. *African Philosophy Through Ubuntu*. (Revised edition). Harare: Mond.

Rawls, J. 1999. *A Theory of Justice*. Cambridge: Harvard University Press.

Teffo, J. 2004. Democracy, Kingship and Consensus: A South African Perspective. In Kwasi Wiredu (ed.) A *Companion to African Philosophy*. Maiden: Blackwell Publishing Ltd, 443-449.

Teffo, L. J. 1994a. *The Concept of Ubuntu as a Cohesive Moral Value*. Tshwane, Pretoria: Ubuntu School of Philosophy.

Teffo, L. J. 1994b. *Towards a Conceptualization of Ubuntu*. Tshwane, Pretoria: Ubuntu School of Philosophy.

Tutu, D. 1988. Sermon in Birmingham Cathedral. April 21, 1988. Transcript published by the Committee for Black Affairs, Diocese of Birmingham, 4-5.

Van Binsbergen, W. 2001. Ubuntu and the Globalization of Southern African Thought and Society. *Quest: An African Journal of Philosophy* (African Renaissance and Ubuntu Philosophy Special Issue), P. Boele Van Hensbroek (ed.) 15(1-2): 53-89.

Wamala, E. 2004. Government by Consensus: An Analysis of a Traditional Form of Democracy. In Kwasi Wiredu (ed.) *A Companion to African Philosophy*, Maiden: Blackwell Publishing Ltd., 435-441.

Wiredu, K. 1996. *Cultural Universals and Particulars*. Bloomington: Indiana University Press.

Wiredu, K. 2001. Democracy by Consensus: Some Conceptual Considerations. *Philosophical Papers* 30(3): 227–244.

Wiredu, K. 2011. State, Civil Society and Democracy in Africa. In Helen Lauer and Kofi Anyidoho (eds.). *Reclaiming the Human Sciences and Humanities Through African Perspectives*. Legon-Accra: Sub-Saharan Publishers, 1055–1066.

Chapter 10

Is Partisan Extremism Inherent in Multiparty Democracy?

Alexander Kwakye

Ghana Education Service

Introduction

Generally, the debate about democracy in Africa proceeds from the fact that the practice of democracy in Africa is bedevilled with a plethora of challenges. Prominent African scholars have observed that multiparty democracy, the system of government widely adopted in Africa, has malfunctioned (Wiredu 2011: 1064; Moshi and Osman 2008; Wamala 2004: 440-1; Teffo 2004: 444). Moshi and Osman (2008; cited in Fayemi 2009: 114) complain that the "Western insistence on multiparty politics does not consider indigenous cultural values which makes multiparty electoral politics degenerate into ethnic or communal conflicts". The basis for this conclusion is the belief that multiparty democracy is inherently susceptible to partisan extremism or adversarial politics (Wiredu 2011: 1064; Wamala 2004: 440-1; Teffo 2004: 444). For this reason, Wiredu and these other scholars reject multiparty democracy as a viable option for polities in Africa. Having expressed doubts about the prospects of multiparty democracy in Africa, these scholars question the conceptual relevance of multiparty politics to democracy, and, as a result, draw the conclusion that democracy does not mandate party politics. If democracy does not mandate multiparty system of politics, plausibly, two options can be considered: either to do away with the faulty system, or to find ways to correct the defects in the system. Opting for the former, these scholars prescribe consensual politics as a substitute to partisan politics (Wiredu 1997: 307; Gyekye 1997: 167; Wamala 2004: 437; Teffo 2004: 445-446).

The following analytical questions come to mind when contemplating on the position that multiparty democracy should be jettisoned because it has failed to yield the expected dividends of democracy in Africa—due to its susceptibility to partisan extremism: is partisan extremism an inherent feature of multiparty politics, and are majoritarianism and consensus mutually exclusive notions, such that the latter could not be brought to bear on the former?

A cursory analysis will be done on these fundamental questions with a view to pointing out the flaws in the call to do away with multiparty democracy because of partisan extremism. It is envisaged that a critique of this prescription will lead us to arrive at a conclusion that political players are not slaves to the system within which they operate. And as such, when we fault the system, it absolves them of any moral guilt.

Faulting Multiparty Politics

Kwesi Wiredu, one of the prominent philosophers in Africa, sees multiparty democracy, the system of government widely adopted in Africa, as antithetical to the spirit of *communalism* (Wiredu 2011: 1060-1). The said communalism is a phenomenon that was pervasive in traditional African societies. Wiredu points out that multiparty democracy has malfunctioned in Africa because it is inherently susceptible to partisan extremism (Wiredu 2011: 1064), a phenomenon that has *overly* "politicised and exacerbated pre-existing dissensions and created new ones with deadly consequences" (Wiredu 2011: 1064). Hence, Wiredu blames multiparty politics for the political instability and many other challenges Africa faces in her pursuit of democracy.

Majoritarianism, the principle that underpins multiparty politics, allows political decisions to be made based on the preponderance of numbers, and for that matter, the party that wins the most seats in a general election is entitled to form a government, whereas the parties that lose stay out of power or become the opposition (Wiredu 2011: 1060). Simply put, in a multiparty majoritarian system, "government becomes government with the consent of only the majority" (Wiredu 2011: 1060).

Besides, Wiredu thinks that the bad fate the minority groups suffer in a majoritarian system denies them the right to have their views substantively represented in governmental decisions (Wiredu 1997: 307). He argues that instituting a political decision procedure such as majoritarianism in a polity keeps some minority groups periodically out of power. This, according to Wiredu, is a violation of the fundamental human rights of the minority groups (Wiredu 1997: 310) because their views or interests are not represented in governmental decisions, thereby creating some political disharmony. Consequently, this *political disharmony* creates rancour, disaffection, and political alienation within the state. That is, the bad fate that awaits minority groups or parties that lose elections under majoritarian democracy is that their *right* to have *decisional representation* is institutionally not recognized. The institutional disregard for the right of the minority (or losers) to have a decisional representation coupled with the fear of losing political power, as I interpret Wiredu's submission, makes multiparty politics confrontational and aggressive. This is because parties who stay out of power see their situation as precarious and as a result, fight aggressively to capture political power. Similarly, the party in power acknowledges that the conditions of being out of power are really bad[1], and for that matter, would not want to relinquish power. This kind of 'I win, you lose,' or 'you win, I lose' anxiety culminates in politics of mutual distrust[2]—a fertile ground for partisan extremism.

The psychological infelicities of losing an election or the fear of losing political power makes multiparty politics excessively partisan or adversarial (Wiredu 2011: 1061). For instance, opposition parties in the desire to capture power, strategically oppose almost every policy proposal emanating from the ruling party. Thus, opposition becomes *obstruction* to state business. Likewise, the ruling party obstinately ignores the views, suggestions, or criticisms on policy issues from the minority parties without any recognition of their possible relevance to the development of the country. Wiredu characterises such a situation as: "…the quintessence of uncooperativeness, leading to an adversarial approach to politics with its manifold severities" (Wiredu 2011: 1061). Such an approach accommodates political conflicts, disaffection, and politics of exclusion, malignment, lack of trust, and the polarization of a country (Wiredu 2011: 1060).

Another difficulty Wiredu identifies with multiparty democracy is that electioneering campaigns, a significant feature of competitive elections, have been known to be so expensive to the extent that "only groups with the command of enormous funds are in a position to present an option to the people" or participate (Wiredu 2011: 1062). The germaneness of this complaint lies in the fact that most of the people cannot meet the cost involved in organizing electioneering campaigns, and this renders otiose the constitutional instrument that grants the 'right to vote and to be voted for' to the citizenry of a country.

A Non-party Politics

Wiredu writes, "If the system in use is such as to cause some groups periodically to be substantively unrepresented minorities, then seasonal disaffection becomes institutionalized. The results are the well-known

---

[1] The condition is bad because the winner takes it all.
[2] The incumbent government sees itself as 'We' and the opposition as 'They'. 'We' are in government but 'They' are in opposition.

inclemencies of adversarial politics. From the Ashanti standpoint, consensus is the antidote" (Wiredu 1997: 307). Using the traditional Akan example of consensual politics, Wiredu demonstrates how a non-partisan approach to politics can help solve some of the recurrent political conflicts or instabilities in Africa. He first dismisses calls for a one-party system by the likes of Nyerere, Kaunda, Nkrumah, etc., as a viable solution to partisan extremism that characterizes multiparty politics in Africa. Besides, he rejects the suggestion that the multiparty system, with the necessary safeguards against the tyranny of the majority, offers a more practical option for pluralistic societies in Africa (Wiredu 1997: 309). Upon rejecting those two suggestions as feasible options, Wiredu suggests that the right solution to the challenges Africa faces in pursuit of democracy is a non-party system based on the principles of consensus. According to Wiredu, a consensual non-party system is ". . . a dispensation under which governments are formed not by parties that win the highest number of votes, but by the consensus of elected representatives. Government . . . becomes a kind of coalition—a coalition— . . . not of parties but of citizens" (Wiredu 1997: 310). People can form a political association to propagate their political ideologies and help to elect representatives to parliament, but these political associations "will be without the Hobbesian proclivities of political parties, as they are known under majoritarian politics" (Wiredu 1997: 310). The reason being that the association having the most elected members will not be entitled to form a government; every representative will be of the government in his personal rather than his or her associational capacity—in other words, independent of party/association affiliations (ibid). Wiredu concludes, "[in] such a non-partisan environment, [there is] willingness to compromise, and with it the prospects of consensus will be enhanced" (Wiredu 1997: 310). Paradoxically, as hinted above, Wiredu's non-party system will not preclude political associations which, in his view, will be needed in a non-party system of government because they will serve as a link between civil society and the state. How? Wiredu explains that under civil society, political associations will serve primarily as a forum for discourse—just like literary associations in civil society—and as vehicles of political education and representation, they will be connected with the state (Wiredu 2011: 1065). By education, Wiredu meant that "[political associations] could be training grounds for the enlargement of political orientations beyond ethnic concerns" (Wiredu 2011, 1065). For this reason, "when ideological or specific policy considerations motivate political associations, tribal antagonisms are likely to be greatly reduced" (Wiredu 2011: 1065).

In a nutshell, Wiredu's primary concern is that there is the need to consider consensual politics as an alternative to multiparty majoritarian politics, and the condition both necessary and sufficient for instituting consensual politics is a non-party approach to governance (Wiredu 2011: 1064). Probably, if it is the case that partisan politics logically leads to adversarial politics, then it can be assumed that the direct opposite of partisan politics, which is a non-partisan politics, implies consensual politics. Hence, according to Wiredu, consensus and a non-party basis of representation amounts to one thing because "a thorough-going adherence to consensus implies a non-party approach to government" (Wiredu 2011: 1063).

Consensual and Majoritarian Rules

Faulting multiparty democracy, Wiredu also denounced majoritarianism, a decisional rule in multiparty democracy in that, majoritarian decisions do not bear the views of the dissenting minority groups, and as such, they are essentially not consensual. For example, outside of Africa, Wiredu lists continental Europe, i.e., countries like Switzerland and Belgium, which he says are constitutional arrangements that have pointed us away from majoritarianism to a designation that can be called "consensual". In Wiredu's view, these countries, however, remain party-based, and the sort of consensus that they aim at is limited; the consensus is one of a kind of understanding among parties. In contrast to the sort of consensus in these countries, Wiredu notes that the sort of polity to keep in mind when we talk about the consensus that he is referring to will be those that are "completely party-less and motivated by a quite radical commitment to consensus" (Wiredu 2011: 1064).

Elsewhere Wiredu also writes, "Electing a representative by a simple constituency vote is a majoritarian procedure, unless there is a score of 100%. Any element of majoritarianism is a loss of consensus" (Wiredu 2011: 1065).

Ostensibly, those two quotations from Wiredu point to the conclusion that consensus and majoritarianism are mutually exclusive notions such that any element of majoritarianism is a loss of consensus. However, this cannot be the case, in that, consensus and majoritarianism, as decisional rules, coincide. They are in fact consociational terms. In this regard, Ani (2013), for instance, asserts that consensus and voting do overlap in practice, and for that matter, voting should be seen as a basic human solution to group decisional intractability (Ani 2013: 5). I interpret 'voting' in Ani's assertion as *majority rule*, and it is this rule that he thinks coincides with consensus. That is to say, in a group intractability, in order to avoid a *gridlock*, the group would, at this point, make a decision to put the matter to a vote. In doing so, the rules of the voting are spelt out clearly. The parties must agree to conditions necessary before any voting can take place. The processes leading to this end involve two decisions that require consensus—(i) to vote on the matter in issue, (ii) the threshold a group requires to win. These two decisions ought to be *unanimous* decisions—consensus. In this light, consensus and majoritarianism should not be seen as contradistinguished variables such that when one is *hot*, the other is *cold*. In this vein, consensus should be understood in two ways, namely:

i.   *a decision* – an expression such as 'This is the consensus of the house' is the same as saying 'This is the decision of the house' (consensual decision);

ii.   *a process or procedure* through which the decision is reached—we hear of consensus building, which is deliberative or dialogic (A decision rule which governs the process of taking a group decision).

The final decision of a group can be referred to as the *consensus* of the group. The deliberative process or dialogue leading to an accepted modus operandi for taking group decisions can be labelled as a consensual rule—a decision rule through which the final decision is taken. It should also be noted that in a group decision making, there is the need for the group to first decide on the accepted level of agreement required to finalize a decision. I intend to call this *pre-consensual rule*—which in most cases, ought to be a unanimous decision. And on the basis of a pre-consensual decision, the modus operandi is established for subsequent group decisions—a group decisional rule is established. A group may agree on, for instance, *absolute consensus* such as *100%* majority votes; or *supermajority* thresholds *such as: 90%, 80%, 75%, two-thirds, and 50%+1* as the agreed level of consensus required to finalize a decision. In this regard, Gyekye writes "In the American democratic system, for instance, decisions on certain matters require, not a simple majority, but two-thirds majority. Such matters include amendment of the constitution, overriding a presidential veto, impeaching the president and some other matters" (Gyekye 2013: 245). Thus, two-thirds majority is the level of consensus required to take those constitutional decisions. Common also to most democratic constitutions that uphold the ideals of consensus are the special provisions made to stipulate the level of consensus required to finalize some special decisions. The 1992 unitary constitution of Ghana, for example, requires not less than a two-thirds super majority vote of no confidence before a sitting president can be impeached by parliament[3]. *However*, due to the fact that the constitutions of the countries known to have adopted consensual politics still allow for party-based politics, Wiredu holds that "the

---

[3] The 1992 constitution on Ghana, article 69 clause 11, page 53. It is also available on: http://www.ghanaweb.com/GhanaHomePage/republic/constitution.php?id=Gconst8.html

consensus *they* aimed at is limited, *in the sense that it is merely*[4] . . . a kind of understanding among parties" (Wiredu 2011: 1064). But, what is noteworthy is Wiredu's admission that there is a consensus—some level of agreement and cooperation among the parties—albeit, it is limited. This admission also supports the fact that consensual decisions could vary with regards to the level of agreement/compromise among the parties or persons involved either in partisan or nonpartisan politics.

Due to the intricacies inherent in the notion of consensual rule, this paper holds that Wiredu's "radical commitment to consensus" (Wiredu 2011: 1064) gives consensus a narrow denotation; because it suggests that consensus and majoritarianism are mutually exclusive notions, and that it is not possible for a simple majority decision or supermajority decision to be forms of consensus.

But as demonstrated above, majoritarian rules—supermajority and ordinary majority—with some qualifications can be said, in principle, to be kinds of decision rules based on consensus—depending on the level of their inclusiveness, tolerance, and compromise. Partisan politics, albeit thrives on majoritarianism, requires consensus as a precursor for sanity to prevail in a general assembly. The relationship between consensus and majoritarianism is not that of mutual exclusion. They are intriguingly interconnected, such that, a majoritarian decision, in principle, can be considered as a product of consensus—a decisional rule.

Excessive Partisanship or Political Extremism

Multiparty democracy allows for partisanship, an inclination to favour one political group's view or opinion as to what is best for a country over other alternatives. But when this inclination is exacerbated—becomes devoid of tolerance and compromise—it leads to an unwillingness to recognize and respect differences in opinions or beliefs—political extremism. At this point, partisanship crosses the line from reasonable to the extreme. When the unwillingness to recognize and respect differences in opinion is exhibited from both sides of the political divide, it culminates in political conflicts of different kinds and shapes. In a nutshell, when a political setting is devoid of tolerance and compromise, it culminates in political extremism.

Kwame Gyekye, another prolific African philosopher, in recounting the woes of political extremism, writes that "excessive political partisanship eliminates negotiation and compromise . . . It breeds politics of exclusion, not of inclusion and accommodation . . ." (Gyekye 2013: 243). It also leads to

---

[4] Emphasis added.

"ideological rigidity" among political parties[5]. However, he disagrees with the view that excessive political partisanship or political extremism is a necessary consequence of multiparty democracy, and the conclusion that the most viable way to deal with the problem of adversarial politics or excessive partisanship is to jettison multiparty politics. Gyekye argues that "it is of course part of the logic of multiparty politics that there should be political partisanship . . . *in that*, political parties have different ideologies and programs, but the logic does not mandate excessive political partisanship" or political extremism (Gyekye 2013: 168; 242). Gyekye asserts that excessive political partisanship is rather a *political behaviour* in which members who share a common political ideology or inclination refuse to change their opinion or position on policy issues despite convincing arguments advanced by the opposing parties. It is a mere refusal to "acknowledge the wisdom in the arguments or proposals of their opponents *and therefore cannot be*[6] . . . a logical or necessary feature or consequence of multiparty system of politics" (Gyekye 2013: 168, 243).

If political postures such as intolerance, the use of intemperate language, electoral violence etc. are in principle products of a political system rather than some moral agents, then we can say that excessive political partisanship is a necessary feature of multiparty democracy. But if we can logically distinguish a political system and the people in the system, then products of people's behaviour within a political system cannot consistently be said to be the product of the political system. Partisan extremism is merely taking an immoderate and uncompromising political standpoint on issues before an assembly for deliberation. Whatever triggers these extremism or excesses in partisan politics, to reiterate Gyekye's position, is the moral disposition of the individual politician. In what follows shortly, I advance an argument by analogy which denies the claim that adversarial politics or partisan extremism is the logical consequence of multiparty democracy.

Absolving Political Players of any Moral Guilt

Negative proclivities such as fanaticism, religious extremism, zealotry, pedantry, dogmatism, ethnocentrism, and stereotyping can operate in contexts as varied as academia, religion, multinational states, etc. People condemn these negative behaviour(s) and blame persons who perpetuate them without necessarily condemning the contexts in which they are exhibited. The reason for doing so is that some people within a social

---

[5] Gyekye 2013, 242.
[6] Emphasis added.

context can behave in a certain manner which might not necessarily be the general behaviour of all the people: because if a particular behavioural pattern or trait is the logical consequence of a particular context, then inevitably, all the people within that context must exhibit that behaviour. For example, it is erroneous to argue that because some ethnic groups or some members of an ethnic group believe in the superiority of their groups, and thereby deride other ethnic groups, ethnocentrism and stereo typing are the logical consequences of ethnic grouping. By reason of the fact that not all those who belong to ethnic groupings are ethnocentric, we can justifiably condemn the social behaviour 'ethnocentrism' and the people who believe and indulge in it without necessarily condemning social groupings based on blood ties—ethnic groups.

Similarly, it is erroneous to argue that because some Muslims indulge in acts of *terrorism* or extremism, Islamic extremism or terrorism is the logical consequence of Islam. Thus, Islam mandates terrorism. This type of reasoning commits a fallacy of *stereotyping* and *composition*. The argument erroneously moves from existential quantification to drawing a universal conclusion, and the fact that there are other members in Islam who are not extremists, makes the generalization faulty. Religious extremism among some Muslims cannot be said to be the logical consequence of Islam because there are Muslims who are not terrorists or extremists: likewise, there are many individuals who are terrorists but not Muslims. In effect, acts of terrorism or Islamic extremism are the products of some people's behaviour rather than a necessary consequence of Islam.

Drawing from the analogies cited above, we can also condemn partisan extremism or adversarial politics without necessarily condemning multiparty politics, the context in which these political behaviours can be exhibited. Besides, a political system and the behaviour of the people towards/within the system are logically distinct, because the product of the people's behaviour cannot, in principle, be said to be the product of the system. Hence, it can be concluded that partisan extremism or adversarial politics are products of some individuals' behaviour, but not the logical consequence of multiparty politics.

Although, it is an undeniable fact that partisan extremism and adversarial politics are found in the context of multiparty politics, but in as much as it is a context being populated by a human with moral tendencies, negative tendencies such as partisan extremism could be exhibited. However, an attempt to mistake partisan extremism and adversarial politics as correlates or logical consequences of multiparty democracy will land the thinker in a fallacy of composition or hasty generalization. What is in issue with regards to the compound words: 'partisan *extremism* and *adversarial* politics' is not the words, 'partisan' or 'politics' but the words *'extremism'* and 'adversarial' attached to them. One can be partisan in a social discourse, but when an individual shows adversity to those who hold a different opinion on national issues, we ought to condemn it. The disposition to go to the extreme politically or the susceptibility to show aggression or hostility to others in any political setting—be it a monarch, aristocracy, a one-party state, or multiparty democracy—is an individual affair. The person who goes to the extreme to push his political ideologies, beliefs or even kill his political opponents because of ideological differences is likely to do the same on religious, ethnic, etc. grounds.

There are politicians who operate in the same multiparty context but are not excessively partisan, and do not exhibit the features of extremism stated above. This suggests that excessive partisanship is a human error rather than a systemic failure. There are, for example, great academics, or religious men and women who are not zealots, fanatics, extremists, and there are also people in the same folds who exhibit these traits. The propensity to treat those who hold different political ideologies as adversaries is, therefore, an individual trait but not a systemic error which ought to be blamed on multiparty democracy. Hence, it is wrong to prescribe that in order for Africa to make significant progress in her pursuit of democracy, multiparty democracy should be jettisoned because it entails partisan extremism. Such a position presupposes an absolution of individuals who indulge in those acts of extremism any moral responsibility or guilt; because it is the political system that has made them so.

The Paradox of Partisan Interest

Another underpinning factor believed to motivate an individual to be extremely partisan is partisan interest: which is the tendency to put one's party's interest above national interest when taking governmental decisions. Let me conceptually unpack 'partisan interest' by looking at what the word party entails. The word 'party' has other senses apart from the sense that *it is an organization to gain political power.* For example, a person involved in legal proceedings can be said to be a party to the case, a band of people associated temporarily in some activity, e.g., we can say, 'They organised a party to search for the lost child. There is something common to these three senses of the word 'party'. That is, *common interest* or a common sense of purpose. The notion of common interest is very essential to the word 'party', and for that matter, in a multiparty set up, it presupposes multiplicity of common interests or divergent party interests. It is a general belief that members of a general assembly vote on issues taking into consideration the interest and ideological inclinations of their political parties. Thus, partisan politics blossom on party interest and when it is exacerbated into partisan extremism it has partisan interest as its precursor. Conversely, a non-partisan approach to government becomes a system of government whereby political representatives vote to accept or reject proposals solely on their merits but not on party interest/ideology.

But, in reality, representatives in an assembly can be motivated by personal interests other than partisan interest when voting on issues before the house. Both partisan interests and personal (selfish) interests could drive members to show adversity to fellow competitors. Those who proscribe multiparty democracy seem to portray partisan interest as the major competing force against national interest; such that in the multiparty context, political players are easily inclined to decide on national issues wearing only their political lenses. Notwithstanding, there is also a fundamental militating factor against national interest: which is the egoistic tendencies of the individual politician. Wiredu's account, for instance, only considers partisan interests and constituents' interests, and takes personal interests for granted (Wiredu 1997: 303-311). Personal interest is also a force to reckon with in a democracy: because individually or collectively, people fight or compete to capture state power not just to implement their plans or policies, but also to enjoy the privileges associated with these political offices. The reason why politicians 'fight' over an opportunity to serve their country is that they want to enjoy the right to exercise political power, control the public purse, and the privileges associated with these political offices. This also explains why there are as many intra-party as inter-party conflicts. Politicians of similar ideological inclinations or shares similar partisan interest compete for positions within their own political party in almost the same adversarial manner as they compete with other parties and with those of different ideologies. Hence, selfish, as well as partisan interests, could drive members to show adversity to fellow competitors.

Moreover, when an agenda borders on the common interests of individual representatives, irrespective of their political differences, unanimous decision is easily attained. For example, when the Ghanaian parliament (2009) was deliberating on how much the state should pay them as their emolument, there were no dissenting opinions from the political divide that perhaps, they were taking too much money for themselves; it was a unanimous decision. There are two distinct common interests at play here, personal interest, and national interest. That is, interests common to all the representatives and interests common to the citizenry. The notion of common interest in this situation should be understood in two ways: one is the aggregate of personal interests common to all the representatives, and the second is interests common to the general people—the wellbeing of the citizenry. Members of the Ghanaian parliament, when deciding on their emoluments, were motivated by interests common to them as a group. The point is that representatives in an assembly, when voting on proposals, can be motivated by *common interests* in two dimensions: the common interests$_1$—common to the individual parliamentarians—and common interest$_2$—common to the general people. When representatives are motivated by *parochial* interests$_1$ in the decision-making process, it does not satisfy substantive representation because, at that point, the representatives only represent themselves. However, when they are motivated by interests$_2$ common to the people they represent, genuine substantive representation is achieved. Hence, it is erroneous to assume that when nonpartisan approach to politics replaces partisan politics, or when we give consensus an edge over majoritarianism, the only motivation or interests that will push representatives to vote in a certain manner on issues is interests of the people. This cannot be the case because representatives can equally vote on issues in a nonpartisan manner, yet the interest that motivated them will not be common to the general public but themselves.

Now, if personal biases and parochial outlooks could still be there to contend with, even in consensual politics, then one can justifiably question the need to jettison multiparty system because individuals can be motivated to be hostile to other members by interests other than party interest.

Conclusion

The call to jettison multiparty democracy implies that partisan extremism or adversarial politics is a necessary feature of multiparty politics; so, when you take away multiparty politics—the faulty system—you necessarily do away with the problem of partisan extremism or adversarial politics—the bane of contemporary African politics. This paper argued in support of the view that partisan extremism is a product of people's behaviour rather than a necessary consequence of multiparty system; because we can conceptually distinguish between a political system and the behaviour of the people within the system. Hence, the call to sanitize African politics so that democracy, as practiced in the continent, will yield the expected dividends, ought to be directed at the African politician and not the multiparty political system. As moral agents, political extremists are morally liable for their acts of extremism, whether the actions proceeded from partisan and/or personal interests.

References

Ani, E. I. 2013. On Traditional African Consensual Rationality. *The Journal of Political Philosophy* 22(3): 342-365.

Fayemi, A. K. 2009. Towards an African Theory of Democracy. *Thought and Practice: a Journal of the Philosophical Association of Kenya (PAK)* 1(1): 101-126.

Gyekye, K. 2013. *Philosophy, Culture and Vision: African Perspectives*. Legon-Accra: Sub-Saharan Publishers.

Gyekye, K. 1997. *Tradition and Modernity, Philosophical Reflections on the African Experience*. New York: Oxford University Press.

Moshi, L. and A. O. Abdulahi (eds.) 2008. *Democracy and Culture: An African Perspective*. Lagos: Adonis and Abbey Publishers.

Nyongo, P.A. 1992. Popular Struggle for Democracy in Africa. In B. Caron, A Gboyega and E. E. Osaghae (eds.) *Democratic Transition in Africa*. Ibadan: Credu

Prah, K. K. (ND). *Multi-Party Democracy and It's Relevance in Africa;* Centre for Advanced Studies of African Society, Cape Town. Available on: *###www.elections.org.za/...rkArea/DownloadAsset.aspx?...*

Teffo, J. 2004. Democracy, Kingship and Consensus: a South African perspective. In K. Wiredu (ed.) *A Companion to African Philosophy*. Maiden: Blackwell Publishing, 443-449.

The 1992 Constitution of Ghana. Available at: www.politicsresources.net/docs/ghanaconst.pdf; http://www.ghanaweb.com/GhanaHomePage/republic/constitution.php?id=Gconst8.html (accessed 22 August 2019).

Wamala, E. 2004. Government by Consensus: An Analysis of a Traditional Form of Democracy. In K. Wiredu (ed.) *A Companion to African Philosophy*. Oxford: Blackwell Publishing, 435-441.

Wiredu, K. 1997. Democracy and Consensus in Traditional African Politics: A Plea for a Non-Party Polity. In C. Eze (ed.) *Postcolonial African Philosophy: A Critical Reader*. Oxford: Blackwell, 303-312.

Wiredu, K. 2011. State, Civil Society and Democracy in Africa. In H. Lauer and K. Anyidoho (eds.) *Reclaiming the Human Sciences*. Volume 2. Legon-Accra: Sub-Saharan Publishers, 1055-1066.

Chapter 11

Wiredu and Eze on Good Governance

By Helen Lauer[1]

University of Dar es Salaam

In West Africa, scrutiny of governance in all its aspects has been the focus of intense debate among academics, revolutionaries and opinion leaders since the mid-nineteenth century (Baku 1990). This is not a new historical development in Africa; monitoring, critiquing, and petitioning a government's treatment of its citizenry, its policies, efficiency, integrity, structural arrangements and institutional practices, might be regarded as a natural progression from the time-honoured ceremonial pillorying of individual royals in authority (Yankah 1998). Social critique has been a ritual mainstay of indigenous West African courts since antiquity (Assimeng 1992).

This essay will explore the widely read controversy between Kwasi Wiredu and perhaps his most influential critic, the late Chukwudi Emmanuel Eze, about indigenous Akan rule by consensus and its potential to strengthen the delivery of Africa's contemporary democratic promises.[2] Ostensibly, these two well-known West African philosophers occupy opposite poles in their respective evaluations of the traditional centrepiece of African governance— i.e., the council of elders advising a selected royal family head in life-long service. Eze's main points of criticism are: (i) Wiredu's arguments in favour of this non-party style of politics can function just as well to defend the single-party platforms of the early nationalists whose monopoly on political power required rigid suppression of democratic freedoms. (ii) Wiredu indulges in misleading romanticism and an excessive rationalism in his normative accounts of pre-colonial Akan society. The paper will treat these two objections in separate sections. A third section will discuss the inherent

---

[1] Originally published in *Philosophia Africana* vol. 14, no.1 (September, 2012): 41-60.
[2] 'Akan' refers generally in West Africa to a wide range of language speakers, those of whom are in Ghana and likely speaking Twi or Fanti or other languages.

mistake of conflating normative analyses with circumstantial and historically factual accounts of African political practice.

One outcome of the overview presented here is that the respective concerns of Wiredu and Eze appear to be compatible on a careful reading. Each of them highlights the urgency of distinct but complementary demands in the overall remit of good governance in a constitutional democracy, be it federalist or republican: Wiredu stresses the current need for effective distributive justice, and Eze is concerned with individual citizens' entitlements to recognition and to freedom of political opposition. I hope to demonstrate a basic congruity between these divergent yet complementary foci of West African political heritage and their relevance to our current economic and demographic conditions. Contrary to Eze's analysis, I will argue that his own vision for furthering "democracy for its own sake" is affirmed by Wiredu's normative portrayal of Akan deliberative counselling (Eze 1997: 320). Along the way, I will stress the nature of political legitimacy as a normative property, an honorific adhering in objects through evaluative reasoning. Once it is made clear that political legitimacy is not an empirical matter of historical fact connected through causal links to those institutions and establishments in which people at different times have invested their confidence, the apparent opposition between Eze's and Wiredu's democratic ideals falls away—or so I shall argue.

Initially, to diagnose a misleading component of Eze's widely discussed critique of the indigenous non-party politics presented by Wiredu, I will demonstrate that Eze seems to overlook what Wiredu himself has actually and consistently claimed about traditional Akan authority in recently published works. I interpret Wiredu's model of Akan political norms in the remote past as a normative reconstruction, for which the absence of authenticating recorded evidence is not germane. I argue that Wiredu's model of one type of pre-colonial African political institution is vindicated not by reference to past events but by moral reasoning in light of current principles of good governance, articulated by West Africans today in their condemnation of despotism, nepotism, bribery and other forms of corruption, lack of national strategic planning and failure of economic vision (e.g. Frimpong-Ansah 1996). More generally, normative reconstructions from within are needed to further political innovation for African contexts and beyond, for reasons I raise in conclusion. These ideal tableaux should not be conflated with empirical models and then misleadingly justified or condemned with sole reference to empirical evidence or to the absence of evidence as in the case of Africa's pre-colonial past.[3] As spelled out in the penultimate section, such confusion may be a second factor responsible for Eze's disagreement with Wiredu's positive portrayal of ancient styles of Akan governance.

On the other hand, in keeping with Eze's concerns, the recent literature in African political analysis features a suspicion that consensual protocols controlled by elites through traditional norms can undermine the inclusiveness and egalitarian ideals of modern representative democracy (Amanor 2006, 2012; Ninsin 2007). This suspicion has developed significantly in the global arena, as well. It has been argued by contributors to American anarchist studies that consensus-building processes often serve to cover authoritarian coercive pressures. Since the eighteenth century, elites have controlled the deliberative process by applying rationalistic criteria to disqualify subordinate group opinions as emotive and subjective, thereby rendering them unfit for public discourse, and in turn, rendering the demands that motivate subordinates' opinions insignificant or illegitimate (Sanders 1997). Mark Lance (2005) explains how consensual procedure systems in a way that stifles individual opposition and minority opinion. Daniel H. Levine, studying civilian-based peacekeeping mechanisms effective in African conflict zones, observes that "the official denial of power is a mask for the operations of fairly rigid power hierarchies" and so consensus-building can be an effective hegemonic tool for side-lining opposition.[4] It is worthwhile exploring whether indigenous councils of elders in Africa's traditional polities exhibit these deterrents to democratic inclusion, as Eze's critique claims.

A Controversy About Consensus

Perhaps the leading contemporary Ghanaian interpretation of democracy as essentially consensual is reflected in the work of the philosopher Kwasi Wiredu (1998, 2001a, 2001b, 2011). Over the last quarter of a century, Wiredu has been advocating the adoption of pre-colonial Akan ideals of good

---

[3] Throughout his widely read *Tradition and Modernity* (1996), it is often unclear when Kwame Gyekye is making an observation about what must occur for causal reasons or as customary rule, and when he is proposing a normative imperative about what should occur. A common complaint is that the African pre-colonial past is too obscure for reliable speculative discussion; see T. Carlos Jacques (2011).

[4] In conversation, University of Ghana, Legon, November 2011. I am grateful to Dr. Daniel H. Levine, Maryland School of Public Policy, for drawing my attention to the literature in the United States critiquing the elitism and hegemony prevalent in many consensus based systems of decision making and political process.

governance modified for contemporary institutional practices. Not all of Wiredu's published works are easy to access, however, which might account for the persistent disparity between the claims he has published about non-party, multi-party, and one-party politics and the claims mistakenly attributed to him by other critics (e.g., T. Carlos Jacques 2011) since Eze (1997, 2000). On the other hand, Eze and others (including historian-economists, political scientists—see Amanor 2006, 2012; Ninsin 2007, 2012) have argued that formal reinforcement of chieftaincy structures and loyalties undermines the development of sufficiently strong and progressive state apparatus to make the latter capable of fulfilling even the most basic of modern democratic ideals (Ninsin 2007, 2012). Chukwudi Emmanuel Eze (1997, 2000) was concerned to protect the development of new African democracies from the resurgence of one-party autocracies, which plagued the earliest years of Independence. Eze's essay "Democracy or Consensus? Response to Wiredu" (1997) is published in a classic anthology that he edited; and a later version of it is also widely available on the internet (2000).

The focus of criticism, which we will examine here begins with Wiredu's approval of indigenous African non-party government, and his advocacy of a modification of the traditional political process which omits political parties and relies instead upon associations which would annex the central apparatus of a modern representative democracy. Wiredu adamantly criticizes the multiparty electoral processes characteristic of modern oligarchies (e.g., the UK and US models) as too expensive and distracting from development agendas that are so critical to modern African citizens' welfare all over the continent (1998: 244).

Historical Realism or Fantasy?

Any commentary on political affairs that refers to Africa's remote past meets with certain obstacles. In the first place, it is moot whether intangible features of public discourse and political relations are accessible to empirical review— unlike ancient Greek public interchanges that were copiously chronicled and analysed at the time.[5] Records preserved orally are notoriously elusive. In some sub-regions of Africa, textual evidence of pre-colonial court proceedings are scant; in other regions, the *a priori* prejudice that Africans have no written history camouflages those manuscripts that do indeed predate European mercantile adventurism and colonial administrations (Kea 2003, 2012). Secondly, speculations about Africans' contested political heritages are

---

[5] Emmanuel Kofi Ackah, Classics section head, in conversation November 2011, University of Ghana, Legon.

especially vulnerable to criticism since they are burdened with essentialist projections of an idyllic, pristine by-gone Africa (Amanor 2006, 2012). The accounts of some early European chroniclers visiting Africa have remained seminal, but others have been proven profoundly misleading (Mudimbe 1988).

Setting aside the questionable veracity of empirical records, the principles of traditional authority are not easily analysed from the cultural and political distance of neo-classic liberalism. The fact is that good governance in Africa may not even be recognizable by an uninitiated foreign assessor. Most of the institutions of indigenous leadership are virtually invisible from outside, in accord with historically established norms to protect them against potentially disruptive intrusion. And conceptually, the key notions of democracy manifest in Africa quite differently from the way they do in modern states influenced by ancient Greek political culture (Opata 1998: 145). Delivering democracy through consensus by a deliberating representative council of elders involves advising a 'chief' who is appointed for life.[6] But the term 'chief' itself evokes the sense of unassailable authority reigning over a dictatorial institution, and this is an approximation of the Akan people's *Nana*, the Dagbon people's *Na*, the Ga's *Matse*, the Ewe's *Dogbe*, the Yoruba's *Eze*, the Igbo's *Igwe* and their other title-holders or *Ozos*, the Hausa's *Sultan*, or Benin's *Oba*. Various connotations are carried by these traditional honorifics evoking the ideal of a political, spiritual, symbolic and practical vessel of communal wealth, a social steward, a common land trustee and custodian, a military leader, and a family head. African primordial systems of governance are non-confrontational, non-competitive. They have developed since the origin of civilization itself featuring consensual decision-making fuelled by the will to accommodate every viewpoint via compromise, rather than the will to dominate via the tyranny of majority opinion (Wiredu 1998). They rely upon very old notions of judicial process, third-party arbitration, and executive authority-by-council sanctioned by the impartiality of ancestral power. Yet the outsider sees only Africa's elected central state bureaucrats who interact in the global arena in the wake of an ethically appalling historical legacy that developed from the origins of today's ruthlessly hierarchical world trade relations.

From within African primordial publics, these modern elected governors of the central state appear epiphenomenal. They come and go; but the

---

[6] I am grateful to Emmanuel Ifeanyi Ani for discussion of chieftaincy titles current in Nigeria, February 4 2012, University of Ghana, Legon. These roles are the spiritual, political, social, ceremonial and custodial leaders chosen by merit for life from among their eligible peers in the royal lineages in African societies. Traditionally they could be deposed by their community for poor performance.

traditional authorities remain accountable to their subjects and more seriously to their ancestors—not for four years but for life—to serve all the needs and concerns of their communities and of future generations. Political power and leadership of this kind is not obtained through votes (Opata 1998: 145) It cannot be assessed accurately by the standards that apply to the exercise of multi-party electoral politics in late-capitalist societies, as exist in the US and UK (Wiredu 1998: 244).

Correlatively, it would be wrong to interpret the governance of a traditional chief and council as undemocratic because the chief is not elected. Ancestrally authorized leadership is not autocratic, nor is it messianic, nor is it benign dictatorship. In principle, if a man becomes a leader by appointment of his ancestors, the dignity and security of his office must be protected at all costs. But at the same time, he loses his individual self; he is no longer an ordinary person with ordinary social claims and supports. He has no friends. He has no hobbies, no proclivities. He becomes instead a vessel for his ancestors, a vessel of service for his people, now and in future generations. If he is Akan and disregards his responsibilities in this capacity, the retribution will come from *Onyame* (God) at the discretion of his ancestors. If his personality infects his views and actions too much, he will be deposed according to the protocols in place for this eventuality, at the initiative of his own people. Even where peoples' conflicting interests require their leader's assertive intervention and executive decision, the chief will go into council with the representative elders, again as a vessel. In principle, he does not rule at will, nor according to his own independent discretion, but always under the advice of his community's elders (Wiredu 1998: 242-243).

So it is the council of elders that plays the central role of authority in decision making and policy formation in West African consensual democratic systems; it remains a common feature of governance among the majority of Akan, Ga, Dagbon, Ewe, the Yoruba, Igbo, Hausa people, and in other sub-regions where traditional authorities function for the majority in systems parallel to the centralized state apparatus. On Wiredu's view, an updating of the central role of this advisory cabinet structure would involve associations in consultation with deliberating elders, rather than political parties competing for votes and winning absolute power in two or four-year bursts.

Reading these features of traditional authority as principles and ideals, not as empirical reports, reveals that Wiredu's normative perspective is consonant with Eze's position—contrary to what Eze's own critique claims, as will be spelled out momentarily. First, a word about the sources relied upon here for illuminating Wiredu's expressed views, as they appear to starkly contrast with the versions of his claims presented by Eze and others (example, Jacques 2011). Wiredu's explicit defence of non-party politics and his depiction of indigenous norms of consensual democracy date back to the (1995) publication titled "Democracy and Consensus in African Traditional Politics." This article became widely accessible online in 2000 and is the chief focus of Dr. Eze's (1997) critique, which is also available on the same website, *Forum for Intercultural Philosophy* <http://them.polylog.org/2/fwk-en.htm>. appears 2000, Wiredu's analysis of Akan political culture was most frequently seen in the final third part of his book titled *Cultural Universals and Particulars: An African Perspective* (1996: 145-190). The most frequent reference by commentators is made to this book and to a seminal paper originally titled "The State, Civil Society and Democracy in Africa," which Wiredu presented at a conference in Abidjan in 1998.[7] Wiredu's views are further adumbrated in two less widely circulated but very effective essays (which were evidently not available to Eze at the time he developed his critique)—these are "Tradition, Democracy and Political Legitimacy in Contemporary Africa" (2001a), and "Democracy by Consensus: Some Conceptual Considerations" (2001b). Wiredu further clarified points about consensual politics, which he made in all of these works, when he delivered two keynote addresses, responded to questions from the audience, and subsequently held private discussions April 15-17, 2009.[8] His views have not varied substantively since those published in 1995.

One of the critics of Wiredu who is representative of the 'alterity studies' genre complains that Wiredu confuses "myth" with "historical truth;" and that a "romanticised, illusory" image of pre-colonial African society as "communal or collectivist . . . inspires Wiredu's work" (2011: 1026-1027). Carlos Jacques charges Wiredu with committing the same "unanimist illusion" as Paulin Hountondji (1996) accused Kwame Nkrumah of making in his romanticized version of pre-colonial Akan societies in *Consciencism*.

Eze also accuses Wiredu of fantasizing that harmony and unity were the hallmark of pre-colonial Akan society (Eze 2000; Jacques 2011). But it is not clear why. In his texts, Wiredu conjectures nothing like a purely harmonious ancient Akan society. On the contrary, he points to "sharp disagreements that prevailed at all levels" and "various loci of disagreement and conflict . . . even within traditional councils" (1998: 246). Wiredu neither exaggerates nor romanticises the success of pre-colonial rule. Rather he remarks upon the

---

[7] Slightly revised, this essay was re-issued twice under the title "Society and Democracy in Africa," in 1999 and 2001. It is reprinted under its original title in 2009 by editors Helen Lauer and Kofi Anyidoho.

[8] At the 7th Faculty of Arts Colloquium held at the University of Ghana, "The Humanities and the Idea of National Identity," which will be published in the forthcoming Proceedings of that Colloquium.

self-evident contrast between notorious despots and celebrated non-despotic rulers of olden days (2001a: 163).

Different Senses of 'Compromise'

Further, Wiredu elaborates that without the known existence of conflicting points of view throughout an ancient Akan community, there would be no need to seek a consensual compromise over what to do through protracted deliberation under the trees: "Deliberation need not always lead to compromise" (1998: 247) and "consensus need not be the end of all debate" (2011: 1061). Against the backdrop of Wiredu's traditional political scenery, the sustained expression of a diversity of viewpoints is essential to representing a community. And of course, this would have to be the case. To stress, as Wiredu does, that the key virtue of traditional Akan politics lay in the elder council members' "will to consensus" (2001a: 171) would be pointless among elders assumed to be manipulable or already in perfect agreement. In this respect, Eze's vision of the value of free speech where "democracy is its own end" (1997: 320-321) is consistent with Wiredu's explication of the raison d'être for deliberation by a representative council. On Wiredu's account, the ideal goal of protracted discussion is not the dissolution of opposing views; he stresses that the goal of consensus-building is the resolve of what *will* be done, juxtaposed alongside the myriad of enduring opinions about what *should* be done or what would be ideal to do. Elders in counsel holding divergent opinions are expected to maintain the integrity of their views, yet share a will to consent in finding the way forward through compromise sufficient to facilitate a plan. "Agreement here need not be construed as unanimity . . . about what ought to be done . . . only about what is to be done" (1998: 243).

Wiredu is consistent in spelling out the definitive contrast between 'compromise' in its concessional sense of relinquishing one's beliefs, capitulating one's values to a coercive opposition on the one hand, versus *decisional* consensus which requires reaching a practical compromise to determine collectively "what *will* be done" to serve all the individuals affected. The latter negotiating process requires that each deliberator sustains their interests in the face of conflict, not abandoning or surrendering them. Wiredu states explicitly that elders in council can compromise in practical matters of determining "what is to be done," without forsaking their differences of opinion "about what is true or false" and what they variously think ideally *ought* to be done (1998: 242; 1999: 35). In order to illuminate how the compromises required for decision making do not entail any suppression whatsoever of divergent beliefs and values, Wiredu took care to delineate these several senses of consensus in all the published texts cited here. Thus Wiredu repeatedly distinguishes "consensus on normative and cognitive issues" from "decisional consensus" (1998: 243; 1999: 33; 2001a: 169; 2001b: 235-237; and his keynote address of 2009 published 2011: 14).[9]

Thus a careful reading of Wiredu's account of consensual procedure in traditional polities reveals that his concerns are consonant with Eze's concerns that in a democracy, there are measures to minimize the risk of suppressing individual points of view. In fact, to Wiredu's way of understanding traditional Akan political ideals, prioritizing individuals' needs and entitlements was, and remains, the very crux and purpose of communitarian ethos. In particular, the consensual decision-making model of the proverbial council presupposes that individuals' divergent interests are all sustained, because in principle they must all be equally recognised and accommodated.[10]

Non-party or One-party Polity

Eze was among the contemporary African political thinkers who remain wholly unconvinced by the communitarian ethos. He did not countenance the "will to consent" that Wiredu attributes to members of traditional deliberative councils as the driving force for progressive political democracy conducive to socio-economic development. Eze found no substantive difference between Wiredu's reasons for rejecting multi-party politics and the early Africanist nationalists' ideological defence of one-party rule. Eze began his critiques (1997, 2000) of Wiredu by categorising him in this camp of African thinkers who rely on a "return to the source model" (1997: 313). According to Eze, the celebrated early nationalists (including Cabral, Ki-Zerbo, Kenyatta, Nkrumah, Nyerere, Senghor, Toure, Sithole) discouraged electoral politics as un-African, and denigrated multiparty activities as a ruse to monopolise popular support and to pre-empt political opposition. They supported traditional communal ethos, as a strategy to forward their narrowly defined ambitions. They proposed that the resurrection of African identity depended upon themselves, to lead a return to the essential, original African harmony and unity that had been trampled by colonialism.[11] And since

---

[9] Delineating three senses of consensus mistakenly conflated by critics was reinforced by Wiredu during discussion at the Legon Faculty of Arts Colloquium, April 15-16, 2009. A revised version of these lectures has been published as "The humanities and the idea of national identity," (Wiredu 2019).

[10] Wiredu in conversation with the author, April 17th 2009, Philosophy Department, University of Ghana, Legon.

[11] T. Carlos Jacques claims that "[t]he single party of the African nationalists was not then a traditional political party. Indeed, but for the name, it is identical to, I would contend, Wiredu's non-party political order" (2011: 1026).

history shows that the myth of lost African unity was used as a rhetorical justification to suppress political association and press freedom, critics regard both models as equally dangerous vehicles of tyranny through the "exclusion of individuals" or groups "who fail to embody the essence of the community" (Jacques 2011: 1029).

Whether it is accurate to analyse the political thought of all the early African nationalists *en masse* cannot be tested in this compass. Notwithstanding, subsequent to Eze's (1997) critique—perhaps as a consequence of it—Wiredu's actual statements in defence of non-party politics cannot be characterised as supportive of the mid-twentieth century nationalists' justifications for one-party rule. In all his essays and in conversation, Wiredu repeatedly and explicitly disparages one-party politics and the ideological fig leaves used by early nationalists to cover their brute stronghold upon power when they suppressed political party opposition (1998: 251; 1999: 41; 2001a: 163-167; 2001b: 240). Wiredu is adamantly opposed to the suppressions of press freedom and political association that make possible the formation of effective political parties. In all versions of Wiredu's seminal essay "State, Civil Society and Democracy in Africa," (1998, 1999, 2001), he explicitly distinguished his non-party vision from one-party politics:

> In concluding this advocacy of a non-party system of politics, I would like to dissociate myself from any concealed hankering after a one-party system. This is especially necessary since some politicians have been known to use the banner of the non-party idea. The fundamental difference . . . is that the [non-party system] embraces the freedom of political association while the [one-party system] execrates it (1999: 43; 1998: 251)

Wiredu also discusses at length the danger of "one-party states" being created "*de facto* . . . by ambitious power seekers . . . under the guise of no-party rhetoric" (2001b: 240). In his arguments for non-party politics, Wiredu actually spells out in greater detail than does Eze the contemporary threats to constructive political process posed by "one-party chicanery" (2001b: 242). At one point in his writing Wiredu described one-party systems as even worse than multi-party systems, since on the latter electoral scene ". . . there is at least an appearance, though often only an appearance, of press freedom. In the unlamented era of the one-party system, not even an appearance of press freedom existed" (2001a: 167).

Wiredu and Eze are both concerned that one-party rule can undermine political legitimacy (Wiredu 2001a: 166; Eze 1997: 318-321). Wiredu illuminates the current temptation to confuse the pretences of democratic deliverance to

Africans with the antics of contemporary "pseudo-democratic power holders" who manipulate "majoritarian rule" and "simulate popular consent" to suit the interests of their "well-financed backers" (2001a: 166, 168).

Whatever shortfalls there may be in Wiredu's outline of non-party political procedure in a modern nation-state, his critique is useful for illuminating the dysfunctions and incoherencies intrinsic to electoral politics as conducted in the US and the UK, where compromise and deferential cooperation are marks of political impotence. The strength and desirability of elected representatives is measured characteristically by their capacity to stall, obstruct, thwart, if not to obliterate the effectiveness of opposition party rivals. Yet in those "culture[s] of conflict," the very raison d'être of a political party vanishes without a robust opposition to pit against and vanquish for four years—at great cost to the social welfare of the citizenry (1998: 246-247). Wiredu depicts multi-party electoral practices as oligarchic, deceitful, and rabidly divisive in ways that Africans struggling in besieged economies today can ill afford.

Political Legitimacy and its Decline

Everyday life in West Africa has become migratory, predatory, culturally complex, and so challenging that individuals are no longer mystified by superstitious beliefs about their "shared and common past and future as it was [formerly] carried forward in the myths of origins" (Eze 2000: par 16). Eze claims that African people no longer believe in the sacred powers of their chiefs, whose authority used to be legitimized by the belief that they are divine links with the ancestors. It was the magico-mythological beliefs in ancestral power that Eze says legitimated traditional African authority. So he concludes that the ancient Akan style of leadership has lost irreparably its former utility (Eze 1997: 318, 2000: par 16). His chief reason is that pre-colonial people's naïve confidence in their own communal unity is irrelevant to the quest for good governance in modern Africa.

Eze further invalidates such naïve confidence in its own right, speculating that the historic African reverence for communal unity was an ideological fabrication espoused by the olden-day power establishment of chiefs, councils of elders, priests and auxiliary conservers of traditional myth and magic who retained an interest in sustaining the status quo:

> If the traditional mythological origins and justifications of consensual politics can no longer hold today (due to secularisation and religious pluralisms, for example) . . . then we may have to (re)invent usable . . . mythologies. For . . . a secular political institution, if it renounces brute force . . . needs some sort of mythology . . . in order to endure (Eze 1997: 318, 2000: pars 16, 19)

Eze proposes to show the irrelevance of traditional rule by recounting examples that display how differently from the pre-colonial days African people now understand themselves and the conflicts in which they are caught up. Eze is impressed that Africans today have been secularised (2001: par 21)—by which he seems to mean they have been enlightened. Conflicts appear insoluble nowadays because the combatants believe, and believe correctly, that their economic interests and survival needs are genuinely and diametrically opposed. Eze cites many examples including the crisis in the Niger Delta where the very existence of the Ogoni people is pitted against the priorities of company shareholders and police employed by Mobil, Dutch Shell and Chevron Oil companies drilling in the area (1997: 318, 2000: par 21).

There are two problems with this analysis. One is that the causal account which depends upon an epistemic shift from superstitious, magico-spiritual beliefs to rational appreciation of modernizing democratic structures seems contradicted by evidence gathered by political economists and historians who have analysed the decline and atrophy of chieftaincy institutions through the twentieth century (Robert Addo-Fening 2012; Kojo Amanor 2006, 2012). Traditional rulers in West Africa lost their subjects' respect and confidence because of their collusion with colonial administrations beginning in the early 1900s, together with the rapidly deteriorating economic conditions this brought about through colonial strategies of indirect rule (Amanor 2006: 160). Traditional elites were pauperized and corrupted in the course of their accommodation, adaptation, and capitulation to colonial intrusion, manifesting in specific types of actions that destroyed the livelihoods of commoners. Chiefs commercialized large tracts of arable common land held in their trust throughout Southern and Eastern Africa to a few landholders; others denied naturally evolving land markets for the migrant farming settlements growing up through West Africa. Chiefs helped control land reserves as holding pens for forced migrant labour; and they organised forced labour for Europeans' export crop production. Individuals who had no historical or ancestral relation to polities were installed as chiefs where no lineages were in ascendance, to help the Queen of England extract African resources and exploit African labour (Amanor 2006: 160). From this analysis of historical economic change, it appears that the decline of African traditional authority's efficacy was not caused by a change in African commoners' notion of political legitimacy; it issued rather as a causal consequence of the material effects of chiefs' actions. Such effects included the penury to which African peasantries were reduced by colonial intrusion, which entailed chiefs' collaboration and independent disempowerment.

In contrast, Eze's causal account of this trend is epistemological. He argues that it is unrealistic to suppose consensual politics was ever really effective in pre-colonial Akan society just because everyone recognised their common interests and shared a "rational belief in the power of reason." Eze chides Wiredu that if he thinks Akan chiefs and their subjects in ancient times "actually" (2000: par 15) had this much contemporary sense so as to believe in the "virtue of the persuasiveness of ideas," (2000: par 13) then he "might need further evidence to make a successful case" of it—by which Eze implies this would be impossible. On Eze's view, debating of the elders was tolerated most likely because these rituals of governance were conducted in the hocus-pocus atmosphere of ancestral power and spiritual forces, so that naïve people believed superstitiously that they were bound in a mystical unity (1997: 316-317). Lévy-Bruhl ([1910] 1966) would have said they held pre-logical beliefs. As Eze reasons, now that Africans are no longer naïve, such institutions will not be able to function.

But on the contrary, as historians have depicted, people's spiritual beliefs remained active, and their expectations of political legitimacy remained robust throughout colonialism, so that through this lens, they witnessed and condemned the colonial perversions of chieftaincy depreciating their political institutions. To pick one instance: in the early 1900s, the people of Bulisa in (now) Northern Ghana were placed under a-historical authorities by ad hoc British appointment. The historian Robert Addo-Fening explains these subalterns' illegitimacy was patently clear from the outset because the public believed these colonial appointees lacked *nam* (2012: 692). This divine endowment of spiritual power and ancestral sanction continues to this day to underpin the exercise of legitimate political traditional authority in the three Northern regions of Ghana as it does in other places throughout the world, e.g., in the Tibetan refugee settlements throughout India and Nepal.

Description ≠ Legitimisation

A second and more trenchant problem with Eze's critique is methodological. Eze overlooks an elementary yet fundamental difference between *empirical conditions* of governance (including the populace's shared views of their leadership at different historical moments) on the one hand, and *normative principles* that legitimate a specified form of leadership (independently of particular times and places and prevailing popular beliefs) on the other. Wiredu's thesis about the legitimacy of Akan consensual politics is normative. In assessing the plausibility of Wiredu's arguments, therefore, the problem is not whether Wiredu has got the pre-colonial facts straight. His account is not about how all royal councils performed their duties in fact. Doubtless there were dismissive elitists who suppressed conflicting interests, and failed in their performance of their duties. No one who condones chieftaincy as an institution today pretends it is not grossly corrupted by individual swindlers in office.[12] And doubtless there were superstitious and magical defenders of royal thrones, as there are today. Lack of evidence for the historical veracity of Wiredu's model is not critical because the *legitimacy* of a society's governing institutions does not depend causally upon what individuals or the majority *actually* believe to be legitimate at a given time. Prevailing public opinion never legitimizes a prevailing system of governance in the sense of legitimacy that concerns Wiredu when he advocates non-party consensus for contemporary Africans and rejects the popular cut-and-thrust of today's most powerful and celebrated multi-party democracies.

Eze doesn't see this. Instead, he writes that Wiredu's otherwise admirable contrast between secular beliefs in reason *versus* ancient ideas about the divine may "undermine the very belief systems that made possible the 'consensual' politics of the past . . ." (1997: 317; 2000: par 18). This misses the normative purpose of Wiredu's reconstruction of Akan political norms. In a minimal sense, of course, popular beliefs and related material conditions 'make possible' the actual practice of consensual politics—in that any governing activity is a socially recognised practice, which means it cannot be carried on without the tacit awareness and complicity of individuals. But the frequency of beliefs throughout a population which sustains an institution is not the same feature of thought functioning in the public domain which normatively *legitimizes* that institution.

If we follow Eze's instructions to reflect upon "what makes one political opinion more persuasive than the other" at a given time (1997: 317, 2000: par 18), we will be committing the fallacy of appeal to the masses. Legitimacy is accorded to a specific system of governance through principles that determine rational bestowal of respect, confidence, and commitment; political legitimacy is not a brute function of numerical mass in public approval. Such principles vary—indeed, they constitute the contrast between political traditions; e.g., the criteria defining honourable behaviour and leadership virtues diverge momentously between African political values and neo-liberal priorities. In

---

[12] Ghana's National House of Chiefs' chairman explained the public's recognition of improper performance of chiefs in an open forum for discussing plans to incorporate formally Ghana's paramount chiefs into the judiciary branch of central government: corruption of traditional offices are recognized openly by their sitting on stools that have not been blackened (i.e. their positions have not been sanctioned ancestrally over generations of recognition, an accreditation symbolized by the ritual pouring of sacrificial blood on a royal lineage head's seat of office). *Chieftaincy in Ghana: culture, development and governance.* Institute of African Studies, University of Ghana, Legon, November 2003.

consequence, more than one set of criteria may spell out the concepts of responsibility, just authority, feasibility, accountability, marital fidelity, material success, impartiality, rule of law, constitutionality, individual civic rights, entitlement to social welfare, just provision of public goods, equal treatment, economic trust, due process, fair trial, protection of person and property.

The Normative Basis of Political Legitimacy

Africans with formal education function with more than one set of these criteria. An example of such incorporation of divergent frameworks is West Africans' familiarity with contrasting notions of justice. The political culture of un-centralised, non-state polities shifts the very notion of justice—the purpose and structure of its pursuit—away from the competitive model of legal arbitration that dominates Western legal systems. When two or more parties in a West African primordial public are in conflict, they seek a neutral party to mediate. If this fails, a formal hearing is sought in an established legal structure presided over by a recognized authority, who might be a chief. When called upon to resolve the conflict, this authority is not expected to establish which party is the winner and which is the loser. Justice in this system is not served by determining who is legally 'right' and who is 'wrong'. Judicial process is not a competition; rather, conflict resolution through these procedures of justice is the "restoration of an equilibrium that previously prevailed before the conflict arose."[13]

Of course, in drawing this contrast between notions of justice as culturally specific, I have presupposed individuals' beliefs and values as contrasting with the commitments and behavioural dispositions of their contemporaries living in another political tradition. So at this point, someone of Eze's persuasion might well ask: what then does legitimizing a model of governance consist of, if not the accumulated beliefs about the constitutive concepts that are shared among the very people who are the living subjects of an actual government in practice? The answer to this lies in acknowledging that being governed is like having a history in R.G. Collingwood's sense (1946). Being governed in a certain tradition constitutes another aspect of what it means to be a reasoning subject, imbued with starting assumptions about individual entitlements, legitimate authority, just treatment, social orderliness and durable obligations.

---

[13] I am grateful for this account to the Ghanaian historian Divine E. K. Amenumey, professor emeritus History Department, University of Cape Coast, Ghana, in conversation July 2003.

Eze complains that Wiredu seems to "suggest that it is the logical power of the ideas presented" which justify a form of governance. Yet the power of legitimacy *is* indeed 'logical', broadly speaking: A set of principles (P) characterising legitimacy of governance provides the deductive antecedents of general descriptive statements (D) that refer to the specific practices and policies comprising a particular system which is thereby deemed legitimate because those descriptive statements (D) follow as semantic entailments from the accepted starting principles (P).[14] To analyse political legitimacy otherwise is to risk confusing a normative relation between a practice and principles that support it, with the contingent relation between cause and effect. Suppose you believe along with Eze that the causes of political legitimacy in olden days resided literally in the fact that certain beliefs occurred to commoners living at specific times and places, and that the effects of their having these beliefs were the subsequent intentions and consequent actions of other people who were the elites ruling over them at some remove from, but still sustained by, the approving, adoring attitudes of their subjects. Such an account of what legitimizes governance is, in itself, a good example of magical and superstitious thinking.

This contrast between normative and circumstantial relations is important to sustain methodologically, so it is worth emphasising. Consider a contemporary example that illuminates the distinction between popular belief and the appropriate basis for legitimizing state authority. When the Cold War folly reached its peak in the 1980s, there was a publicized American policy whereby Born Again government appointees were issued official ID cards entitling them to emergency evacuation by helicopter transport out of the Washington DC area in the event of a nuclear attack (Larry Josephson 1985). The bulk of Christian fundamentalist voters *believed* their chosen few representatives would be moved up to heaven literally in a Holy Rapture, away from the hellfire of a nuclear apocalypse. These convictions were encouraged by frequent public appearances of their President Ronald Reagan with the original TV-evangelist Billy Graham. Yet as strong and pervasive as was the American Silent Majority's belief that God inspired their president to build a programme of nuclear proliferation, the *fact* that this popular confidence yielded a powerful voting

---

[14] Of course, the sense of semantic entailment intended here between P and D is notoriously problematic, but no moreso here than, for example, in the reason given by an agent for his own intentional action, or in the relation promoted so comprehensively in Carl Hempel's deductive nomological model of incomplete explanation, wherein an *explanandum* statement describing an event E follows from the set of statements S *explanans* in the sense that S provides good reason for believing E was likely to occur (1974: 96-97).

block did not legitimize the Star Wars programme in any *normative* sense. Of course, the programme indeed might have been legitimate, but that would be due to considerations other than its mass appeal. The popularity of Zionist extremism may be *causally* responsible for the *occurrence* of a terrorist attack in a busy downtown market of the Gaza strip, but it cannot *cause* that action to be *legitimate* or not. The legitimacy of a political policy or institutionalised behaviour is not linked to our thoughts about it in any causally sequential order. The link is rather, for want of a better word, logical—or normative in some sense broader than 'logical' usually connotes.

This moral or ethical sense of political legitimacy as an objective property of institutions is in some way independent of particular circumstances and cultural conditioning. The political legitimacy that Wiredu attributes to consensual democracies is a quality supervenient upon historical conditions, demographic factors and geographic location.[15] It is the sense in which South Africa's former governmental structure of apartheid was not legitimized by the temporal fact that the system had been established for generations; nor could it be legitimized by the demographic statistical analyses presenting the pass laws and segregation policies as overwhelmingly popular among voting South Africans at the time, and internationally condoned.[16] Of course, legitimacy is a virtue whose attribution is warranted and justified differently by distinct social groups. Political legitimacy might be an objective feature of the social world whose recognition varies with the observer's frame of reference. Obviously this realist speculation about the nature of political legitimacy requires more investigation than can be pursued here (Sayre-McCord 1988: 256-281).

African Philosophers Assessing African Politics

Disagreement about the political legitimacy of traditional African modes of governance and their relevance to modern democratic institutions is hardly unique to Wiredu and Eze (example, Awoonor 2011). The foregoing discussion has focussed upon Wiredu's depiction of traditional consensus-based leadership, which has survived the centuries despite the invasive colonial perversion and corruption of indigenous authority. This review of Eze's

---

[15] Wiredu (2011: 1064) regards consensual democratic features as characteristic of other African heritages besides the Akans of Ghana, e.g. "the Bugandans of Uganda, the Zulu of South Africa, but exemplars can be multiplied."

[16] Samuel P. Huntington (1968) and the Feierabends (1966) presented statistical arguments for categorizing apartheid South Africa in the mid twentieth century as a 'satisfied' society. Serge Lang (1998: 5-18) staged a moving anti-apartheid challenge to these "political opinions passed off as science."

objections compelled us to consider afresh the standards that Wiredu and Eze each employ for according legitimacy, and the reasons why one of them urges reliance upon non-party politics while the other holds a strong preference for democracies featuring multi-party politics. Wiredu's arguments for non-party consensual governance are chiefly utilitarian, not sentimental, contrary to his critics' say-so. But my portrayal in itself does not vindicate Wiredu's model, which falls short of providing a practical programme for replacing multiparty competitions in large populations.

We found that in essence, Eze and Wiredu concur in their parallel concerns to promote good governance by pre-empting despotism, preserving free speech, encouraging diversity of opinion and with it political contestation, while avoiding the ruthless profligacy and power lust which are reinforced in the major league politics of oligarchic democracies. They both recognise that Africans stand to benefit from norms of governance that have not been perverted by the excesses of capitalism. They disagree about whether a modification of traditional norms of consensus could provide a feasible alternative to the expensive contests and short term seizure strategies for gaining exclusionary power demonstrated in the world's high profile democracies today (Wiredu 2001a: 162).

I have tried to show that Eze's published reasons for opposing Wiredu on this point: (i) preambled Wiredu's clear disparagement of one-party politics in published work dating from 2001; and (ii) conflated empirical conditions with normative justifications for judging a political programme's practicality as opposed to its legitimacy. Possibly in consequence of this conflation, Eze's critique reveals a misapprehension of Wiredu's agenda for constructing a tableau for framing contemporary Africans' assessment of their political alternatives and their economic conditions, an assessment based on inherited, enduring democratic values that Eze himself espoused in his critique, viz. his concern for free speech, for unimpeded political disputation, for the sanctity of political recognition, and for the duty of government to practice inclusive stewardship. Nevertheless, Chukwudi Eze's critique of traditional African politics demonstrates the critical importance of impassioned scholarly dialogue in order to positively influence changes in political culture—not only for the African continent's future, but in the global arena as well.

Conclusion

An important corrective in African studies is the painstaking job of distinguishing carefully reasoned normative models depicting selected indigenous values and principles, from facile, hackneyed brand-imaging of a bygone idyllic Africa. For what is at stake here is the general utility of academic debate as a source of inspiration and clarification actualising the near and distant political future. This is a legacy of critical theory which very clearly emerged with the intellectual dawn of Africans' formal Independence in response to colonialism in the early twentieth century (Max Assimeng 1992: 1-56) and which continues in the current period of African renaissance humanities scholarship and research (Falola [1996] 2012).

Wiredu's retrospective modelling and the controversy it provokes are not just reflections of African nostalgic sentimentality: there are historically specific, epistemically substantive reasons to keep alive the African retrospective and controversy about appropriate political leadership in the models of governance indigenous to Ghana and Nigeria, Senegal, Sudan, Rwanda, Somalia, South Africa, and within other newly emerging democracies on the continent. Perhaps the most effective and compelling aspects of indigenous rule must remain hidden from the international gaze to have remained intact and effective throughout the colonial ordeal—hidden in the sense that their utility and intrinsic values may not be recognisable by foreigners first hand, nor readily articulable in the international languages of former colonizers. So it is specifically African voices that need to be heard and provided the post of authoritative experience in the global discourse about good governance.

The capacity to reflect upon and to critique (for instance) West African political ideals is part of an inheritance specific to people who share an inside, tacit knowledge of at least two kinds of political culture.[17] Schooled in the international languages of their former colonizers, citizens of post-colonized West Africa typically adjudicate between divergent systems of justice, competing norms of feasibility, incompatible senses of propriety, contrary moral codes and multiple definitions of family and civic allegiance. Thus African intelligentsia assess current events from a wider, richer repertoire of political experience than do their counterparts whose exposures to the constraints of poverty are shaped in large measure by capital-controlled digital images. African perspectives overlap instructively with some Western political theorists who promote an ethics of care, who take seriously the demand for fair trade and distributive justice on a global scale, and who are especially committed to formulate antidotes to the dominant free-market value orientation that ratifies the level of violence and inequity characteristic of the current global economic order. So it is that African intellectuals can bring historically specific understandings and capacities for building global

---

[17] It exists on the "boundary or frontier" between two kinds of political culture. Again I borrow Alasdair MacIntyre's image for the location of a person "growing up as a full member of two linguistic communities" (1987: 388).

justice as an on-going deliberation over generations. But this is the subject of another discussion (Lauer 2017).

***

University of Ghana, Legon, February 2012

Updated with minor revisions, University of Dar es Salaam, Tanzania, January 2019

References

Addo-Fening, Robert. 2012. Chieftaincy, Colonialism and the Atrophy of Traditional Governance in Ghana. Reprinted in H. Lauer and K. Anyidoho (eds.) *Reclaiming the Human Sciences and Humanities Through African Perspectives.* Accra: Sub Saharan Press, 683-702.

Amanor, K. S. 2012. Custom, Colonial Ideology and Privilege: the Land Question in Africa.14th Annual Pan African Anthropological Association Conference, Institute of African Studies (IAS), University of Ghana, Legon, 2nd–6th August, 2004. Reprinted in H. Lauer and K. Anyidoho (eds.) *Reclaiming the Human Sciences and Humanities Through African Perspectives.* Accra: Sub Saharan Press, 279-288.

Amanor, K.S. 2006. Customary Land, Mobile Labor and Alienation in the Eastern Region of Ghana. In R. Kuba and C. Lenz (eds.) *Land and the Politics of Belonging in West Africa.* Leiden and Boston: Brill, 137-160.

Assimeng, M. 1992. *Foundations of African Social Thought: A Contribution to the Sociology of Knowledge.* Accra: Ghana Universities Press.

Awoonor, K. 2011. Democracy, their Democracy: our Portion of the Discourse. In H. Lauer and K. Anyidoho (eds.) *Reclaiming the Human Sciences and Humanities Through African Perspectives.* Accra: Sub Saharan Press,1036-1044.

Baku, D.E. K. 1990. History and National Development: The Case of John Mensah Sarbah and the Reconstruction of Gold Coast History. *Institute of African Studies Research Review* New Series 6(1): 36-55.

Collingwood, R.G. 1946. Human Nature and Human History. *The Idea of History.* Reprinted in Patrick Gardiner (ed.) *Philosophy of History.* Oxford Readings. Oxford: Oxford University Press, 17-21.

Eze, E. C. 1997. Democracy or Consensus? Response to Wiredu. In Emmanuel Chukwudi Eze (ed.) *Postcolonial African Philosophy: A Critical Reader.* Oxford: Blackwell, 313-323.

Eze, E. C. 2000. Democracy or Consensus? Response to Wiredu. Revised online in the *forum for intercultural philosophy* series. <http://them.polylog.org/2/fee-en.htm>. Accessed March 13, 2009.

Falola, T. 2012. Nationalising Africa, Culturalising the West, and Reformulating the Humanities in Africa. Keynote Address of International Conference on Rethinking the Humanities in Africa, Obafemi Awolowo University, Ile Ife Nigeria, June 13-14, 2006. In H. Lauer and K. Anyidoho (eds.) *Reclaiming the*

Human Sciences and Humanities Through African Perspectives. Accra: Sub Saharan Publishers, 31-45.

Feierabend, I. K. and L. Rosalind Feierabend. 1966. Aggressive Behaviors within Politics 1948-1962: A Cross-National Study. *The Journal of Conflict Resolution* X(3): 249-271.

Frimpong-Ansah, J. H. 1996. *Flexibility and Responsiveness in the Ghana Economy: Post Decline Atrophy Syndrome.* The J. B. Danquah Memorial Lecture Series no. 29. Accra: Ghana Academy of Arts and Sciences.

Hempel, C. G. 1974. Reasons and Covering Laws in Historical Explanation. Reprinted in Patrick Gardiner (ed.) *The Philosophy of History.* Oxford: Oxford University Press, 90-105.

Hountondji, P. 1996. *African Philosophy: Myth and Reality.* Trans. Henri Evans. Bloomington: Indiana University Press.

Huntington, S. P. 1968. *Political Order in Changing Societies.* New Haven: Yale University Press.

Jacques, T. C. 2011. Alterity in the Discourse of African Philosophy: a Forgotten Absence. In H. Lauer and K. Anyidoho (eds.) *Reclaiming the Human Sciences and Humanities through African Perspectives.* Accra: SubSaharan Press, 1017-1030.

Josephson, L. 1985. *In the Rapture.* Radio documentary on the Reagan administration produced for Pacifica Radio WBAI, broadcast and distributed on tape in New York City.

Kea, R. 2012. Intellectual life and Scholarship in the Islamic Western Sudan during the Seventeenth and Eighteenth Centuries: a Political and Social View. In H. Lauer and K. Anyidoho (eds.) *Reclaiming the Human Sciences and Humanities through African Perspectives.* Accra: Sub-Saharan Publishers, 726-745.

Kea, R. (2003). Science, Technology, and Learning: Eighteenth Century Moliyili (Dagomba) and the Timbuktu Intellectual Tradition. In H. Lauer (ed.) *History and Philosophy of Science for African Undergraduates.* Ibadan, Nigeria: Hope Publishers, 238-270.

Lance, M. 2005. Fetishizing Process. *Institute of Anarchist Studies.* (Washington DC: Georgetown University). Accessible online <http://zinelibrary.info/files/Fetishizing%20Process.pdf. >

Lang, S. 1998. Political Opinions Passed Off as Science: The Huntington Case. *Challenges.* NY: Springer-Verlag.

Lauer, H. 2017. Global Justice as Process: Applying Normative Ideals of Indigenous African Governance. *Philosophical Paper*s 46(1): 163-189, http://dx.doi.org/10.1080/05568641.2017.1295621

Levi-Bruhl, L. 1910/1966. *How Natives Think.* Transl. Lilian Ada Clare. New York: Washington Square Press.

MacIntyre, A. 1987. Relativism, Power, and Philosophy. Reprinted in Kenneth Baynes et al. (eds.) *After Philosophy: End or Transformation?* Cambridge: MIT Press, 385-411.

Mudimbe, V.Y. 1988. *The Invention of Africa.* Bloomington: Indiana University Press and London: James Currey.

Ninsin, K. 2012. Ghana at 50: Tribe or Nation? *Ghana Speaks* Lecture/Seminar
Series of the Institute for Democratic Governance (IDEG). Commissioned
and delivered initially in Accra: Ghana@50 Jubilee Lecture series, March.
2007. Reprinted in Helen Lauer and Kofi Anyidoho (eds.) *Reclaiming the
Human Sciences and Humanities through African Perspectives.* Accra: Sub-
Saharan Publishers, 1116-1141.

Opata, D. 1998. The Beautiful Interpreters Are Not yet Here: The Poverty of a
Metaphysics of State and Civil Society in Africa. Special Issue: Proceedings of
the International Interdisciplinary Colloquium: State and Civil Society in
Africa. *Quest,* 12(1): 135-150.

Sanders, L. 1997. Against Deliberation. *Political Theory* 25(3): 347-377.

Sayre-McCord, G. 1988. Moral Theory and Explanatory Impotence. In G.
Sayre-McCord (ed.) *Essays on Moral Realism.* Ithaca: Cornell University
Press, 256-281.

Wiredu, K. 1995. Democracy and Consensus in African Traditional Politics: A
Plea for a Non-Party Polity. *The Centennial Review* 39(1) Winter: 53-64.
Reprinted online at *Polylog: Forum for Intercultural Philosophy* 2 (2000)
http://them.polylog.org/2/fwk-en.htm#f7. Accessed October 24, 2019.

Wiredu, K. 1996. *Cultural Universals and Particulars: An African Perspective.*
Bloomington: Indiana University Press.

Wiredu, K. 1998. The State, Civil Society and Democracy in Africa. Delivered at
the international colloquium of the same name at University of Abidjan-
Cocody, Ivory Coast, July 13-18, 1998. First printed under this title in a special
issue of the colloquium proceedings in *Quest. An International Journal of
Philosophy* XII (1) June. 1998: 241-252. A version appears as "Society and
Democracy in Africa." 1999. *New Political Science.* 21(1): 33-44. This second
titled paper was reprinted in *Explorations in African Political Thought:
Identity, Community, Ethics.* T. Kiros (ed). New York: Routledge. 2001. It was
reprinted again as "The State, Civil Society and Democracy in Africa." In H.
Lauer and K. Anyidoho (eds.) *Reclaiming the Human Sciences and Humanities
through African Perspectives.* Accra: Sub-Saharan Publishers. 2011, 1055-1066.

Wiredu, K. 2001a. Tradition, Democracy and Political Legitimacy in
Contemporary Africa. *Rewriting Africa: Toward Renaissance or Collapse?*
Japan Centre for Area Studies JCAS Symposium series no. 14. Osaka, Japan:
National Museum of Ethnology, 161-172.

Wiredu, K. 2001b. Democracy by Consensus: Some Conceptual
Considerations. *Philosophical Papers* 30(3): 227-244.

Wiredu, K. 2011. The Humanities and the Idea of National Identity. In H.
Lauer, N. A. A. Amfo and J. A. Anderson (eds.) *Identity Meets Nationality:
Voices from the Humanities.* Selected Proceedings from the Seventh Annual
Faculty of Arts Colloquium April 15-16th 2009. University of Ghana, Legon.
Accra: Sub-Saharan Publishers, 1-17.

Wiredu, K. 2019. The Humanities and the Idea of National Identity. Revised
version in H. Yitah and H. Lauer (eds.) *Philosophical Foundations of the
African Humanities through Postcolonial Perspectives.* Leiden: Brill, 103-119.

Yankah, K. 1998. *Free Speech in Traditional Society.* Accra: Ghana Universities
Press.

Notes on Contributors

Alexander Kwakye (Mr)

Teacher, Ghana Education Service, Accra, Ghana

Bernard Matolino (PhD, UKZN)

Associate Professor, School of Religion, Philosophy and Classics, University of KwaZulu-Natal, Durban, South Africa

Dennis Masaka (PhD, UNISA)

Lecturer, Department of Philosophy and Religious Studies, Great Zimbabwe University, Masvingo, Zimbabwe

Edwin Etieyibo (PhD, Alberta)

Professor, Department of Philosophy, University of the Witwatersrand, Johannesburg, South Africa

Emmanuel Ifeanyi Ani (PhD, Nnamdi Azikiwe University)

Senior Lecturer, Department of Philosophy and Classics University of Ghana, Ghana

Helen Lauer (PhD, CUNY)

Professor, Philosophy and Religious Studies Department, University of Dar es Salaam, Tanzania

Husein Inusah (PhD, University of Ghana)

Senior Lecturer, Department of Classics and Philosophy, University of Cape Coast, Cape Coast, Ghana

Martin Asiegbu (PhD, Catholique Université de Louvain)

Senior Lecturer, Department of Philosophy, University of Nigeria, Nsukka, Nigeria

Munamato Chemhuru (PhD, University of Johannesburg)

Senior Lecturer, Department of Philosophy and Religious Studies, Great Zimbabwe University, Masvingo, Zimbabwe

Victor C. Nweke (Mr)

PhD Student, University of Koblenz-Landau, Koblenz and Landau, Germany

Vitumbiko Nyirenda (Mr)

Masters Student, University of the Witwatersrand, Johannesburg, South Africa

Index

www.ingramcontent.com/pod-product-compliance
Lightning Source LLC
Chambersburg PA
CBHW072128020426
42334CB00018B/1711